Understanding UML: The Developer's Guide

With a Web-Based Application in Java™

• •

Understanding UML:
The Developer's Guide

ers, Inc.

Sponsoring Editor	Diane Cerra
Production Manager	Yonie Overton
Production Editor	Edward Wade
Editorial Assistant	Antonia Richmond
Cover Design	Ross Carron Design
Text Design, Illustration, and Composition	Sybil Ihrig, Helios Productions
Copyeditor	Judith Brown
Proofreader	Ken DellaPenta
Printer	Courier Corporation

Designations used by companies to distinguish their products are often claimed as trademarks or registered trademarks. In all instances where Morgan Kaufmann Publishers, Inc. is aware of a claim, the product names appear in initial capital or all capital letters. Readers, however, should contact the appropriate companies for more complete information regarding trademarks and registration.

Some of the generic discussion of OO development in Chapter 2 and the OO development model used in Chapter 3 were originally used in *An Introduction to Object-Oriented Modeling*, a book on OMT notation that Paul Harmon wrote for Popkin Software & Systems Inc. in 1996. Material in these chapters is copyrighted by Popkin Software & Systems and is used with the kind permission of Popkin Software & Systems Inc.

Morgan Kaufmann Publishers, Inc.
Editorial and Sales Office
340 Pine Street, Sixth Floor
San Francisco, CA 94104-3205
USA

Telephone	415-392-2665
Facsimile	415-982-2665
Email	*mkp@mkp.com*
Web site	*http://www.mkp.com*

Order toll free   800-745-7323

02 01 00 99 98   5 4 3 2

Library of Congress Cataloging-in-Publication Data

Harmon, Paul.
    Understanding UML : the developer's guide : with a Web-based application in Java / Paul Harmon, Mark Watson.
      p. cm.
    Includes bibliographical references and index.
    ISBN 1-55860-465-0
    1. Object-oriented methods (Computer science) 2. Computer software—Development. 3. UML (Computer science) 4. World Wide Web (Information retrieval system) I. Watson, Mark, 1951-   .
II. Title.
QA76.9.O35H36   1997
005.2'76--dc21   97-41284
                         CIP

Dedication

To the many methodologists who have contributed to an understanding of object notation. To Grady Booch, James Rumbaugh, Ivar Jacobson, and the others at Rational Software Corporation who initially created the Unified Modeling Language, and to all the others who have helped them. To Mary Loomis and Jim Odell and the many individuals and companies who worked with the Object Management Group's Object Analysis and Design Task Force to standardize the final version of UML. As a result of their difficult, multiyear effort, we now have a standard notation for the next generation of software development.

Contents

Acknowledgments

Many people have helped make this book possible and need to be given some credit for its existence, although they are, of course, innocent of its imperfections, which derive solely from its authors. In the beginning there was Myrna Kasser of Popkin Software who convinced the lead author that he should write a book providing an overview of OMT. Myrna, Manager of Research and Technical Communication at Popkin, noticed that Popkin Software's customers complained about the traditional methodology books and wanted a simpler overview that could get them started on their first OO development effort. She, along with many other people at Popkin Software, including Lou Varveris, Ron Scherma, and Mark McGreggor, all contributed to this effort in many ways. Then there was Diane Cerra, the Senior Editor at Morgan Kaufmann who got excited about the idea of doing an introductory book on UML and focusing on Java applications. Her enthusiasm translated into a contract and then constant encouragement until we submitted the manuscript. Next, we need to thank Jim Odell, the cochair of the Object Management Group's Analysis and Design Task Force, and one of the leading OO methodologists, who not only kept us up on how the OMG standardization effort was coming but read the manuscript and provided good advice. We want to thank Jon Hopkins of Rational Software Corporation who helped me understand some confusing points about UML notation. Others who read the manuscript and made good suggestions include Curt Hall, Bob Harmon, Bill Morrissey, Pooks Rutherford, and two anonymous readers. We also want to thank Edward Wade, Production Editor at Morgan Kaufmann, and Judith Brown who copyedited the manuscript. Finally, of course, the authors have to thank their families for providing encouragement even while we ignored them to spend evenings and weekends working on the manuscript.

Introduction

This book is for those who want a simple introduction to the use of an object-oriented (OO) methodology. Reading this book should give you a good overview of how to use an OO notation to analyze and design applications. At the same time, it can serve as an introduction to the newest OO notation, the Object Management Group's Unified Modeling Language (UML). And, since our example involves a Java application designed for the Internet, this book can be used by those who know Java and want to learn how to use an OO approach to analyzing and designing new Java applications for the Internet.

We describe the notation that has just recently been introduced and standardized by Rational Software, Microsoft and the Object Management Group (OMG), and others. This notation was specifically designed to supersede earlier OO notational conventions such as the Booch notation, the Object Management Technique (OMT) or Rumbaugh notation, and Jacobson's OO Software Engineering (OOSE) notation.

We'll use the UML notation to develop a simple application that will be written in Java and designed to be accessed over the Internet. This is a type of application that will become

increasingly common in the next few years. As Internet applications become more complex, developers will need to analyze their applications before they begin to develop them. The
fact that Java is an OO language and that there will increasingly be class and component libraries and tools to support
Java/Internet development means that there will also be a
growing need for Java/Internet developers to understand OO
analysis and design techniques.

An introductory book like this can't take the place of larger,
more detailed books on OMG's UML that will be published
later. It can, however, do a better job of explaining the basics,
showing how all the pieces fit together, and helping you walk
through an example of a simple Java/Internet application
development effort.

1.1 Development of UML

In the process of developing UML, two things happened. First,
the methodologies that were an integral part of the Booch,
Rumbaugh, and Jacobson systems were separated from the
notation. The UML does not specify a methodology (a series
of steps to follow to develop an application). Instead, UML simply provides a set of notational conventions that a developer
can use to describe or model an application. When you actually start to develop an application, however, you need some
kind of sequence to follow, just to understand why you might
want to use one diagram rather than another at any point in
the development process. Hence, we provide a generic
methodology that is used to develop a simple distributed
Internet application. We have tried to keep our methodology
separate from the UML notation so that you'll understand
what the OMG standardized on and what we are adding.

The second thing that occurred along the way to standardization was the addition of metamodeling elements. In general, when you are developing an application, you only use a

subset of the notational elements. If you are developing a more complex application, you might require more specialized notational elements. If you are going to create an OO modeling tool that supports the UML notation, on the other hand, you need to be sure that elements in one diagram are always kept consistent with elements in other diagrams. In other words, you need a very precise, abstract specification of the relationships between all of the elements. This high-level specification is called a metamodel. The distinctions, for example, between class and type or between class and the stereotype of a class aren't important for most developers who are writing small or midsized OO applications. They are very important, however, if you are designing an OO repository and need to keep track of the kinds of elements that any user might want to store in the repository. UML is a very detailed notation that is accompanied by a precise metamodel.

In fact, UML is more precisely specified than any previous OO notation. Thus, UML will perform better when implemented on OO modeling tools or stored in OO repositories. UML is also the product of several committees and includes lots of things that are only used under rather specialized circumstances. Indeed, at first glance, the UML notation appears to be quite a bit more complex and intimidating than the earlier Booch, Rumbaugh, or Jacobson notations. In fact, if you ignore all the metanotational elements and the many features included for more specialized applications and focus only on those elements needed for basic OO analysis and design diagrams, the new notation is more elegant and much simpler than the earlier notations. In this book we'll focus only on the basic UML notational elements that you will need to develop beginning applications. As you become more skilled in using UML, you will probably want to study a more comprehensive book and learn some of the more complex notational conventions. In the meantime, however, you can use what you learn in this introduction to UML to create all the basic diagrams you will need for most of the projects you will probably undertake while you are first learning to use UML.

1.2 Using UML to Develop Applications

Anyone who has been programming for any length of time has either been involved in, or at least heard about, a project that was overanalyzed: The development team worked with a consultant or a modeling tool for months and created a very detailed design. Then, when they switched to the programming phase, they quickly found that the design couldn't be implemented. So a group of hackers had to start from scratch and put something together at the last moment to save the project.

Similarly, most experienced programmers have either been involved in or heard of a project that was launched after only a cursory analysis phase and soon ran into so much trouble that the project had to be abandoned.

There has to be a middle road—something between overanalysis and underanalysis—that will make it easier and more efficient to develop good applications. We aren't prepared to say that we know exactly what that middle road is, but in writing this book, we've tried to aim for a balance.

We think it's especially important to try to lay out a middle path for programmers who are just beginning to develop Java applications. Some Java programmers are new to distributed programming and are going to find that it takes more analysis than they may have used for programs they have written in the past. Even if you don't like to do a lot of analysis, if you are going to use an OO language for the first time, you owe it to yourself to spend a little time considering what a good OO design might look like. And if you are a more experienced developer who is working on a more complex application, you will definitely want to spend the time to consider how an OO application should be designed to work well on the Internet.

In an earlier book on OMT, which has been well received, the lead author used an example that involved an automated teller machine (ATM). The ATM example was used because several OO methodologists had used it. In the end, it proved less than satisfactory, however, because real ATM systems are quite different from the simpler models that were used to illustrate OO notations. Moreover, the design problems were very complex.

To assure that we played fair this time, we first analyzed a problem then designed and implemented a Java application, both by writing Java code and by creating diagrams in an OO modeling tool. We carried the application all the way through to code that will run on the Internet to be sure that our analysis and design models would lead to an application that could really be implemented. We'll explain the analysis effort that resulted in the initial object model. Then we'll consider the kinds of issues we focused on during the design phase and explain how this led us to modify our application. Finally, we'll provide you with the code generated both by hand and by means of the modeling tool so you can examine the resulting application in detail.

In other words, this book is designed to be a realistic introduction to UML and to analysis and design. We created it to help guide real developers as they tackle OO Internet applications.

1.3 How This Book Is Organized

In Chapter 2 we'll briefly consider the basic concepts of object technology, just to assure that we all have a common vocabulary for what follows. If you are already familiar with OO concepts, you can probably skip this chapter.

In Chapter 3 we'll provide an overview of a simple, generic OO development methodology. We won't present a formal methodology. Instead, we'll simply describe an informal, iterative approach to OO development that underlies most of the formal OO methodologies. We'll use this informal overview as a way of explaining how the diagrams and the various notations we'll be discussing in later chapters all fit together.

We'll consider UML in more detail in Chapter 4. We'll describe all of the diagrams you can develop using UML and how each of those diagrams works with each of the others. Next, in Chapter 5, we'll briefly discuss some of the features of the Java language.

In Chapter 6 we'll consider what OO modeling tools are and how they are useful for most notation-based analysis and design efforts. Then we'll introduce Popkin Software's popular OO modeling tool, which we will use to illustrate how modeling tools can help develop our application.

For a simple application like the example we'll be discussing in this book, it's probably faster to do it by hand. As you approach more complex applications, however, using an OO modeling tool can simplify an application development effort. In this book we'll illustrate both approaches.

We'll take a break from considering OO development in Chapter 7 and consider how you might develop a business process model of our simple sales application. In effect, we'll undertake a small Business Process Reengineering (BPR) analysis using IBM's LOV (Line of Vision) process analysis diagrams. This will provide an overview of the small application we will build throughout the rest of the book. It will also provide an idea of how you can move from a workflow model of a business problem to an OO model.

In Chapter 8 we will introduce use cases and show how our problem would be modeled using them. Then we will extend that analysis by using one of the UML stereotypes—ideal object models. Use case analysis is a popular way of analyzing the overall requirements for a system. It also provides a good way of generating the scenarios you will need to use throughout the rest of the development process. Ideal object modeling is a good way to develop an initial analysis of the objects that will be needed for an OO application.

We'll take a second break from considering UML notation in Chapter 9 and consider an informal way of developing an overview of what classes will probably be needed in a model. Specifically, we'll discuss CRC cards and use them to analyze our simple sales application. CRC stands for Classes, Responsibilities, and Collaborators. You can use this method on your own, or with a group of end users, to identify the main business classes you will need to create for your application.

In Chapter 10 we'll introduce the basic concepts and the notation used with UML class and object diagrams. Then we'll use that notation to diagram our sales example. We'll show

how it could be done if you were drawing the diagrams by hand and how it would be done if you were using an OO modeling tool.

Chapters 11 and 12 follow up with descriptions of the concepts and the notation of UML sequence, collaboration, state, and activity diagrams. We'll see how our sales application could be modeled using these diagrams. We'll also consider how we could develop the four types of diagrams in an OO modeling tool.

Chapter 13 moves on to design. We'll consider some of the things that you should think about during the design phase of a development cycle, and in Chapter 14, we'll consider the issues involved in determining the architecture of a system. We'll introduce the UML documentation, package, and component diagrams and then use them to model the design for our SalesWeb application. Finally, we'll see how these implementation diagrams can be used in an OO modeling tool.

In Chapter 15 we'll expand the object model we developed during the analysis phase of our effort. We see how to add infrastructure classes to our various UML diagrams. We'll also consider the problems of creating user screens or Web pages, accessing data, and other more specialized concerns. We'll briefly touch on coding and testing and then consider how all these things could be done in an OO modeling tool.

Appendix A provides the Java code for the example and information about how to acquire the Java code and Popkin Software's OO modeling tool with the sample application that we will develop in the course of this book. Appendix B, the Job Aid, provides a summary of all the basic UML symbols. Appendix C contains a table that shows how UML notation compares with equivalent notation in Booch and OMT. Appendix D lists organizations and products mentioned throughout the book.

Finally, a bibliography lists some books and Web sites that can help you explore the topics we discuss in detail. Unfortunately, since this is one of the first UML books, we can't provide lots of pointers to advanced books on UML, but most leading OO methodologists will be publishing advanced books in the near future.

The Vocabulary of Object Technology

In this chapter we'll review the basic vocabulary that developers use when they talk about OO languages and applications. If you already have a good grasp of object basics, you may want to skip this chapter. For others, however, we want to provide a very brief overview of the essential elements of object technology.

2.1 What Are Objects?

An object is a complex data type that contains other data types, usually called attributes or variables, and modules of code, usually called operations or methods. (UML uses attributes and operations; Java calls them variables and methods.)

The attributes and associated values are "hidden" inside the object. Any other object that wants to obtain or change a value associated with the first object must do so by sending a message to one of the first object's operations. (A message is

9

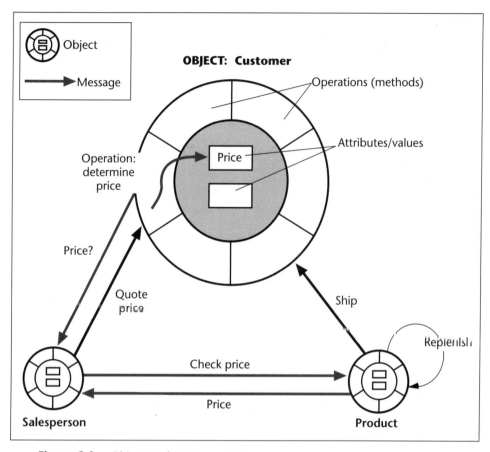

Figure 2.1   *Objects and message passing.*

object-speak for a function call.) Each object's operations manage its own attributes. This is called encapsulation. Encapsulation means that objects don't know or care how other objects store or process data. One object sends a message to an operation associated with a second object. One of the second object's operations, in turn, replies or takes action. We often say that the first object requests that the second object perform some task for it.

Figure 2.1 provides an overview of objects and message passing. We've used a special way of diagramming objects that shows the attributes in the middle of a circle surrounded by cells that represent operations. This way of diagramming objects dramatizes encapsulation and stresses that attributes can only be accessed by the object's own methods.

To appreciate an OO approach, you should contrast it to conventional programming. A conventional software system is basically composed of (1) a block of procedural code, the program, and (2) data, which is independent of the procedural code and is stored in files or tables. In a conventional application, all of the procedural code is stored as a single block, and any changes in the program must be carefully made to assure that changes at one point in the code don't have unwanted side effects elsewhere. Similarly, since the procedural code calls the data, any changes must be carefully made to assure that one procedure doesn't change the data in inappropriate ways before another procedure can use the data. It's possible to modularize a conventional program—that's exactly what the structured methodologies tried to do—but the very nature of the procedural approach guarantees that modularization will usually be limited and that subsequent modifications will be difficult.

Figure 2.2 contrasts a conventional application and an OO application. Unlike a monolithic procedural application, an OO application is modularized in the sense that each object is independent of every other object. Moreover, the procedural code contained in each object is modularized into several independent operations. A message usually only triggers a single operation. If a change needs to be made, the developer often only needs to change one operation. If changes are made to the internal data structures associated with one object, a developer can be confident that all the procedural code changes that will need to be made will only involve operations associated with that same object.

The basic idea of an object can be used in a number of ways. In some situations, the object becomes the fundamental unit of the system. In this case, all of the basic concepts used in an application, including bags, strings, numbers, and addition, are all represented as objects. This occurs in a language such as Smalltalk. (In Java, most of the basic structures are objects, but there are some exceptions, such as char, booleans, int,

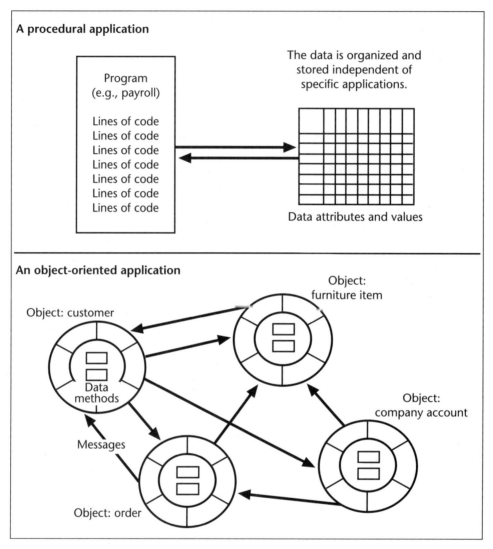

Figure 2.2   *A procedural application vs. an OO application.*

long, float, and other computational elements that are used as primitives.)

Objects may also encapsulate more complex groups of attributes and methods or even other objects. Thus, we can use objects to capture the various elements of a graphical user interface. In this case, icons, windows, scroll bars, and tools all become objects.

At a still higher level, an object can encapsulate all of the attributes and methods that make up business elements. These business objects include things like employee, machine, product, plan, customer, and so on. Using objects of this kind, models of the company and its activities can be developed. At this level, the OO metaphor comes very close to reality, and we speak of employees sending messages to customers, or sending requests to update corporate plans, or to cause machines to generate products. Each of these higher level objects are, of course, made up of more basic objects.

Objects can also be used to encapsulate existing programs. Thus, if a company needs to continue to use a large legacy system—say, the application that handles the company's payroll—the entire application can be placed "inside" an object, and access to the system can henceforth be managed by operations associated with the "legacy object." In fact, although we speak of the application as being "placed inside" an object, normally an object simply serves as an interface to the legacy application, taking messages directed at the legacy application, causing the application to run, and then sending the results back to other objects. In a similar way we can "encapsulate" databases with objects that stand between other objects and the database. The database object receives messages requesting information from a database, converts them into SQL, and sends the SQL to the database. Later, the database object formats any information it receives from the database into a message format and sends it back to the objects that originated the request.

The variety of different ways that object concepts can be used might make them confusing, at first. Once the basic concepts are understood, however, object technology becomes a powerful aid in thinking about computing. The same basic concepts can be used at many different levels of abstraction and in many different situations. In fact, objects are gradually becoming the great unifying concept underlying all software systems.

2.2 Objects, Classes, and Instances

When we get ready to develop an OO application, we need to talk more precisely about how we use the term *object*. Indeed, one of the common sources of confusion for those new to OO development comes from the fact that different languages and different methodologists use this and other terms differently. As most developers start using UML, we hope they will begin to standardize on their use of two important terms: *classes* and *objects*.

Classes are templates that have methods and attribute names and type information, but no actual values; and objects are generated by the classes and actually contain values. Some classes are very abstract and are simply used to provide structure for other classes. Most classes, however, are templates that are used to generate the objects that actually do the work when an application runs. When you compile an OO application, you save information about classes. Classes later generate objects when the application is run.

An object has values associated with it. Some developers use the term *instance* as a synonym for object. Most developers use the term *instantiation* to refer to the process whereby an object (instance) is generated by a class. UML specifies that there can be instances of classes that are other classes (i.e., subclasses) or instances of classes that are called objects. Thus, we will try to avoid using the term *instance* altogether and use class, object, and occasionally, instantiation. We won't talk of instances because they have no precise meaning in UML.

When we create an OO system we focus primarily on the classes that will be needed by the application. In effect, we design the application at the class level. When the system is actually run, objects are generated by classes as they are needed to contain the state information (i.e., attribute values) that is processed by the system. A single class, like *employee*, can have hundreds of instances in existence at the same time. When an object receives a message, it accesses the methods defined in its parent class to find the operation it needs to use to process

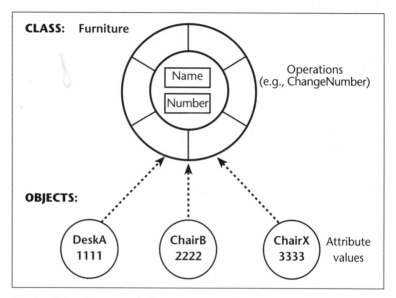

Figure 2.3   *Classes and objects.*

the message. Specific values derived from message passing are stored within objects. When objects are no longer needed by an application, they are eliminated. Figure 2.3 illustrates the relationship between three objects and their parent class.

In Figure 2.3 the class *Furniture* describes the set of all instances of furniture items. It specifies that they have names and item numbers and operations to instantiate a new item or to change an item's number. An object of the *furniture* class would have values for the name attribute and for the item number, as shown.

2.3 Message Passing and Associations

As a generalization, operations are associated with classes. Classes, however, don't normally send messages to each other; objects send messages to each other when the system is actually running. Thus, a static diagram pictures classes and only shows the logical associations between classes. It doesn't show the movement of messages. An association between two classes usually means that the objects of the two classes can send messages to one another.

Some authors discriminate between class operations (static methods) and object operations. In most OO languages, when one object wants to send a message to another, it begins by sending a message that is received by a class that uses a class operation to generate an object to deal with the message. Later, when the object is no longer needed, the class uses another operation to eliminate the object. Similarly, a developer will sometimes place operations and even store data in classes to keep track of certain things—the number of objects that have been generated by the class, for example. In modeling OO applications we normally only focus on the attributes and operations that are inherited by the objects and ignore the "class operations" that handle the creation and destruction of objects or that track the existence of the number of objects. Throughout the remainder of this book, a reference to an operation will always be a reference to an "object operation."

Objects can "contain" other objects. These objects are often called composite objects. In some cases, this means that a message is sent to one object that acts as the coordinator for several objects, but it may mean that one object is actually contained within another. These part–whole relationships are also called aggregations. We might have a car object that was made up of a motor, drivetrain, interior compartment, wheels, and so forth. These objects might, themselves, be made up of still smaller part-objects. Thus, if I sent a message to a car object asking about its oil level, it would, in turn, send a message to the engine object, which would probably pass another message to the oil subsystem. Eventually an object would be found that contained the value needed, and it would then be passed back up the chain.

2.4 Class Hierarchies and Class Inheritance

Classes can be arranged in hierarchies so that more concrete classes inherit attributes and operations from more abstract classes. In class hierarchy diagrams, the arrows always point from the class or object inheriting to the higher level class from which the attributes and operations are derived. (See Figure 2.4.)

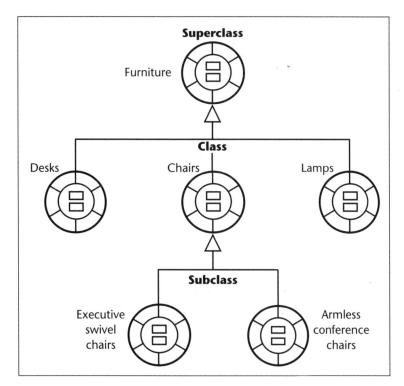

Figure 2.4   *Class inheritance.*

By adding new attributes and methods or changing the code associated with inherited methods, more concrete classes can be created. Thus, we might begin with a class that describes employees and then create two subclasses that are each specialized so that one represents hourly employees and the other represents full-time (or exempt) employees. Because we reuse most of the code that is associated with the *employee* class and only need to add a few refinements to the subclasses for hourly and full-time employees, OO development tends to go faster than conventional programming, once a developer has accumulated a library of commonly used classes. When an OO developer begins a new application, he or she usually begins by looking for previously developed classes that contain most of the general code needed for the new application.

Relative to any specific class in a hierarchy, classes that are above the class in the hierarchy—classes the specific class inherits from—are called parent or superclasses, and classes below the specific class are called children or subclasses.

Some OO languages, such as C++, allow a class to inherit from more than one superclass. If this occurs, it's called multiple inheritance. Java, like Smalltalk, only supports single inheritance. But Java also supports interface inheritance, which we'll consider a little later in this chapter.

Figure 2.5 illustrates an example of single class inheritance and specialization. Until now we've been drawing classes as circles with the operations around the outside and the attributes in the center. This model of a class always reminds us of some kind of simple biological organism, and it works well as a way of illustrating how attributes can be encapsulated inside a wall of operations. These diagrams (which we always think of as Taylor diagrams because David Taylor has done so much to popularize them) are good for introducing objects, but they aren't very efficient to draw and they don't scale up to classes with lots of attributes. Thus, in Figure 2.5, we've switched to UML class notation. The large box represents the class and is subdivided into three sections. In the top section we indicate the class name. In the next section we list the class attributes, and in the lower section we list the names of the operations supported by the class.

Consider Figure 2.5. In this case, the *Furniture* class has one attribute and one operation. The *Chairs* class is a subclass of *Furniture*, and therefore it inherits both the attribute and the operation. (We've put the inherited attributes and operations in brackets to remind you that in a real UML diagram they wouldn't be shown. When you look at a real UML diagram, you just assume that anything shown in a superclass is also

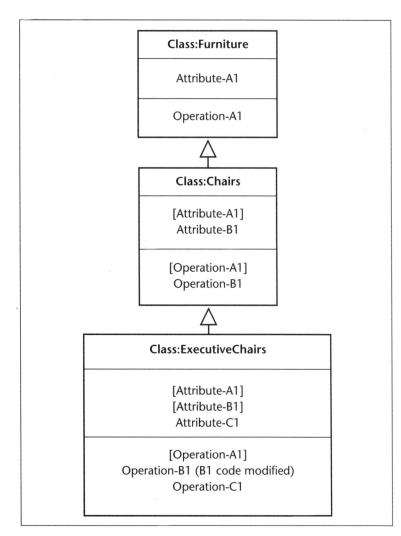

Figure 2.5   *Class inheritance and specialization.*

available in any subclasses.) The *Chairs* class also has a unique attribute and operation of its own. The *ExecutiveChairs* class inherits from both the *Furniture* and the *Chairs* classes. Classes lower in a hierarchy always inherit all the attributes of all the classes above them in the hierarchy. The UML model only shows the operation names, but in a real application, once the code is written to implement a specific operation, both the name and the code are inherited down through the class hierarchy.

Assume that when a developer created the *ExecutiveChairs* class, he or she wanted it to perform just like its parent classes, except that *ExecutiveChairs* would (1) need to keep track of one additional attribute, (2) need one additional operation, and (3) have to perform one operation in a slightly more specific manner. Thus, the developer created the *ExecutiveChairs* class and then added a new attribute and a new operation. The developer also kept the operation name inherited from the *Chairs* class but changed the code associated with operation B-1 so that it performed in a slightly different way than it did in the *Chairs* class. This illustrates the use of inheritance—the creation of a new class that inherits attributes and operations from parent classes. It also illustrates operation specialization where an operation's code is modified so the operation will perform in a more specialized way as a subclass. The developer specialized operation-B1 because he or she knew that instances of the *ExecutiveChairs* class would receive messages addressed to operation-B1 and didn't want the instances to perform in the manner specified by the operation code linked to the name, operation-B1, that was associated with the *Chairs* class. By specializing operation-B1, the developer assured that any instance of the *ExecutiveChairs* class would use the new version of operation-B1, while any other instance of the *Chairs* class would use the old version.

When we actually begin to create UML class diagrams, we won't repeat the attributes and operations that are inherited as we did in Figure 2.5. Normally, to determine all of the attributes and operations of a specific class, you'll need to check both the attributes and operations particular to that class and then also check all of the attributes and operations of any superclasses that that class inherits from. Under those circumstances, if you see an operation name repeated in a subclass, you can be sure that that operation will be a specialized operation.

2.5   Public, Private, and Protected

Now let's qualify what we just said a little more. In most OO languages, including Java, the developer can specify whether an attribute can be accessed by other objects or only be accessed by the operations associated with the specific class (and its subclasses and objects). An attribute that can only be accessed by its own methods is called a private attribute. This is the normal situation and the one we have been assuming in everything we have said above. The alternative is a public attribute. A public attribute would be an attribute that could be modified by operations associated with any class. This would violate encapsulation and should almost never be used in Java programming. So, unless otherwise specified, all attributes referred to in this text are private attributes.

Operations can come in three flavors: public, private, and protected. A public operation is one whose name is exposed to other objects. Thus, a public operation is an operation that can receive messages from other objects.

A private operation is an operation that can't be accessed by other objects. In effect, it's an operation that is only used by other operations associated with the same object for some internal purpose. Imagine you have an object that provides some complex calculation. There is a public operation called ReturnCalculationResult. Whenever I send a message to that operation from an external object, the method is fired, and eventually, the result is returned to the object that sent the query. Now consider that I may not want to write the calculation as a single block of code. And I may need to use several attributes (or even some complex data formats) to keep track of intermediate results. Thus, I create several private operations, termed CalculateStep1, CalculateStep2, and so on.

These operations are private; no outside object knows of their existence.

If I were to decide to change the way I performed the calculation, I would leave the public operation name, Return-CalculationResult, as it is since other objects in my system would depend on it to obtain results they needed. Public operations are promises that my object will perform certain activities when asked. Once established, you should avoid changing them, since other objects in the system have operations that expect to be able to send messages to them. On the other hand, since no one knows of the private operations, I can change them as needed, without needing to change anything else in my system.

Protected operations are a special case. Only subclasses directly descended from the class that contains a protected operation know of its existence and can use it.

When we speak of operations throughout the remainder of this text, we will be referring to public operations, unless otherwise specified. In creating our example, we may very well use private operations, but if we do, we'll be very specific in referring to them as private operations.

One more detail: An operation signature refers to both the operation name and the parameters that must be passed with the message in order for the operation to function. (I might send a message to evoke the Add operation to an object that carries out arithmetic functions for my system. I would need to send, along with the operation name, the numbers to be added; thus, *Add (2, 3)*. The two numbers, in this case, are parameters. In describing my Add operation, I would need to specify the types and number of integers I could send along with the name, Add. When we build interfaces, we specify the public operation names and their parameters. The parameters are important because they assure that the operation will function properly. In addition, they occasionally allow the compiler or interpreter to discriminate between two operation names that are otherwise the same. In fact, if you consider our example in Figure 2.5, you will see that we changed the code associated with operation-B1 in *Class-C*. If an interpreter were trying to decide if a message being sent to operation-B1 were to be sent to *Class-B* or to *Class-C*, it would check the parameters associated with each name to help it decide. In other words, it would check their signatures.

2.6 Interface Inheritance

Interface inheritance isn't as simple or as powerful as class inheritance, but it offers some advantages by avoiding design problems that often occur when programmers use multiple inheritance. Java, for example, supports single class inheritance, but multiple interface inheritance. ActiveX doesn't support class inheritance at all, but does support interface inheritance.

An interface, as it's used when you talk about interface inheritance, is a set of operation signatures (public operation names plus parameters associated with the operation). In more practical terms, an interface is a special type of class—an abstract class—that has a set of operation signatures. A system can have many different interface classes. Java provides a whole library of interface classes. Each interface class can have one or many operation signatures associated with it.

If a class is said to support a specific interface, that means that the developer has incorporated the interface class into the class that is said to support it. This could be represented as an aggregation, as we have indicated on the left side of Figure 2.6. Or the interface class could actually be shown inside the class that supports the interface. In fact, in Java, a single class often supports several different interface classes, so the notation on the left is more efficient. The actual code, however, looks more like the representation on the right, since the interface classes are included in the code specification for the class. An efficient shorthand, for complex diagrams, is to note when standard interface classes are supported by using a "lollypop" symbol to indicate which interface is supported. The lollypop notation is borrowed from Microsoft diagrams where it is used to show that one ActiveX or OLE component is included within a compound document.

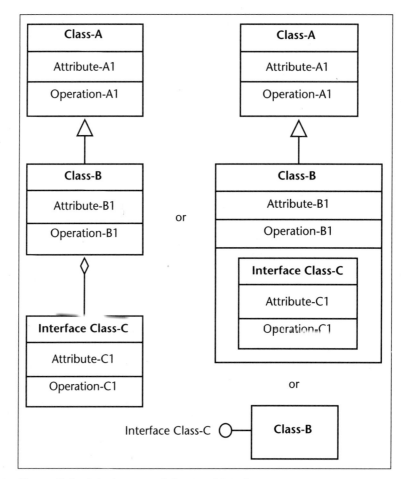

Figure 2.6 *Inheritance and the use of interfaces.*

In most cases an interface class provides operation signatures. The developer is responsible for writing the actual code that will implement each of the signatures included in the interface. In some cases, though not in Java, the developer gets both the signatures and the code to implement them. The former allows the developer more flexibility, but the latter is easier if the interface can be implemented without any changes.

As a general rule, interfaces are predesigned to solve specific problems. By incorporating an interface, you guarantee that your class will be using the exact set of operation signatures that some other class will send messages to once the application is implemented. For example, Java has a thread interface class that provides all the Java threading capability. A class that wants to use threads doesn't need to add any new threading functionality or be a subclass of the thread class. Instead, it can merely implement the interface. This provides the class with all the threading capability it needs.

2.7 Polymorphism

Polymorphism means that the same operation will behave differently when it is applied to the objects of different classes. It also means that different operations associated with different classes can interpret the same message in different ways. Thus, for example, an object can send a PRINT message to several objects, and each object will use its own PRINT operation to execute the message.

Languages vary a great deal in their ability to support different kinds of polymorphism. Java, for example, is more flexible than C++, but not so flexible as some other OO languages.

Typed languages, for example, are less flexible than untyped languages. Say you specify that a *Customer* class will have an attribute called *name*. You might simply specify the attribute name, and leave it at that. Or, you might go ahead and specify that the *name* attribute could only take a value that was a string. If some method tried to associate an integer data type with the attribute name, it would be rejected by the compiler. Similarly, you might want to specify that when an operation passed a message to another object, asking for a person's name, that you would only want the target object to return a string. If developers have to spell out all the data type constraints for all of their classes before the system will compile (or can be interpreted), then the system can't handle certain situations and is therefore less flexible. On the other hand, certain kinds of errors won't occur if the developer has predetermined the data type of each attribute and operation.

C++ is a strongly typed language. It requires that the programmer indicate the data type of each attribute and operation in advance. Smalltalk, on the other hand, is weakly typed. You can omit specifying the data types of attributes if you wish. Thus, in Smalltalk, you could easily write a handwriting recognition application that allowed a user to enter a sales price either by spelling out the number or by entering numerals. If there were no data type associated with the *Sales-Price* attribute, it would accept either value. Smalltalk is more flexible and supports a greater degree of polymorphism.

Java is a nice compromise. It is strongly typed, like C++; you must specify the data type of each attribute and operation in Java. On the other hand, Java, unlike C++, is completely OO and supports the object data type, which C++ doesn't. Since you can easily modify an object, in effect, you can quickly create a new data type that will do whatever you want it to do.

2.8 Beyond the Basics

Object technology is much more complex than we have suggested here. Moreover, each language and each notation supports several variations on the general themes we have discussed. We don't want to go into any more detail at this point, however. We've given you enough to make sense of what we'll be saying in subsequent chapters. If you would like a more detailed discussion of any aspect of object technology, we recommend that you read one of the introductory texts listed in the bibliography at the end of this book.

A Simple Object-Oriented Methodology

There are many different kinds of OO applications being developed. Some are developed in OO languages. Others are being developed with OO modeling tools. Some applications rely on preexisting class libraries, while other applications are developed from scratch. Some applications are designed to handle report generation. Others are designed to be distributed on the Internet, like the example we will consider in this book. Some other applications are designed to handle high-speed transaction processing situations, while still others are designed to control oil refineries in real time. Each of these different types of applications suggests a different developmental approach. The object models used in each type of application, however, can be recorded using the same notation. Different types of applications may require special extensions of the basic UML notation to denote special features of the application, but the basic notation is all the same.

When Grady Booch, James Rumbaugh, and Ivar Jacobson of Rational Software Corporation began to work on a common

OO notation, they made a decision to separate notation from methodology. A notation allows an analyst to describe the problem. In effect, a notational system is a modeling language. A methodology, on the other hand, prescribes a series of steps and actions to take in order to develop an application. A methodology tells a developer what to do, how to do it, and in what order it should be done.

Someone following a methodology will use a notation system when he or she wants to describe a problem, but there is no necessary connection between a specific methodology and a notational system. The three methodologists at Rational Software felt that the time had come to create a common notational system. They did not feel that it was time to create a common OO methodology.

When the OMG decided to try to standardize some elements of OO analysis and design, they also decided to call for the standardization of OO notation and to avoid trying to standardize the steps by which an OO application should be developed.

In this chapter we will describe a generic approach to OO development. Our approach is not a complete OO methodology. We are simply describing a generic approach that highlights the main features that most OO methodologies have in common. Our overall OO development model provides a very general set of developmental phases and allows us to discuss when different diagrams might be used during a generic application development effort.

In addition to describing a simple, generic approach to development, we will consider two alternative ways of actually developing an application. In one case we will discuss writing a program in Java code. In the second, we'll discuss developing the application diagrams with an OO modeling tool and then use the tool to generate the Java code.

As we've stated earlier, this book is designed to introduce you to the new UML notation. It is not designed to teach you a specific OO methodology. Once you have completed this book, you will need to turn to other books if you want to learn a detailed, step-by-step approach to creating a real OO application. Having said that, we'll now describe a very informal approach to creating an OO application.

3.1 An Iterative Approach to Object-Oriented Development

Figure 3.1 provides an overview of what we'll simply call an iterative approach to OO development. Others might call it a cyclical or spiral model, and still others might say that it described a Rapid Application Development (RAD) model. The essence of this approach is that you develop an application by successive approximations. First you develop a core application—an initial prototype. Then you refine the prototype, improving and extending it. Depending on the complexity of the application, you may go through many cycles or iterations.

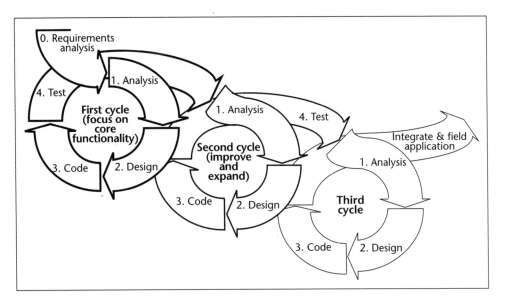

Figure 3.1   *An iterative approach to OO development.*

Some methodologists use the term *prototype* to refer to a single application that is developed prior to developing a complete application. Others use prototype to refer to any of several approximations that are developed in order to gradually expand and enhance a core application into a full-blown application. We'll use prototype in this second sense. Thus, we would say that each cycle results in a prototype and that you keep developing approximations or prototypes until you finally get an application that you regard as complete.

You begin by defining the scope and requirements for the entire project and creating a high-level description of the entire application. You document what the system will do, who will use it, and what constraints or performance criteria it will need to meet to be judged successful. The requirement statement serves as a "contract" between the users who request the system and the developers who agree to build it. Next, you will probably lay out a high-level object model of all the business objects that will be required for your application.

Following this, once you have a good idea of the entire scope of your application, you select a portion of the entire application to develop first. Some people suggest you should begin by developing the hardest part of the application first. If there is any uncertainty about whether the application can be developed or not and you tackle the trickiest part and succeed, then you will be confident you can do the remainder. For example, many large system development efforts fail because developers design systems without adequately considering all the infrastructure issues involved in actually deploying the system. Thus, developers of large OO systems often develop an initial prototype system that doesn't do much, but demonstrates that it can interface with all the infrastructure elements it will need to deal with in order to assure that the overall infrastructure design is adequate.

In other cases, a portion of the system that supports some of the functionality that the end users are most interested in is developed first to assure that the system will satisfy the end users. However you approach it, there should be some overall plan that determines what part of the application you will develop during the first prototyping cycle, the second cycle, and so on. Obviously, this can change. As you develop your first approximation, you may identify problems that require you to revise your overall design. Still, when you begin, you should have some idea of the cycles you plan to go through as you successively approximate your final product.

3.2 Phases of a Development Cycle

To repeat: During your initial requirements effort you develop an overview of the entire system. Then, in your initial analysis phase, you subdivide the system and select a portion of it to develop during the first cycle.

During analysis you focus on designing an ideal or logical system that satisfies the requirements statement without being overly concerned with implementation considerations. During design you modify your work to take real-world constraints into account. During the design phase you design a concrete, physical system. During the coding phase you write code. Then you test the initial prototype. In some cases you will be testing to see if the prototype satisfies user needs, and in other cases you will be testing to see how it will work in the environment in which you expect to field the system. In some cases you will be able to field the first prototype of the application and solve at least a portion of the problem.

After you are satisfied with the first prototype, you proceed to the second analysis phase. In this round, you begin by reexamining your overall analysis in light of what you learned as you developed the initial prototype. Usually, you will want to make at least some modifications. In other cases, you will decide, as a result of testing the prototype, that you should completely redesign the basic class model or even switch to a completely different application architecture before you continue. This may sound discouraging, but it's far better to throw away a prototype and start over than to develop a complete application and then discover it won't do what it's expected to do.

Once you have settled on the overall application architecture you will use during the second cycle, you're ready to expand your first prototype or to begin to prototype another portion of the application. This is how iteration works: you build a prototype, test it, modify and extend it, test it some more, and keep going around until you have completed your entire application and are ready to field it.

Figure 3.2 provides a more detailed look at the first iteration cycle. In this illustration we've focused on a single cycle, and we've added some details.

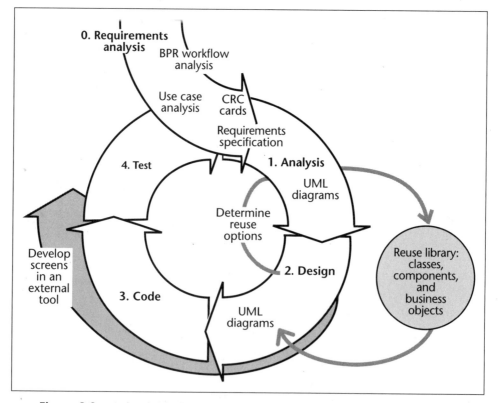

Figure 3.2   *A detailed look at one cycle of the iterative approach to OO development.*

3.2.1 *Requirements Analysis*

Our first cycle is unique because it begins with a requirements phase that precedes the analysis phase. In effect, the requirements phase is a kind of front-end analysis. Different things can occur during this preliminary phase. Some companies begin with a formal Business Process Reengineering (BPR) study. Others create scenarios, use cases, or CRC cards to help get an overview of the problem. In any case, this initial state ends with some kind of requirements specification—a document that provides an overall description of the application to be developed.

BPR means many things to many people. For some it describes a process whereby the entire company is studied and then redesigned. For others it is a synonym for undertaking a software front-end analysis. We intend to use it to mean something between these extremes. For our purposes, a BPR study is undertaken by a joint committee that includes some business managers, some users, and some people from the company's information systems group. The purpose of the BPR study is to take a broad look at a company process. The existing business process is examined, and alternatives are considered, costed, and compared. The goal of a BPR effort is to determine whether there are ways to reorganize the process in order to significantly improve the way the tasks are done, the quality of the product, or the satisfaction experienced by the customer. When you think of a BPR effort in this way, software development is only a part of an overall BPR effort. Product redesign, job redesign, and major changes in the way work flows through the organization are all just as important as changes in the software systems used in the process. Thus, a BPR effort will likely result in changes in many different aspects of a company process. Some of the changes, however, will call for the development of new software.

If you undertake a BPR effort and identify software that needs to be developed, or if you are simply assigned a software project, once you begin to focus on defining the scope of a specific software development effort, you will probably want to undertake a use case analysis. Almost all formal OO development efforts begin with at least an informal, high-level use case analysis. And, if you wish, you can extend this initial use case analysis by breaking the application up and doing finer grained use case diagrams of the various subsections of the application. In addition, you can use ideal object models to convert use cases into rudimentary class diagrams.

Whether you begin with a BPR analysis or explore the problem by creating use case diagrams and descriptions, sooner or later you will want to write a formal requirements statement. The requirements statement can be a one-page overview, or it can be a very complex document. Its overall purpose is to say what the new software system will do. Requirements statements are often accompanied or supplemented by scenarios describing specific sequences that follow users from when they make inputs until they obtain outputs from the system. Many developers undertake use case analysis simply because they consider it a particularly effective way to generate scenarios.

Another way of developing an overview of your system and actually developing an analysis of the classes you will need in your system at the same time is to use an informal approach referred to as CRC cards. In this case a group works together to construct scenarios and to simultaneously identify the classes that will be needed to implement the scenarios.

A good requirements statement should provide a sufficiently complete description of the application to be developed to enable the developers to consider how the application can be modularized. This isn't important for small applications, but if the application is large at all, then it's best to develop it by means of successive approximations. To do this, the complete application is subdivided, and the first effort focuses on developing a prototype of only a portion of the complete system. This approach would not work very well if you were using a conventional procedural language, but it works well when you undertake an OO approach because it's much easier to modify and expand an OO application.

3.2.2   *The Analysis Phase*

Once you begin the OO analysis phase, there are five groups of UML diagrams that you can use. These diagrams constitute the OMG UML notational system. In addition, each of the basic diagrams can be modified or extended in various ways to handle special problems. Some diagrams, for example, the class diagram and the sequence diagram, are used over and over throughout the development effort and keep getting expanded and refined. Others, for example, the collaboration diagram and the state diagram, are only used when you encounter particular problems and need to define a specific object or interaction in more detail. We'll provide an overview of all the UML diagrams in Chapter 4 and then consider each in more detail in later chapters.

You will notice that we have not laid out a specific series of steps. We have mentioned several types of different approaches to front-end analysis, including BPR, CRC cards, and others, that are not formally included in the UML system. We'll consider all these techniques, but we don't expect that you'll use them all. In effect, we're presenting you with several alternatives. There's no one right way to do OO analysis. We'll simply show you how the various methods and diagrams work and leave it to you to decide what combination works best for you.

Analysis versus Design

In traditionally structured "waterfall" methodologies, gurus used to insist that developers maintain a rigid distinction between analysis and design. Analysis was when you figured out what the application should do. Design was when you decided how to do it. By keeping analysis and design separate, you kept your options open. And you avoided situations in which you created systems hampered by the constraints imposed by some unspoken, but assumed, system design. In reality, things were never as neat as the gurus would have liked. It's hard to undertake an analysis in the abstract. The real business situation always does, in fact, impose some constraints, and only fools ignore constraints that they know they will have to live with when they start writing code. So a sharp distinction between analysis and design has always been more a goal than a reality.

In OO systems development, the split between analysis and design becomes even harder to maintain. If you undertake a BPR project, you often end up agreeing to an architecture for the new software system before you've even begun to analyze the nature of the specific application. More important, if you develop an overview of your system and then break it into modules so you can prototype one module at a time, you are already assuming some kind of design. And, of course, when you do iterative or cyclical development, as we recommend in this book, you will be constantly shifting between analysis and design. Moreover, it will get even more complex as companies begin to rely on class libraries and reuse software components that already incorporate design assumptions.

Having said all that, we still recommend that when you are in the analysis phase of a project, and especially during the first analysis phase, when you are conceptualizing your first general object model, that you think of the classes in your model as abstractly as you can. There are many different ways to do the same thing. Design always imposes efficiency considerations that require you to modify good class models in ways an OO purist wouldn't recommend. Still, in the early phase of each cycle, when you are focused on the class diagram, try to create the cleanest, most logical model possible. Clean models make it easy to see whether you've considered everything that needs to be included. Later, during design, you can always figure out how to rearrange your model to make it more efficient.

One of the advantages of a cyclical approach that moves from analysis to design and then, when you begin the next cycle, returns to analysis, is the opportunity that it affords developers to reconsider what they have done during the design phase and clean it up. In large system development efforts there is a natural tendency for things to get complex. Complex applications, however, are harder to maintain. Thus, something you should do during each analysis phase is review what you have done to date and see if you can simplify your application. Sometimes this simply involves cleaning up the names being used. In other cases it involves remodularizing the system or revising a group of class associations to provide a cleaner way of handling a problem. (Smalltalk developers talk of "refactoring"—a process during which they step back and reconsider the overall structure of an application and then modify it to make it easier to understand.)

UML offers a number of ways of modeling system architectures. In some cases you will use UML package diagrams just after you do use case analysis. In other cases, you won't consider packaging until you get to design or development. In this book we'll try to avoid talking about architectural issues till we get to design, even though it will prove impossible in some situations. In those cases we'll simply admit that we are making assumptions and hope we can make them without committing ourselves to too much before we understand the full scope of the application.

Business Objects versus Infrastructure Objects

In analyzing and designing an OO application, you'll avoid a lot of confusion if you make a distinction between classes that refer to real things in the company environment—which we'll call business objects—and classes that are used to facilitate software processes, which we'll call infrastructure objects.

Business objects are the kinds of things that end users talk about, and they are the classes that you will want to identify during your initial analysis effort. Business objects include things like employees, sales orders, accounts, machines, rejection slips, and company sites.

Infrastructure objects are classes that the developer creates to assure that the software works. Users don't usually know or care about these classes. Infrastructure classes do things like put windows on the screen, manage the sequencing of other classes, transfer data between a server application and a database, and provide a time stamp for orders. You usually identify a few infrastructure classes during the initial analysis phase, but most infrastructure classes are ignored during analysis and are identified, instead, when you reach the design phase and begin to consider where different parts of the application will reside.

Different developers use different terms, but the important thing to keep in mind is that the initial analysis models should focus primarily on objects that represent real things in the corporate environment. Classes that handle data transfers and bookkeeping tasks should be largely ignored during the initial analysis phase and then considered in detail during the design phase.

One of the misleading things about some analysis books is that they focus almost entirely on analysis and therefore on business objects. This might seem to suggest that OO applications have a relatively small number of very high level classes. In fact, most OO applications have a few high-level business classes and more infrastructure classes that actually handle all the behind-the-scenes work.

In this book we'll begin by focusing on the business objects that are developed during the analysis phase of any development effort. Then, when we turn to the design phase, we'll consider what additional classes will be needed to actually implement the application we are building and offer some advice on how to identify and model infrastructure classes.

3.2.3 *The Design Phase*

Design begins when you shift your focus from the logical relationships between objects to the physical layout of your systems. Unlike earlier methodologies, where you usually had to shift to an entirely new notation to record design decisions, an OO notation is unchanged when you move from analysis to design. Indeed, that's one of the reasons it's so easy to slip back and forth.

In design, you simply extend the diagrams you used in analysis and add information. Specifically, you add infrastructure objects to the business objects you developed during analysis. You also get much more specific about how operations will accomplish specific tasks. And you make concrete decisions about the physical layout of your system, what hardware you will use, and how your software will get modularized and which modules will be placed on which machines.

In addition to extending the system in the ways we've mentioned, you'll want to develop users' screens, Web pages, and any other interfaces required by your system. In OO systems, you also need to face some serious "buy versus build" decisions. Can you incorporate existing classes into your software? Can you reuse components? All these practical issues need to get sorted out during the design phase.

Screen and Other Interface Development

In some application development efforts, the code for the application interface is developed right along with the rest of the application. The windows are objects of classes created specifically to provide an interface to the application. In other cases, special tools are used to develop interfaces. Java provides its own interface development framework—the Abstract Windowing Toolkit (AWT). Other interface tools are tailored for specific operating system environments. Some OO modeling tools provide special interface development facilities. Or the developer might use supplemental tools, such as Visual Basic, or PowerBuilder for interface development. Or you might use an HTML interface tool if you are developing a Web application. In effect, the screen development effort is often done in parallel with the basic development effort. If the application is to be produced in several iterations, screens are typically developed for each prototype as it is designed and coded. We've indicated this in Figure 3.2 by showing a secondary arrow that begins during the design phase and continues past the coding phase.

Reuse and Components

In addition to other considerations, in all OO development efforts, there is the question of reuse. Most companies that have been involved in OO development efforts have at least some components that they use for interface development.

In your first OO projects, we recommend you ignore the possibility of creating classes for reuse. Concentrate, instead, on developing an object model that works for your specific project. Use other classes and components from the Java Development Kit (JDK) or other class libraries, as appropriate. After you have used and modified classes a bit, you will begin to understand how to generalize a design and create classes for reuse. It's not trivial, however, and if you try developing classes for reuse while you are still trying to understand how to create classes and reuse existing class libraries, you will probably find yourself overwhelmed.

While you shouldn't worry about creating classes for reuse too early, you should begin to use existing classes and components as soon as possible. The reuse of existing classes will significantly reduce the time it takes you to develop an application.

When OO developers start talking about the reuse of class libraries, environments, components, or frameworks, the conversation is usually rather imprecise. No one has a very clear idea of how to classify the different types of objects developers commonly reuse. Similarly, no two people seem to use the word "component" in the same way.

Figure 3.3 illustrates some of the ways that the terms *object* and *component* can be used. Remember that an object can be a single entity with attributes and operations, or it can be a composite object that contains several other objects.

An OO language, such as Java, provides a class library that includes classes ranging from simple classes to specialized language classes. These are collectively known as the Java Development Kit, which we'll consider in more detail in Chapter 5. Sun, which produces Java, also provides some additional sets of classes for more complex problems. Some tool kits include classes for windows development.

In general, programmers tend to call classes used for windows development, components. Java's Abstract Windowing Toolkit (AWT) is a collection of JavaBeans. Java applets function as a kind of component. JavaBeans is Sun's official component model, just as ActiveX is Microsoft's component model. Some developers might argue that components aren't

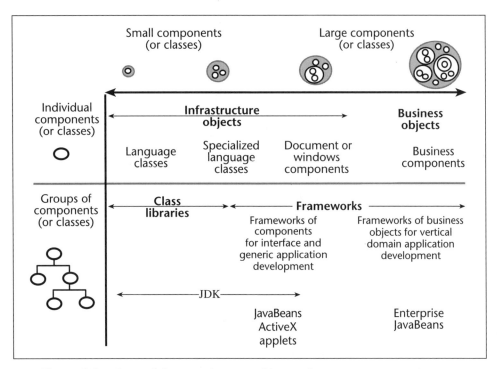

Figure 3.3   *Some of the ways the terms* object *and* component *are used.*

always classes, and that's certainly true in the case of ActiveX. Sometimes components are programming modules that simply have "classlike" interfaces.

Large classes or components that equate to a basic business concept, like employee, account, or machine, are often called business objects or business components. This is the area most companies focus on when it comes to developing classes for reuse. In fact, there are still some theoretical concepts to work out in this area. On the other hand, most programmers get lots of practical reuse out of language class libraries and mid-sized classes or components. Sun has recently introduced an expanded component model, called Enterprise JavaBeans, which is specifically designed to use for business objects.

In general, when people speak of groups of classes or components, they use the terms *library* or *framework*. We're sorry there are so many terms that more or less mean the same thing, but that's the way it is. Don't let it confuse you too much.

Sun makes its Java class library, JDK, available for free. Most OO language tools, such as Cafe and J++, include additional class libraries for windows development and for linking to databases, and so on.

Some companies have also begun to develop libraries or frameworks of business objects that can be reused. If you have class or component libraries available, you will need to determine whether any components or business objects already exist that you can use. If components are to be used, the design effort changes from designing new objects to identifying and modifying preexisting objects. At the moment, most companies practice a combination of both.

Just as we can distinguish between business objects that describe actual entities and processes in the company environment from infrastructure objects that are simply used to handle the details of programming, we can also distinguish between components that function as business objects and components that provide infrastructure services. Most components currently available are designed to handle infrastructure details. In the future, however, companies are likely to develop components that capture the functionality of an employee class or a machine class. These high-level components will make it possible to snap together high-level analysis models without having to write code and should significantly reduce the time it takes to create new applications. At the moment, however, developers usually need to create the business objects for the initial analysis model and can then use components to reduce the effort during the design phase.

Some vendors and companies group components or business objects into sets that work together, and they often use the term *frameworks* to describe these sets of components or business objects. Thus there can be component frameworks designed to handle infrastructure issues—such as a framework to make it easy to link to any of several databases and generate SQL code as needed. Other component frameworks are made up of a mix of high-level business components and infrastructure components and deal with things like payroll systems or factory floor scheduling.

IBM has developed a complex, layered set of Java components to aid companies in large–scale application development. The initial release of the overall collection of components, referred to as the San Francisco Project, is pictured in Figure 3.4. In effect, IBM has completed the foundation and utilities layer and the common business object layer, as well as a set of APIs that lie between these two layers. IBM has also completed one of the business process frameworks: the general ledger framework. Source code is available for the general ledger framework. The initial delivery consists of some 3100 Java classes, including some 23,700 methods and 275,000 lines of source code. Full installation requires 250MB of disk space. Binary code is available for the foundation and common business object layers.

IBM expects that companies using the foundations and a business process component such as general ledger will have

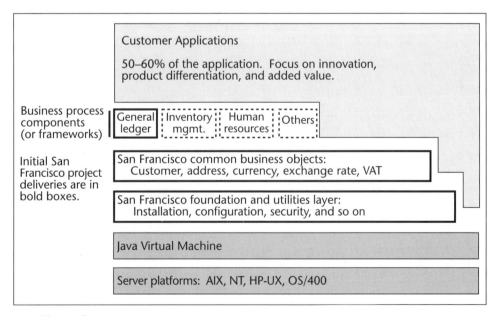

Figure 3.4   *The components in IBM's San Francisco Project.*

40% of the application complete. Moreover, since all the IBM components have been extensively tested, IBM hopes this approach will allow companies to avoid lots of the infrastructure problems that typically plague new developers when they attempt distributed applications.

If companies are interested in developing business objects or business-level components for reuse in subsequent projects, they must be especially careful in developing their initial classes to assure they will have the generality required for extensive reuse. Most companies find that if this type of effort is to be undertaken, a separate individual should be appointed to take responsibility for identifying, polishing, and storing classes for reuse. Moreover, most developers who try to develop classes for reuse find that they must do it on two or three different application development efforts before they understand what kind of general classes they need. Suffice it to say that this task is beyond the scope of this book.

We have indicated the use of components in Figure 3.2 by adding a component and business object library to the right of our development cycle. An arrow begins in the design phase and leads to the library and back to the design process to suggest that developers should look for components and business class libraries during design. We'll consider many of these issues in more detail in Chapter 13 when we return to design issues.

3.2.4 *The Coding Phase*

The next phase in the development cycle begins when you start writing code. During the design phase you will have specified all the objects in the system, and you probably will have identified all the attributes and most of the operations. You may even have written pseudocode to specify what each operation will do.

In OO development, the class structures and names that you have created during the analysis and design phase become code elements during the coding phase. Thus, once again, there is no sharp break between design and coding. It's simply a matter of getting more specific about how each operation is going to be carried out and finally expressing the operations in an OO language.

If you are doing your development in an OO modeling tool, at this point you could generate code and it would include all your class structures and the names, data types, and other information you have specified about the attributes and operations. During the coding phase you need to complete the actual code required to implement each operation and write any specific code needed for interfaces or linkages.

We won't consider coding in any detail in this book, although we will provide the annotated code for the sample application that we will discuss throughout the book so that you can see how we carried that specific application from design to code.

3.2.5   *The Testing Phase*

The final phase in the cycle involves testing the code you have developed to see if it functions properly. Depending on the nature of the first prototype, testing may be a formal affair or it may involve fielding your prototype application and determining how users react to it.

Once again, we won't spend much time on testing, since it is well described by others and has little to do with UML notation, as such. The important thing, for our purposes, is simply to remind you that, in an iterative development cycle, testing leads right back to analysis and design. You test your prototype, and then, according to what you find, you change your original model, or you begin to expand and enhance it, and the cycle begins again.

Of course, each subsequent cycle is a little more confused, from a traditional perspective, than the last because some analysis, design, and coding has already been done. On each subsequent cycle, you examine all the analysis and design work you did in previous cycles and then extend it. In many cases you will find yourself working, once again, with the same diagrams you used in the previous phase and simply modifying objects to provide more functionality.

4

The Unified Modeling Language

I n this chapter we'll present a very general overview of the UML notation. We'll describe each UML diagram in a superficial way and consider how you might use each diagram during the application development process.

4.1 UML Symbols

Before looking at UML diagrams, it might help to consider the nature of the symbols used in the diagrams. UML symbols are of three basic types: core (or first class) symbols; more or less specialized extensions to the core symbols, called adornments; and very specialized symbols, which are termed stereotypes. The core symbols are broadly divided into two groups: modeling symbols and relationship symbols.

We've illustrated the relationships between some of the common UML symbols in Figure 4.1. Notice that class, state, and use case are core model elements and association and dependency are core relationships. You can adorn a class by adding information about its attributes and operations. If you want to use really specialized versions of classes, you are into the range of stereotypes, as, for example, OOSE's control and entity classes. In a similar way, a straight line is an association. Placing a diamond on the line—an adornment—indicates that the association is an aggregation. Adorning the line with numbers indicates how many instances are involved in the relationship.

Since this book is an informal approach to UML, we won't discuss all the UML symbols in detail. Nor will we draw sharp lines between core elements and adornments. As a rule of thumb, symbols used in different diagrams tend to be core symbols. We will introduce most of the UML core symbols. We won't begin to introduce all of the adornments or the stereotypes. We will always note when symbols are stereotypes. That said, let's consider the different sets of UML diagrams.

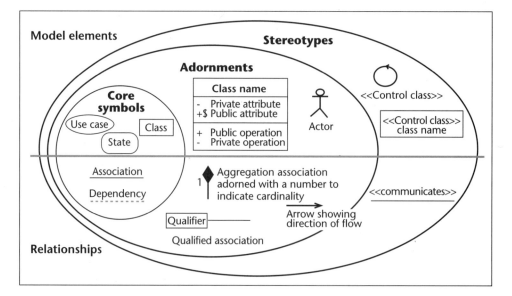

Figure 4.1   *UML notational symbols.*

4.2 **UML Diagrams**

Five different groups of UML diagrams offer five different ways of looking at the same problem. By creating the diagrams in each group, you can analyze a problem from different perspectives. The UML diagrams are grouped as follows:

- Use Case Diagrams
  - Use case diagrams
  - Use case descriptions
  - (OOSE) Ideal object models
- Static Structure Diagrams
  - Class diagrams
  - Object diagrams
- Interaction Diagrams
  - Sequence diagrams
  - Collaboration diagrams
- State Diagrams
  - State diagrams
  - Activity diagrams
- Implementation Diagrams
  - Package diagrams
  - Component diagrams
  - Deployment diagrams

A complete UML analysis and design documentation set consists of all of the UML diagrams you have developed. We'll consider each group of diagrams, in turn.

4.2.1 *Use Case Diagrams*

The UML *use case diagram* can be used to describe the main processes in a system and the interactions between the processes (use cases) and external systems or individuals, called actors. Once the use case overview is developed it can be expanded to show more detail, including subprocesses and processes that are sometimes added to other processes. To define an interaction between a use case and an actor, you write a generic scenario, called a *use case description*. The use case description is a series of sentences describing each step in the interaction. The use case description is subsequently used to generate specific scenarios and interaction diagrams.

Although not an official part of the UML notation, there are extensions for the UML notation that allow developers to define *ideal object models*, which were originally defined in Jacobson's OOSE methodology. In effect, an ideal object model suggests some of the high-level classes that will be needed to implement a use case. When using ideal object models, you usually develop one for each use case. Ideal object models provide a nice intermediate step to make the transition from use cases to class diagrams easier.

4.2.2 *Static Structure Diagrams*

The UML *class diagram* is one of the two central diagrams in UML development. The class diagram shows the classes that will be included in your application and the relationships between classes. You create other diagrams primarily to refine your understanding of what is going on in the class diagram. Moreover, there are several class diagrams—a high-level class diagram that identifies a few classes and the basic relationships between them and then a whole series of more complex class diagrams that incorporate more and more information. Indeed, if you are creating a very large system, you will probably divide your system into modules, called packages in UML, and do one class diagram for each package.

UML does not define a specific object diagram but, in fact, uses informal object diagrams. In some cases you create object diagrams to show the interaction of a set of objects. In other cases, objects are added to class diagrams to show how specific objects will be used within the context of the overall class model. The most common type of object diagram in UML is called a collaboration diagram, which we'll consider in the next section. You only do object diagrams when you encounter special problems and need to analyze how a specific set of objects will function. In many cases, it's easier to develop a prototype and test your assumptions than to worry about diagramming object interactions.

4.2.3   *Interaction Diagrams*

The *sequence diagram* (or event trace diagram or interaction diagram) shows the relationships between specific objects. The sequence diagram represents objects as vertical lines and shows how messages are sent between the various objects. (The messages are sometimes called events. Technically, the line shows a message passing between two objects. An event occurs at the instant when the target object responds to the message.) A sequence diagram allows you to study how a set of objects interact in time. You do not need to do sequence diagrams for every set of objects that interact, but most OO developers rely on sequence diagrams second only to class diagrams. When in doubt about how some set of objects will interact, prepare a sequence diagram.

A sequence diagram should correspond to a specific scenario. Sometimes developers prepare sequence diagrams from scenarios and then compare them to the class diagram to see how they correspond. At other times, developers prepare sequence diagrams right after preparing use cases and scenarios and then use them to prepare the class diagram. There is no correct order in which to do this, except that you need to know the classes in your system before you can prepare a sequence diagram, so most developers begin by preparing at least a very informal class diagram before starting on a sequence diagram.

A *collaboration diagram* is a cross between an object diagram and a sequence diagram. Some or all of the objects from a scenario are shown as they would be in an object diagram. Then, instead of showing lines that merely link the objects, arrows are inserted and numbered to illustrate a specific sequence of events. By following the numbered arrows, you can follow the movement of messages during the course of a scenario. Thus, like a sequence diagram, one collaboration diagram describes a specific scenario.

4.2.4 *State Diagrams*

A *state diagram* (or Harel diagram) provides a very detailed picture of how a specific object changes states. (A state refers to the value that is associated with a specific attribute of an object and to any actions or side effects that occur when the attribute's value changes.) Imagine an object with an attribute called color. Each time you flicked a switch, the value of the attribute would change, always going from red to blue to white and then back to red. If you wanted to document this specific activity, you would use a state diagram. Many systems are developed without the use of state diagrams. On the other hand, they are indispensable if you are working on real-time process control applications or systems that involve concurrent processing.

According to Rational's UML documentation, an *activity diagram* is a special type of state diagram. We've included it within the general state diagram group, just as the UML documentation does. But we have to tell you that this only makes sense in a narrow, logical way. A real state diagram describes a detailed picture of how a specific object changes state. An activity diagram, on the other hand, describes activities and flows of data or decisions between activities. In effect, activity diagrams are the diagrams used in most workflow analysis tools. Activity diagrams provide very broad views of business processes. Or they can be used to break out the activities that occur within a use case. Activity diagrams commonly show many different activities that will be handled by lots of different objects.

4.2.5 *Implementation Diagrams*

Implementation diagrams capture design information. Once again, we've grouped three diagrams in this category, just as Rational's UML documentation does. First, *package diagrams* are used to show how classes can be divided into modules and to indicate high-level relationships between packages. Packages are used strictly for logical modularization. If we had our choice, we'd include package diagrams with class and object diagrams.

Component diagrams are used to show how code is actually divided into modules. In many applications there is a one-to-one relationship between package diagrams and component diagrams. The package diagram shows the logical divisions, and the component shows that you actually went ahead and implemented it as you had proposed via the package diagram. Of course, you might have changed your mind during design and moved some classes to a different module when you actually compiled the code, and in that case, the component diagram would be different. Component diagrams are not normally used to represent smaller components, such as ActiveX or JavaBean components, used in user interface design.

The third type of implementation diagram, *deployment diagrams,* are used to describe the physical architecture of the application. Nodes in a deployment diagram usually represent hardware platforms. It is common to place component diagrams on top of deployment diagrams to indicate which modules of code will go on which hardware platforms.

4.2.6   *The Diagramming Process*

In all cases, if you are working on a large system, you will need to prepare many different versions of all of these various UML diagrams to capture all of the information you need for a full understanding of your system. The important thing is that you don't have to develop all of the possible diagrams before you can begin to develop code and test your assumptions by running a prototype version of your system. You begin by limiting the system you want to develop during your first iteration and then only develop the diagrams you need to understand your first prototype system. After testing the prototype, you revise your diagrams to capture what you have learned, and then you expand existing diagrams and prepare new diagrams to analyze your second prototype, and so on.

4.3 Additional Diagrams and Notations

In addition to the UML diagrams we have just described, we use and explain three other types of diagramming notations in this book: LOVEM (Line of Vision Enterprise Methodology) BPR workflow diagrams, CRC cards, and ideal object diagrams.

Increasingly, companies are using some kind of BPR analysis to take a broad look at their business processes before they focus on specific software development efforts. Most BPR projects document the results of their effort by means of workflow diagrams. A LOV diagram is a stereotype of a UML activity diagram.

One of the most popular workflow diagramming approaches is the *LOVEM* BPR workflow diagrams (or Rummler-Brache diagrams) that IBM and others use to show how activities flow from customers to others inside an organization. They are a popular way for BPR specialists to analyze existing business processes and to determine how those processes might be streamlined. We've included LOVEM diagrams to show how a workflow analysis might complement a UML software development effort.

CRC cards are literally 3-inch x 5-inch cards that some analysts use to help them work with users to identify the initial classes in an application. This technique, though informal, is popular because it is so simple and because it usually gets good results. It's an especially useful way to get a group of people thinking in an OO way. We've included a chapter on CRC cards primarily to provide some additional help for those new to OO development.

We have already mentioned that *ideal object models* are a special kind of diagram used in Jacobson's OOSE methodology. They weren't directly incorporated into the UML notation. Ideal object diagrams are a stereotype that falls between use case diagrams and UML class diagrams. They provide one more good way for new developers to quickly see what classes might be needed for a specific application.

4.4   A Generic Approach to Object-Oriented Development

Figure 4.2 illustrates one way of looking at the relationships between the various diagrams. The figure assumes you begin by using BPR, use cases, or CRC cards to identify the overall structure of your problem and to develop some scenarios. It also assumes that you will develop a requirements statement that states what your finished system will do.

Once you have created your requirements statement, Figure 4.2 suggests which UML diagrams you will use to analyze, design, and develop your application. The bold arrows suggest major paths. Most developers create at least one use case diagram and several scenarios. They also create several sequence and class diagrams. The sequence and especially the class diagrams are at the heart of your analysis and design effort. They just keep getting more elaborate as you understand your application better. The other diagrams are used less frequently. Each has special functions and tends to get used according to the specific type of application you are developing. Again, there is no set order in which you use any specific diagram. Large systems development efforts often generate hundreds of diagrams and use all of the various diagramming types. Small systems often get by with two or three class diagrams, two or three sequence diagrams, and nothing else. Most application development efforts, of course, fall in between these extremes.

Neither the OMG nor Rational Software advocates a specific development methodology. Indeed, Booch, Rumbaugh, and Jacobson have each recommended different methodologies. And many other OO methodologists recommend still other developmental sequences.

4.5   A UML Notation Job Aid

Throughout the chapters in which we talk about UML diagrams, we'll be introducing lots of names and diagramming conventions. To make it easier to remember the conventions

Figure 4.2   *Relationships between various UML diagrams.*

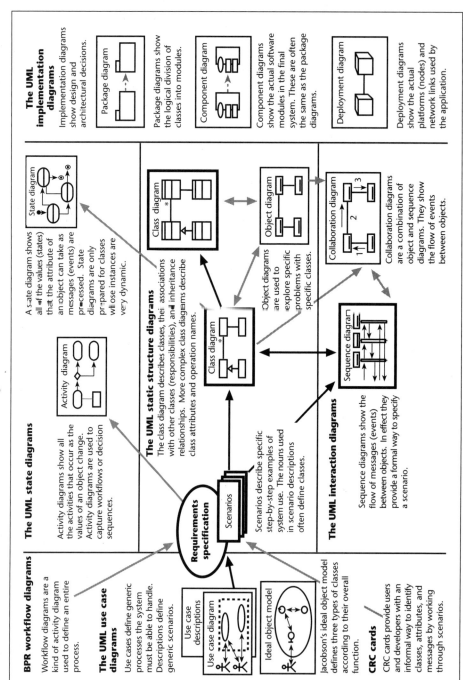

BPR workflow diagrams

Workflow diagrams are a kind of activity diagram used to define an entire process.

The UML use case diagrams

Use cases define generic processes the system must be able to handle. Descriptions define generic scenarios.

CRC cards

CRC cards provide users and developers with an informal way to identify classes, attributes, and messages by working through scenarios.

Jacobson's ideal object model defines three types of classes according to their overall function.

Use case descriptions

Use case diagram

Ideal object model

Requirements specification

Scenarios

Scenarios describe specific step-by-step examples of system use. The nouns used in scenario descriptions often define classes.

The UML state diagrams

Activity diagrams show all the activities that occur as the values of an object change. Activity diagrams are used to capture workflows or decision sequences.

Activity diagram

State diagram

A state diagram shows all of the values (states) that the attribute of an object can take as messages (events) are processed. State diagrams are only prepared for classes whose instances are very dynamic.

The UML static structure diagrams

The class diagram describes classes, their associations with other classes (responsibilities), and inheritance relationships. More complex class diagrams describe class attributes and operation names.

Class diagram

Class diagram

Object diagram

Object diagrams are used to explore specific problems with specific classes.

Collaboration diagram

Collaboration diagrams are a combination of object and sequence diagrams. They show the flow of events between objects.

The UML interaction diagrams

Sequence diagrams show the flow of messages (events) between objects. In effect they provide a formal way to specify a scenario.

Sequence diagram

The UML implementation diagrams

Implementation diagrams show design and architectural decisions.

Package diagram

Package diagrams show the logical division of classes into modules.

Component diagram

Component diagrams show the actual software modules in the final system. These are often the same as the package diagrams.

Deployment diagram

Deployment diagrams show the actual platforms (nodes) and network links used by the application.

while you prepare your initial diagrams, we've prepared a job aid with the basic symbols on it and included it in this book as Appendix B. If you are going to prepare diagrams by hand, you can photocopy it and use it as a job aid when you begin preparing UML diagrams. If you use an OO modeling tool, the tool will probably provide palettes of UML notational elements that will serve as a job aid when you go to draw the diagrams within the tool environment.

Coding Applications in Java

There are many ways to develop an application. You could begin and do the entire application by hand, drawing each UML diagram with a pencil on paper and then working with a programming tool to create code for the application. If you were doing a Java application like the case study we will use in this book, you might develop the Java code directly. Or you might develop the Java code with one of the popular Java visual programming environments that have been introduced and are designed to be used in conjunction with Internet development (e.g., Borland's JBuilder and Latte, Microsoft's Visual J++ Pro, Symantec's Cafe, Rogue Wave Software's Jfactory, or IBM's VisualAge for Java). These tools usually support both Java development and HTML browser interface development.

If you have a large application, or you are going to produce several different Java applications that will share common elements, you might consider using an OO modeling tool (e.g., Cayenne's ObjectTeam, Rational's Rose for Java, Platinum

Technology's Paradigm Plus, Popkin Software's SA/Object Architect, or Select's Select Enterprise). With a modeling tool, you create the UML diagrams using a drawing environment within the modeling tool product. Once you are satisfied with the UML diagrams, you have the modeling tool product generate the actual code you need for your application.

For a small application, most programmers will probably find it easier to program directly in a language. Once the application begins to get complex, however, and several developers intend to work on the same application together, an OO modeling tool has distinct advantages. Similarly, if the application is likely to change a lot during the development process or if you plan on using lots of classes that you have already used in previous applications, then an OO modeling tool becomes an option you should consider.

In the process of developing the example used in this book, one author programmed the application directly. The other developed the same application using Popkin Software's OO modeling tool, SA/ObjectArchitect. In subsequent chapters, when we describe the use of UML and the development of the application, we'll begin by describing a specific diagram in UML. Next we'll consider how we could use that diagram to develop our sample application. We'll begin by discussing the development effort as if we were developing the application directly, drawing the diagrams and then creating the Java code in a programming environment. Then we'll review how we would have accomplished the same task using Popkin Software's SA/Object Architect.

The application we'll develop in this book, by itself, isn't complex enough to justify using an OO modeling tool. In spite of that, you'll see how the modeling tool simplifies the development task by automatically generating new diagrams from earlier diagrams. Moreover, it insists on consistency that a developer using an informal method might easily ignore. Later, he or she might have to spend additional time checking and rechecking names to debug inconsistencies. Clearly, the author who worked directly in Java had an easier time of it on the simple application we describe. He drew the UML diagrams quickly and then wrote Java code. If we were going to develop several applications, each involving sales orders and customers, however, the author with the diagrams already in the OO modeling tool would have a distinct edge when it came to generating new applications that reused parts of the older applications. The developer using the OO modeling tool would end up producing new applications much faster than the developer dealing with programming code.

In this chapter we'll consider Java as an OO programming language and provide some suggestions for approaching application development from a programmer's perspective. Then in the next chapter, we'll consider how Popkin Software's OO modeling tool works.

5.1 Java As an Object-Oriented Language

This is not a book on Java programming. We don't rely on your understanding Java to use this book. We provide Java code, but you can understand the UML diagrams even if you don't know any Java code. In this section we'll simply provide a high-level discussion of Java as an OO language just to assure that programmers who are unfamiliar with Java understand its key features.

Java was designed by James Gosling in 1990. (Gosling had earlier written the original source code for UNIX emacs.) As everyone probably knows by now, in 1990 Sun was looking for a language to use in developing TV set-top systems for a cable venture they were considering. When that venture was put on hold, the language was set aside. In 1995, when Sun became actively engaged in Internet development, the language, renamed Java, was revived.

In 1990, when he was first designing the new language, Gosling looked at all the popular OO languages, including C++, Smalltalk, Eiffel, and Objective C, and identified problems with each. Sun then asked Gosling to create a new design that combined the best features of each OO language while

C++	Java	Smalltalk
Developed by AT&T as the next generation of the C language in the 80s.	Developed by SUN for use on the Web in the early 90s.	The earliest commercially popular OO languge was developed at Xerox PARC
Hybrid. Combines OO and procedural features.	OO, but it has a C-like syntax.	It's consistenly object-oriented.
It's strongly typed.	It's strongly typed. Object is a data type.	It's not typed.
It's compiled.	It's interpreted. You need a run-time engine. You can use a just-in-time compiler to make it run faster.	It's interpreted. You need a Smalltalk run-time engine to run it. You can use a just-in-time compiler to make it run faster.
Supports multiple inheritance. No interface inheritance.	Single inheritance. Supports multiple interface inheritance.	Supports single inheritance.
No garbage collection. You must specify how instances are created and destroyed.	Automatic garbage collection.	Automatic garbage collection.
	Applets can be called from HTML and executed on Web browsers.	It saves an image of the application.

Table 5.1   *A comparison of C++, Java, and Smalltalk.*

meeting the requirements Sun had set for the new language. The new language had to be efficient, portable, and secure.

Java draws heavily on C, although it is closer to Objective C than C++ in many ways. Many of C++'s more complicated features have been removed. Java is an interpreted language. It also incorporates garbage collecting and dynamic linking (from Lisp and Smalltalk), interfaces (from Objective C and OMG's Interface Definition Language or IDL), packages (from Modula), concurrency (from Mesa), and exceptions (from Modula-3). Table 5.1 compares some of the key features of

Java, Smalltalk, and C++ that we'll consider in this brief overview.

Java was publicly introduced in May 1995. Initially Sun positioned Java as an ideal language in which to develop applets that could be downloaded to add more functionality to Web pages. Later, Sun began to emphasize that Java was a platform-independent language and that an application developed in Java could be fielded on any platform that had a Java Virtual Machine (JVM—a Java interpreter). As companies decided that the Internet provided the best possible way to develop distributed applications, Java proved to be the right language for the times. Currently, Java is in the process of superseding the other OO languages and seems likely to become the preferred language for new systems development by the end of this decade. All major Internet browsers now support Java, as do nearly all hardware platforms. Thousands of Java applets are now available for reuse, and dozens of tools support Java development.

5.1.1   *Java Language Basics*

Java's basic syntax is very similar to C and C++ and is easy to learn, if you already know C or C++. More important, if you don't know C or C++, Java is easier to learn than either of those languages. Many typical C statements are used in Java. For example, Java has the normal C if-else, for, and return statements, as well as declarative and assignment statements, and it uses { and } to enclose blocks of code. Here, for example, is how you would write a small Java program to put "Hello World!" on the screen:

```
class helloworld {
    public static void main (String args[ ]) {
    System.out.println("Hello World!");
    }
}
```

The helloworld class contains a single operation called main. (Java calls operations, methods, but we'll stick to operations, which is the preferred UML term.) The main operation makes use of the Java *top* class by calling the `println` operation of the `out` object. `System.out.println` is an operation invocation. The programmer didn't need to create an *out* object. It is included in the Java class library that comes as part of the JDK, along with the interpreter. `Out` is an object instantiated from the `System` class that deals with output operations.

Like C++, Java supports public, protected, and private access. Java is a strongly typed language and supports the following types: boolean, byte, char, short, int, long, float, and double. Unlike C++, however, arrays and strings are objects in Java. Thus, all arrays have a length associated with them, and their bounds are checked both at compile and run time.

Because all variables are strongly typed and there is no pointer type, Java is more secure and Java developers are protected from some errors that C or C++ developers often fall into. In C, where a pointer is inherently not strongly typed, it simply refers to an address that stores data of an arbitrary type. Pointers can thus take on any given type, and even worse, most types can be converted to functions as a pointer. This means that a C program that appears to be doing one thing might actually be doing something else. In other words, pointers leave C programs open to security problems that are avoided in Java.

Unlike C++, Java's data types are independent of the underlying platform. Moreover, most data types are objects. Because objects can be subclassed, a developer can quickly create any new data type needed for a specific type of application. This gives Java much greater flexibility than C or C++, which are limited to their defined data types. Unlike C and C++, Java's numeric types are independent of the underlying hardware and operating system.

Like Smalltalk, Java is an interpreted language and requires an interpreter or run-time engine, which, as mentioned earlier, Sun calls the Java Virtual Machine. The JVM is, in effect, a software emulation of a hardware architecture on which Java Bytecode is executed. Before Java can run, the JVM must already be installed on the Web browser or the operating system. (The JVM is written in C and Assembler.) An example of Java's machine independence is that Java is always a 32-bit language, regardless of whether the Java code is executing on a 32- or a 64-bit CPU.

Because Java is interpreted, applications that are being developed can be tested and revised without requiring a compile and run cycle. This makes Java development a lot easier than C/C++ development. When a Java application is complete, it is "compiled" into what Sun calls Bytecode. Later, the JVM interprets the Bytecode when it executes the program. By installing a just-in-time (JIT) compiler along with the virtual machine, you can compile as the code is interpreted and eliminate the need to reinterpret anything already interpreted. This makes actual execution much faster.

Java also lacks a preprocessor, goto, typedefs, structs, unions or enums, pointers, functions, and implicit coercions and has only limited casting. There are no header files in Java. There are no make files. Every class has its own .class file.

Like Smalltalk, Java supports garbage collection. Thus, the language automatically handles storage allocation and the elimination of unnecessary objects. Developers don't have to write operations to create and delete objects in Java. And, since developers don't have to deal with freeing memory, several types of memory errors are eliminated. The Java garbage collector achieves reasonably high performance by running in the background whenever the CPU is idle.

Again, like Smalltalk, Java only supports single inheritance in class hierarchies. Like Objective C, ActiveX, and OMG's IDL, however, Java supports the multiple inheritance of interfaces. In other words, the interface (which indicates which operations a class can respond to) is separate from the object. The developer can define what interface classes a given object will implement.

For example, Java has a *thread* class that provides all the Java threading capability. An application that wants to use threads, but doesn't need to add any new threading functionality, needn't be a subclass of the *thread* class. Instead, it can merely implement the runnable interface, which defines a single operation, run. This provides the class with all the threading capability it needs. In Java, threads are a fundamental part of the language. The *thread* class is in the java.lang class library. It is threading that allows a Java applet to put an image on a Web page while simultaneously playing music.

Finally, Java allows you to embed C and C++ code inside a Java application.

5.2 The Java Development Kit

A key thing to remember about Java, which is also true of other interpreted OO languages such as Smalltalk and Objective C, is that it is almost impossible to distinguish between the language, its interpreter, and the class libraries that are used to create and execute code. Figure 5.1 illustrates the JDK

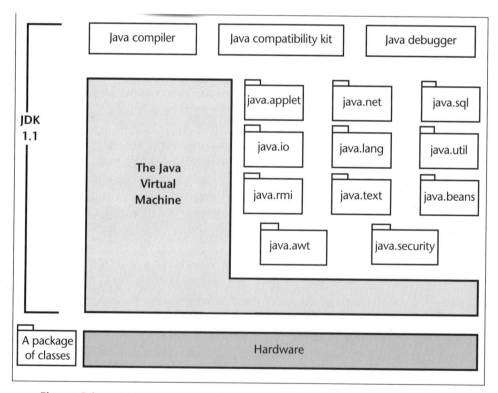

Figure 5.1   *The Java Development Kit 1.1.*

(version 1.1), which includes the interpreter, compiler, class libraries, and debuggers.

Java divides its class libraries into groups that it calls packages rather than frameworks. We've represented each package of classes (and associated interfaces) in Figure 5.1 with a little file folder, which is the UML symbol for software packages. Packages, in turn, can be subdivided as necessary. The Java Remote Method Invocation (RMI) package, for example, is divided into four subpackages: java.rmi, java.rmi.server, java.rmi.registry, and java.rmi.dgc.

Even though the Java class library is organized into packages, it is, in fact, a single class hierarchy, and any specific class can be traced back to the ultimate class, *object*, which resides in the java.lang package. In effect, the class *object* tells every other class how to be a class or object. Packages can contain either classes, linked by inheritance to *object*, or interfaces. As we've already noted, an interface is a limited sort of class that provides a set of operation names.

When a programmer writes Java code, he or she usually begins by identifying one or more Java classes in the library to subclass. For example, the RMI package contains classes and interfaces that support linking Java classes on different platforms. We'll consider the specifics of this later in this chapter. Suffice it to say that if I want a Java class on one machine to send a message to a Java class on another machine, I will use the RMI package to help facilitate it. Specifically, I will subclass classes like *RemoteObject* and *RemoteStub* or use interfaces like *RemoteCall Interface* to provide code I will need. (See Figure 5.2.)

5.3   The Java Platform

Because Java is an interpreted language, it requires that the JVM be available whenever a Java program is to be run. This has been provided for by all the major operating system vendors, who have incorporated the JVM in their operating systems. Moreover, since Java depends on classes derived from the Java class library included in the JDK, those classes also need to be available to any Java application when it runs. The

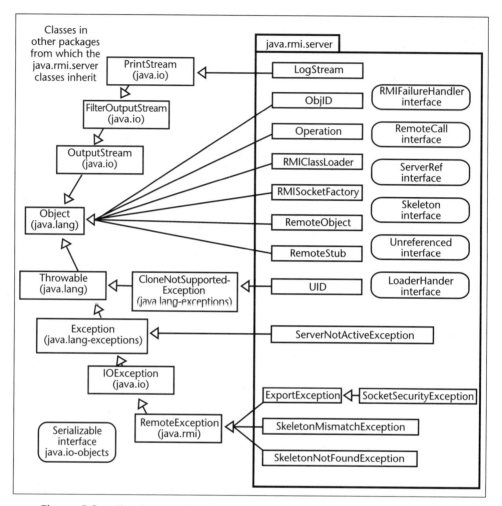

Figure 5.2   *The classes and interfaces in the java.rmi.server package and their relation-*
ship to other classes in the JDK library. (Note that the interface notation
used here is not UML notation.)

entire set of Java elements that are available on any platform
that runs Java are sometimes called the Java Platform. (See
Figure 5.3.)

If you glance at Figure 5.3 you see that the JVM, which
includes the interpreter and the class libraries, sits underneath
an additional set of classes that are designed to handle things

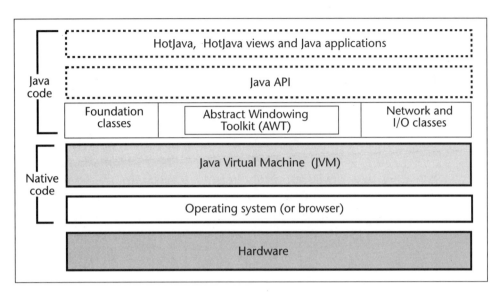

Figure 5.3 *The Java Platform.*

like graphics, windowing, and so on. In other words, the JVM contains the Java interpreter and the core Java language classes, while the Java Platform includes a broader set of classes and utilities to help use them. All operating system vendors have implemented the JDK. Some, such as Microsoft, have not yet implemented all of the Java Platform. (The complete Java Platform for Windows environments can be downloaded from the Sun Web site.)

We'll consider some of the packages in the Java class library and the higher level utilities for developing screens and linking with databases when we get to design.

5.4 Compiling and Interpreting Java

In a recent interview, James Gosling, the lead designer of Java, said that the "biggest issue with Java for most applications is performance." He noted that in many cases Java worked just fine, but in some cases it failed to perform well enough, in part because of systems problems (moving data to and from disk drives), in part because of poor implementations of the JVM, and in part because of the current compiler and interpreter technology, which Sun is working to improve. Obviously, Java faces the same problems that have faced others who have used interpreted languages, including Smalltalk, and Objective C developers. And, of course, Sun is in a position to take advantage of everything vendors of those languages have learned about how to speed up interpreters.

To clarify this, consider Figure 5.4, which illustrates the relationship between the Java "compiler," the Java interpreter, and the JIT compiler. Figure 5.4 illustrates the role of the Java

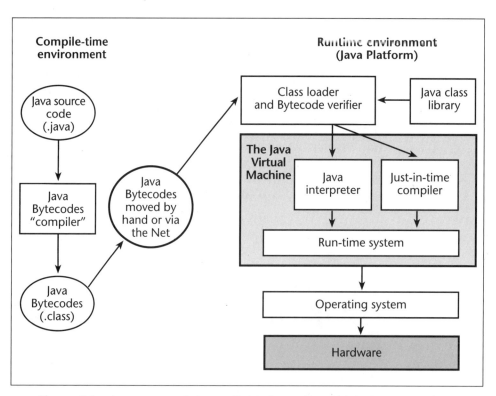

Figure 5.4   *Java source code is compiled to Bytecodes, which is then executed at run time. (After Java OS White Paper by Sun.)*

Bytecodes compiler and the JVM in changing source code into run-time code. Although it is not shown in Figure 5.4, keep in mind that the Java source code and the Java compiler are contained within the JDK. Thus, the code is created and compiled on the developer's platform, using the JDK, and then transferred to another platform, which also has its own JDK, where it is loaded with whatever Java classes are needed and then interpreted or run through the JIT compiler.

We put "compilers" in quotes to remind you that we are dealing with an interpreted system. Normally a compiler takes source code and converts it into machine code with a knowledge of the hardware chip on which the compiled code will be executed. The Java compiler compacts code less than a normal compiler would to generate Bytecodes. When Bytecodes are loaded on a machine with a JVM, they are interpreted as the code is executed. In some cases a JIT compiler may execute the Bytecodes, in which case any links established during a session will be remembered and less interpretation will be required. Thus, a JIT compiler executes the code a little faster than a straight interpreter would. The actual interface to the underlying chip is provided by the JVM. Although the Bytecodes are not compiled with a knowledge of the underlying hardware, the JVM itself must be machine specific and know how the underlying hardware works.

5.4.1   *Applets versus Applications*

Java is designed to support two separate execution modes. You can write Java code and then deliver it as either a Java application or a Java applet. In either case Java is platform independent and runs on top of the JVM.

In the application mode, the Java application depends on the presence of a Java class, *main*, that provides a lot of needed functionality. Equally important, a Java application can access and use any resources on the host platform. Thus, a Java application could access data stored in a database on the same machine.

In the applet mode, Java does not depend on the presence of the Java class, *main*, but relies, instead, on a special class

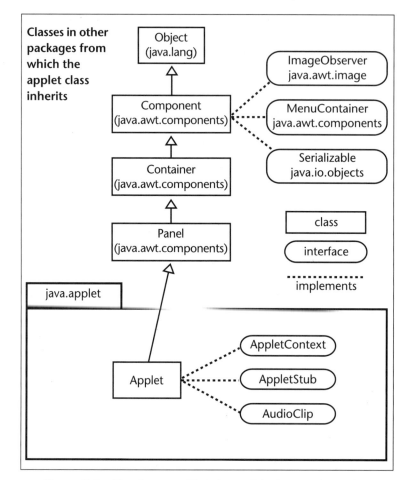

Figure 5.5 *The classes and interfaces of the java.applet package.*

called *applet.* (See Figure 5.5.) Applets are downloaded over the Internet and executed inside browsers that include the JVM. An applet cannot access any resources of the host platform outside the browser. In effect, an applet is a special type of component designed to be executed on browsers with the JVM.

Unlike applications that rely on a main operation, an applet may have explicit init, start, stop, and destroy operations. A Java applet has a permanent existence on a host server, where it is stored but does not execute, and has only a temporary existence on a client, where it is executed but not stored.

Tags referencing applets can be embedded in HTML code. When a user loads a Web page with such a tag, the browser automatically proceeds to download the applet(s) from the server. The Java applet can only function if the JVM is already a part of the browser.

Here, for example, is the Java applet and HTML code we would write to call the *HelloWorld* applet on a browser:

```
import browser.Applet;
import awt.Graphics;
class HelloWorld extends Applet {
      public void init() {
            resize(150,25);
      }
      public void paint(Graphics g) {
            g.drawString("Hello World!",50,25);
      }
}
```

And then you would write the HTML code:

```
<HTML>
      <HEAD>
      <TITLE> A Demo Program </TITLE>
      </HEAD>
      <BODY>
      Here is the output of my program:
      <APPLET CODE="HelloWorld.class" WIDTH=150 HEIGHT=25>
      </APPLET>
      </BODY>
      </HTML>
```

It's possible for a given Web page to refer to several different applets, all of them retrieved from the host and then executed on the browser. These independent applets are able to interact on the client's Web page.

The Java class library contains many classes that are useful for developing either applets or applications. The java.lang package, for example, contains language types, threads, exceptions, and so on. Java.util contains hash tables, vectors, and cache. Java.awt contains the Abstract Windowing Toolkit for writing user interfaces, and java.network contains sockets.

Some operations used in applets—for example, the operation for loading images, getImage()—are unavailable to developers creating regular Java applications. Application developers must use the Java Toolkit to obtain and implement equivalent operations.

5.4.2 *JavaBeans*

Sun's JavaSoft subsidiary released its JavaBeans component specification in 1997. Unlike the applet specification, which defines a browser-specific component, JavaBeans is a generic approach to creating reusable components. JavaBeans can range in size from a few classes to complex business objects. They can also be used to encapsulate legacy applications or other components, such as ActiveX. Sun refers to the JavaBeans used as business objects or to encapsulate applications as Enterprise JavaBeans.

Since the announcement of JavaBeans, IBM and Apple, which had been supporting an alternative component model, OpenDoc, have dropped that model and joined with Sun to extend JavaBeans. Microsoft's ActiveX is the major component model that JavaBeans will have to compete with. In effect, there are two parts to the JavaBeans standard. One part is the component model. The second part is a way of encapsulating other components, such as ActiveX.

Microsoft's ActiveX component model is specific to the Windows environment. If a Java developer incorporates ActiveX components in his or her code, it probably won't run on other platforms. Thus, unless you are sure that your application will be strictly confined to a Windows environment, you should probably use JavaBeans.

Microsoft is making a major effort to convince Java developers that they should use ActiveX components. Moreover, there are many excellent ActiveX components on the market, and your company may already have a library of OLE or ActiveX components. Getting developers to incorporate ActiveX into Java code, however, is just Microsoft's way of destroying the portability of Java. If you have preexisting ActiveX components you want to use in an application, encapsulate them in JavaBeans. An ActiveX component inside a JavaBean will work just as well as it would otherwise. And you will be assured that your application will execute on whatever platform you load it on, or in whatever browser it's downloaded to.

Sun plans to incorporate IBM's JavaBeans Migration Assistant for ActiveX—a utility that converts an ActiveX control into a JavaBean that is 100% pure Java—in the next version of the Java Platform. The technology is referred to as "bean dipping."

A JavaBean component can easily encapsulate an OLE or ActiveX component and make it available on any platform whose operating system contains the JVM. At the same time, Sun has developed an ActiveX control, called the JavaBeans Bridge for ActiveX, that lets JavaBeans run in legacy ActiveX containers such as Microsoft's Office and Visual Basic. There are also tools that let you convert Visual Basic, which is used by most ActiveX developers, into Java code.

JavaBeans can communicate with other Java objects via RMI or with non-Java objects via OMG's Common Object Request Broker Architecture (CORBA) which can access objects regardless of the language they are written in or the platform they reside on. OLE/ActiveX components, at the moment, are limited to communicating with other ActiveX components via Microsoft's Distributed Component Object Model (DCOM). The OMG and Microsoft are working on building a bridge between DCOM and CORBA.

Classes to support JavaBeans have been built into the latest JDK 1.1. There is, in addition, a JavaBeans Development Kit (BDK), which includes source code and documentation, sample beans, a test container in which to evaluate bean behavior, and support for generating runtime beans for applications or creating beans for applets. The BDK can be downloaded from Sun's Web site: *java.sun.com/beans*.

We recommend several good books on Java programming in the bibliography if you want to learn more about Java, the Java Platform, or JavaBeans.

Development with an Object-Oriented Modeling Tool

You may remember when Computer-Aided Software Engineering (CASE) tools were popular, in the 1980s, and imagine that all the OO CASE tools disappeared at the end of that decade. Those earlier OO CASE tools that were primarily designed to develop traditional COBOL applications for mainframes have, indeed, largely disappeared. Or you may be completely unfamiliar with OO CASE tools. In fact, there is a new generation of OO development products, called either OO CASE tools or OO modeling tools, that offer developers an excellent way of developing UML-based applications. Most vendors now prefer to call them OO modeling tools and we'll use that designation.

OO modeling tools are software environments designed to facilitate the development of notation-based applications. They depend on diagrams that allow the developer to represent the analysis and design of the application. Once the developer has created diagrams to represent the application, the OO modeling tool then generates some or all of the code for the application.

OO modeling tools rely on OO notations, support OO methodologies, and generate OO code. There are a number of popular OO modeling tools. During the past half-dozen years, while a number of different OO methodologies have been competing with each other, most OO modeling tools supported several OO methodologies (e.g., Booch, Rumbaugh, Martin and Odell, Jacobson) and generated one or more of the popular OO languages, such as Smalltalk or C++. Now, with the standardization of UML, all of the popular OO modeling tool vendors are in the process of introducing new versions of their products to support UML. (For a while, at least, most will support UML in addition to other methodologies and allow users to convert diagrams they may have developed in notations other than UML.) Similarly, the popularity of the Internet and Java has led most vendors to introduce versions of their products that generate Java code and HTML. And, perhaps most important of all, objects and components seem likely to make OO modeling tools the environment of choice for developers who want to assemble applications from preexisting components or business objects.

We believe that OO modeling tools offer a superior way to develop large OO applications. Before trying to justify that statement, let's take a very high level look at how OO modeling tools work.

6.1 Object-Oriented Modeling Tools

Figure 6.1 provides an overview of a generic OO modeling tool. We have overlapped the various tools and utilities that make up the whole to suggest that different tools have different ways of arranging the various capabilities included within the tool.

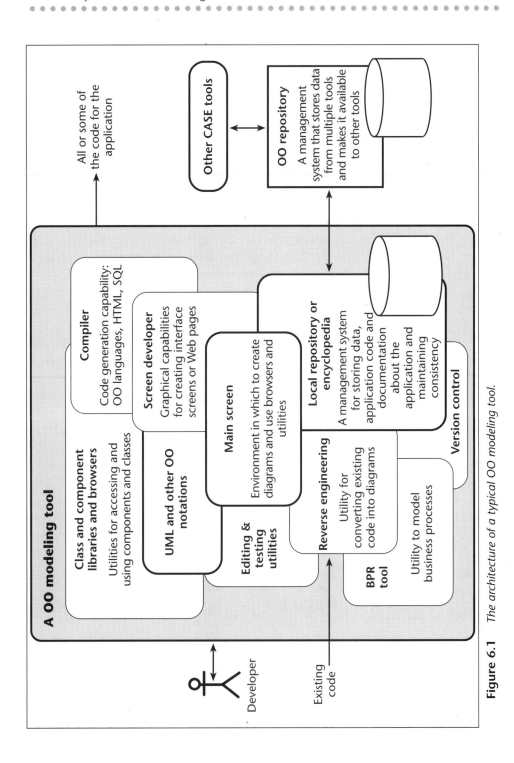

Figure 6.1   *The architecture of a typical OO modeling tool.*

In the center we show an environment that is usually presented as the main window of the tool. It provides the developer with a view into the tool and the various menus that allow the developer to access other capabilities. This environment lets the developer access special windows in which to create different types of UML diagrams, for example. If the tool supports multiple OO notations, it may allow the developer to change a diagram from one notation to another. When the developer moves from one diagram to another, the tool will usually "suggest" some of the structure necessary for the subsequent diagram. The tool can do this because it stores all the information about the application in a local repository (or encyclopedia). The repository management tool assures that names and diagrams are kept consistent. Moreover, most tools can use information in the repository to generate at least parts of new diagrams from information they already contain about other diagrams.

In addition to supporting the development of OO diagrams, most OO modeling tools include facilities for developing screens (or Web pages). Most of these facilities rely on internal, or externally accessible, collections of GUI components or classes.

OO modeling tools also provide editing and testing utilities and compilers. Some modeling tools can run applications from the tool environment, while others simply generate code that can be run anywhere. Most OO modeling tools can generate all types of code, from C++ and Java to HTML and SQL.

Some OO modeling tools provide reverse engineering utilities that can convert existing code into diagrams. This is important if you create diagrams and then generate code and subsequently modify the code. In that case, you want to be able to put the code back into the modeling environment and recapture any changes you have made. Similarly, BPR facilities provided by OO modeling tools allow the developer to model business processes in workflow diagrams and then convert them into object models within the OO modeling environment.

Finally, most OO modeling tools provide some kind of version control. This allows several developers to work on a single application simultaneously. Depending on how the control is set, a single developer can either select a module of the application to work on and lock it so no one else can access it, or several developers can work with the same module and then modify it according to some set of priorities.

The heart of a modern OO modeling tool is its repository. This is where the definitions, diagrams, and documentation for an application are maintained. The repository maintains internal consistency and alerts the developers to any potential problems. All OO modeling tools have their own repositories. Some use flat files, some use relational databases, and some use OO databases.

Recently, IBM, Microsoft, and Unisys have all introduced generic OO repositories that can store information from multiple tools. All three repositories support UML, and most OO modeling vendors have announced they will support these repositories. Microsoft has based its repository on the Common Object Model (OLE, ActiveX). IBM and Unisys are both supporting an Object Management Group effort that will result in a standard OO repository model. Any of these repositories guarantees companies that if they use one OO modeling tool today and decide to use another, later, that they will be able to port their earlier applications to the new tool.

Let's see if we can summarize the advantages of OO modeling tools. They aren't especially useful for small, one-of-a-kind applications, because it requires an effort to learn how to use an OO modeling tool effectively. On the other hand, if you are faced with a large, complex application, and especially if you are trying to develop an application with a team of developers, OO modeling tools can significantly reduce the time it takes to develop the application, while simultaneously improving the quality of the result.

The tools decrease development time, once you know how to use them, because they provide an automatic way to move from one diagram to another and from diagrams to code. Moreover, since they manage the entire application, they assure that names and data types are maintained in a consistent manner. Similarly, they provide an orderly way for different developers to work on different versions of the application while staying in sync with each other. Moreover, as developers increasingly use components and business objects for application development, OO modeling tools provide the ideal way to coordinate the development of diagrams and the insertion of components and business objects into the overall application.

One of the reasons the older OO CASE tools failed was because IBM failed to deliver a universal repository (the AD/Cycle Repository) that it had promised by 1989. IBM failed because the world of software development was changing so fast that no one knew what would be needed by the mid-1990s. IBM started working on its repository in the mid-1980s. It was designed to support OO CASE tools that generated COBOL for mainframe applications. By the late-1980s, however, companies were moving from mainframes to client/server applications, to OO languages, and to windows-based graphical user interfaces. IBM's basic design simply wasn't flexible enough to handle all the extensions and enhancements that companies began to ask for. On top of that, as companies moved from COBOL-based mainframe applications to client/server systems, the market for tools to develop mainframe applications collapsed.

Now, well past the halfway mark of the 1990s, the world of software development seems to be settling down around a new paradigm. Development will increasingly be done with OO languages like Java. A wide variety of different platforms will be networked by TCP/IP, and the Internet will be used to solve distribution problems that frustrated earlier client/server developers. Applications will be more graphical and will depend on components to make interface development easier. And corporate applications will increasingly rely on the reuse of business objects to facilitate large-scale enterprise development.

In recognition of this, the object repositories recently introduced by IBM, Unisys, and Microsoft can do exactly what IBM had wanted to do at the end of the 1980s. Today, a company can develop an application in UML and Java, incorporating JavaBeans and ActiveX components, and store the resulting product and documentation in an object repository. Later, another OO modeling tool can withdraw some or all of that application and modify it for use in another application. This combination of a new, standard OO notation, UML, OO modeling tools, an active components industry, and new OO repositories has laid the foundation for a new generation of OO modeling tools development. The fact that OO repositories and libraries of components and business objects already exist, guarantees companies that this time the OO modeling products will be able to live up to their potential. This is why, in addition to discussing the use of UML in the development of a Java application, we decided to illustrate how UML could be used with an OO modeling tool to develop the same application.

6.2 Popkin Software's SA/Object Architect

There are a number of good OO modeling tools on the market. We chose Popkin Software's tool, SA/Object Architect, for a variety of reasons: first, we think it's one of the good OO modeling tools currently available. Second, one of the authors had recently developed a book on the OMT methodology using SA/Object Architect. He was familiar with the tool and found it easy to use. Since it also provides complete support for UML and Java development, it seemed an obvious choice to use for this book as well.

In addition, unlike most of the OO modeling tools, SA/Object Architect not only supports UML, but also supports Business Process Reengineering analysis, CRC card analysis, database modeling and design, interface development, and schema engineering and reengineering. As you will see as you read this book, we believe that, depending on the scope of the system, more than just UML may be required to do a complete analysis, design, coding, and testing effort. It's more efficient and productive to be able to do as many of these tasks as possible in one tool. It eliminates the time required to keep a lot of extra balls in the air at once, and you don't have to worry about whether you remembered to synchronize Tool A with Tool B after the last set of changes.

Popkin Software has been producing tools to aid in the analysis and design of systems since 1986 and sells a number of tools you can use for object modeling, data modeling, and process modeling. The tools all use the same repository, so in large companies, teams doing different kinds of projects can all have access to the same business rules and enterprisewide definitions no matter what the specific tool and design may be. More information on Popkin Software is available in Appendix D.

Our goal in illustrating UML development with Popkin Software's SA/Object Architect product is not to promote Popkin Software's tool, as such, but to show how any good OO modeling tool can be used to facilitate more rapid development of UML applications.

In the remainder of this chapter, we will introduce you to the SA/Object Architect environment. Once again, our goal is not to provide a detailed introduction to SA/Object Architect, but to provide you with an overview of how any of several OO modeling tools work. Rather than provide an abstract description, which is always a bit harder to understand, we'll describe one specific environment, SA/Object Architect. Most other OO modeling tools work the same way, although each handles specific tasks in a slightly different manner. The point is to show how you can use an OO modeling tool to develop UML diagrams quickly and then use those diagrams to generate code.

6.2.1 *SA/Object Architect: An Overview*

If you bought a copy of SA/Object Architect, loaded the software on your computer, and then opened the SA/Object Architect icon, you would arrive at the main screen, which would appear as it does in Figure 6.2. We won't go into all the items on the SA/Object Architect menu. Instead, just to provide you with a high-level orientation, we'll consider how we want to use the SA/Object Architect tool and then consider some of the menu items we would use to accomplish each task.

Our overall task will be to use our generic, iterative OO methodology to create a Java Web application—the Watson's

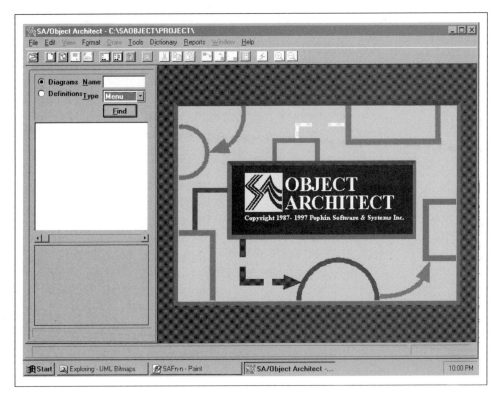

Figure 6.2   *The SA/Object Architect main screen.*

SalesWeb system. We've broken that task up into six general steps:

1. Create an encyclopedia.
2. Analyze the application by creating UML diagrams.
3. Design interface and database linkages.
4. Use SA/Object Architect consistency-checking tools to find problems.
5. Generate the code needed for the SalesWeb application.
6. Complete the application.

Step 1: Create an Encyclopedia

To begin the actual development process, we start by creating an encyclopedia for our SalesWeb application. (SA/Object Architect, like several other OO modeling tools, calls a local repository an encyclopedia and reserves the word *repository* for an external data management system such as Microsoft's Object Repository.)

The SalesWeb encyclopedia will be the repository for all the diagrams, code, and other information that we will enter about our SalesWeb application. In effect, we'll create a special database to contain the SalesWeb information. As we create new diagrams, SA/Object Architect will check with the information already in our database to assure that it's consistent with what we have already entered. And when it comes time to generate the Java code for the actual application, SA/Object Architect will use the information in the data dictionary to generate the code. In fact, SA/Object Architect doesn't store diagrams, as such. It stores information and creates the diagrams as needed.

You create a new SalesWeb encyclopedia by clicking on the File heading and then choosing Encyclopedia. This opens a dialog box that will provide us with a hierarchy of SA/Object Architect encyclopedias. (SA/Object Architect uses a different encyclopedia for each application, although it's easy to copy between them if you need to.) We'll create a new SA/Object Architect encyclopedia and name it "SalesWeb." (See Figure 6.3.)

We won't take advantage of it in our example in this book, but SA/Object Architect makes it easy to reuse code from previous application development efforts. Thus, if you had already developed an earlier version of the SalesWeb application, you could begin the new version by simply creating a new version of the old encyclopedia and then start by editing the diagrams from the older application. Or, if you had never developed a SalesWeb application before, but had an earlier application that had at least some classes that you thought you might be able to reuse in the SalesWeb application, you could create a new encyclopedia and then transfer data from other encyclopedias into the new one. In this case you wouldn't

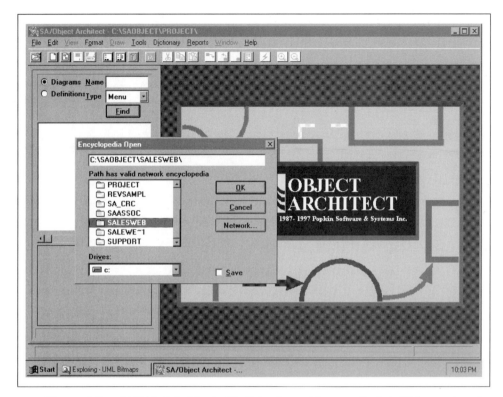

Figure 6.3   *SA/Object Architect with dialog box set to open the SalesWeb encyclopedia.*

have complete diagrams, but you would at least have specific classes that you could begin by reviewing and editing.

After creating an encyclopedia, we need to tell SA/Object Architect what kinds of things we intend to store in the encyclopedia. (See Figure 6.4.) We will configure SA/Object Architect to allow us to use UML notation. (SA/Object Architect supports several OO and non-OO notations, so we'll have to explicitly request UML diagramming symbols.) Similarly, we have to tell it what kind of code we want to generate. We'll choose Java and HTML. We could also configure SA/Object Architect to allow several developers to work on the development project simultaneously. In our case, however, since there will only be one developer creating the application, we'll configure SA/Object Architect for single-user development.

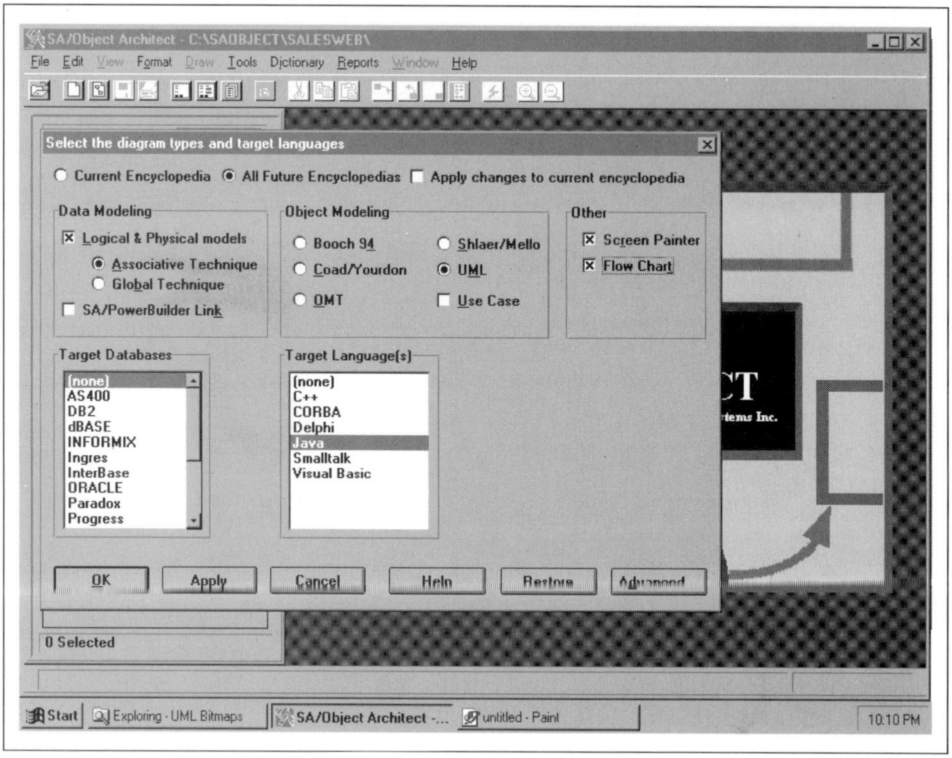

Figure 6.4   *SA/Object Architect dialog for setting the characteristics for an encyclopedia.*

All these configuration tasks are accomplished by pulling down various menus, opening dialog boxes, and selecting settings.

Step 2: Analyze the Application by Creating UML Diagrams

The second step is the heart of our SalesWeb analysis and design effort. We create UML diagrams to describe the problem. In fact, as you will see when we actually develop some diagrams, as we place an element in a diagram, we are required to define it for the encyclopedia. Thus, if we want, we can not only place a box on the screen to represent a class, but also specify some of the class's attributes and operations, indicate whether they are public or private, assign them a data type, and so on.

Because all of the diagrams we will create will be stored in the encyclopedia, we will often be able to move from one diagram to another without having to start over again from scratch. For example, if we begin by creating a use case diagram, and then move to a sequence diagram, we can automatically convert some of our use case elements to sequence diagram elements. Similarly, if we create a class diagram, we can then move to a sequence diagram, and our encyclopedia will already contain the names of the classes we identified in earlier class diagrams.

We won't go into the details of how we create UML diagrams or how we move from one diagram to another at this point. We'll consider the generation of diagrams and what gets transferred from one diagram to another when we consider specific UML diagrams in subsequent chapters.

If we had already done a previous application or if our company had a database of business objects, we could use those in our application. Similarly, we will be able to use Java classes and components when we create screens for our application.

Step 3: Design Interface and Database Linkages

We will handle the interface and database linkages, when the time comes, by using JDK classes. SA/Object Architect also has a screen painter that would allow us to create Windows screens and then embed them in our application, if we wanted to do that. Creating database linkages involves setting criteria for the encyclopedia and using appropriate database components when it comes time to generate application code.

Step 4: Use SA/Object Architect Consistency-Checking Tools to Find Problems

Developers working in Java can always use the Java Bytecode compiler to find out whether they have introduced any illegal constructs into the code, but that's an awkward way to do checking. And it doesn't check UML for consistency.

SA/Object Architect provides tools to check our code. Some of these tools work constantly in the background. Thus, whenever we try to create and link classes, SA/Object Architect watches us and protests when we try to create illegal constructs.

Step 5: Generate the Code Needed for the SalesWeb Application

To generate Java code in SA/Object Architect, you simply instruct the encyclopedia to generate code. SA/Object Architect generates skeletal Java code. If you have written pseudocode within the textual property boxes associated with an operation, then SA/Object Architect will insert that into the skeletal Java code. In other words, you'll have the classes, attributes, and operation names. If you've written pseudocode, you may have the Java code with the operation names. If not, you will need to write the code to complete the operations as you would if you were coding by hand.

Step 6: Complete the Application

You would now be ready to run your Java application and test it with users. In an ideal world, you would never modify the code you generated with SA/Object Architect. If you wanted to change the code, you would change the UML diagrams and then generate new code. In reality, however, you may find yourself modifying the Java code that you have generated as you test it. At the moment, SA/Object Architect does not support the reverse engineering of Java code. In other words, it doesn't take Java code and use it to update the encyclopedia. SA/Object Architect does this for other OO languages and will undoubtedly add this capability for Java in the future.

Even if you can reverse engineer Java code, once you test your application and begin to see how it needs to be redesigned, you can quickly edit the diagrams in the SalesWeb encyclopedia and then generate more skeletal Java code.

6.2.2 *Putting It All Together*

With this overview in mind, we'll begin to consider UML diagrams and create an application. As we create each diagram, we'll return to SA/Object Architect and see how each diagram is created. Later, when we get to design, we'll see how we handle database linkages and screen creation in more detail.

Business Process Reengineering

At this point, we want to describe in more detail the case study that we can use throughout the remainder of the book. Rather than describe a company and a problem in the abstract, we decided to assume that the company put together a BPR team to analyze their problem. We are going to further assume that they were using IBM's LOVEM diagrams. This will provide you with information about the software problem we'll use as a case study in the remainder of this book and will also show how UML and BPR can work together.

We'll begin with a brief overview of BPR. Then we'll consider IBM's LOVEM diagrams and how they can be used to capture workflow sequences. After that, we'll introduce our hypothetical company, Watson's Furniture, and use LOVEM diagrams to analyze how Watson's handles their problems now and how they plan to change the way they do business. This will result in a description of the software system that Watson's will want to develop using OO techniques.

7.1 What Is Business Process Reengineering?

As we've already mentioned, BPR means different things to different people. The current interest in BPR began in 1990 when two important articles were published. Michael Hammer wrote "Reengineering Work: Don't Automate, Obliterate" (*Harvard Business Review,* Cambridge, MA, July–Aug 1990), and Thomas Davenport and James Short wrote "The New Industrial Engineering: Information Technology and Business Process Redesign" (*Sloan Management Review*, Summer 1990). Since then Michael Hammer joined with James Champy to write *Reengineering the Corporation: A Manifesto for Business Revolution* (HarperCollins, New York, NY, 1994), and Thomas Davenport wrote the more thoughtful book *Process Innovation* (HBR Press, Cambridge, MA, 1993). In addition, there have been a number of other books on BPR published in the last few years. The best are listed in our bibliography.

Hammer, the best known of the BPR consultants, originally made a lot of provocative statements and got a lot of media attention. He often suggested that companies should throw out what they were currently doing and begin over again, developing completely new systems that took advantage of the latest computer techniques. In most cases, of course, that radical approach hasn't worked. Most companies simply can't afford the time or the dislocations involved in radical reengineering. In the last few years, Hammer has turned down his rhetoric quite a bit and joined the more sensible BPR advocates who simply urge companies to be bold when they redesign processes.

Most BPR theorists begin with the premise that companies aren't very well organized. Even well-run companies are organized into hierarchies based on functional departments. This organizational structure grew up with the industrial revolution and emphasizes breaking up work into simple jobs. (Remember how Adam Smith, in *The Wealth of Nations*, argued that several pin makers, each specializing in doing only part of the job, could make a lot more pins, working as a team, than each man could if he tried to make complete pins, working entirely by himself?) In the last hundred years, BPR gurus maintain, the emphasis on functional decomposition and hierarchical organizations has gradually become dysfunctional. Jobs have been so subdivided that it's hard for anyone to have an overview of what a group is supposed to be doing or why it's important. Departments tend to develop their own procedures, and they don't always cooperate very well with other departments within the same company. Departmental managers tend to want to protect their turf. Departments do try to maximize their own efficiency, but unfortunately, what works well within one department is often detrimental to the efficiency of other departments and to the overall processes that create and deliver products and services to customers.

More important, from a computer systems perspective, departments have tended to use computers to automate departmental procedures. It's a commonplace to observe that billions of dollars were spent on computer systems in the 1980s, with next to no increase in productivity. Indeed, with a few exceptions, companies automated procedures and hired more people at the same time. In the worst case, the mainframe architectures, with their centralized, hierarchical approach to computing, may have encouraged corporate departments to use computers ineffectively. Whatever may have been true in the past, BPR theorists argue that computers can now be used to facilitate much more efficient ways of organizing the flow of work.

7.1.1 *Business Processes*

In recent years, organizational theorists have emphasized that it's more efficient to conceptualize business organizations in terms of processes. A process, as used in BPR, refers to a stream of activity that begins with the acquisition of resources (e.g., people, capital, supplies from vendors) and ends by producing a product that customers want. Processes are typically called workflows. In effect, a process cuts across a hierarchy chart in a horizontal manner. (See Figure 7.1.)

To successfully sell widgets, a company must somehow coordinate activities from the purchasing department, from

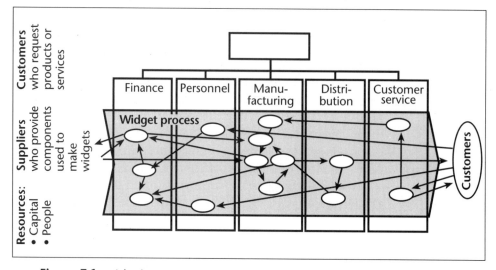

Figure 7.1   *A business process cuts across several departments and includes every activity involved in providing a service to a customer.*

sales and marketing, from manufacturing, inventory, and shipping. Each vertical department handles a portion of the overall process. Traditionally, for example, departments have passed paper to each other to stimulate and document actions. Thus, sales passes sales orders to manufacturing and to accounting. Manufacturing or shipping tells accounting when it has produced the widgets and shipped them to the customer and requests that accounting check to see that the company gets paid, and so on. For purposes of checking what went on in a transaction, lots of paper is passed more than once. Most processes aren't very efficient, in large part because no one has the responsibility for managing the process as a whole.

When you get serious about analyzing a company (or enterprise) to identify its processes, you find that some processes fit the definition we gave above and have external customers, while others are internal and have internal customers. Thus, a company's information systems (IS) department normally gets requests from internal departments and delivers systems (products) to these internal customers. It's also common to distinguish between less important processes and the core processes that actually earn companies most of their profits. In fact, analyzing organizations in terms of processes makes it possible to develop new accounting systems that measure costs and profits in more useful ways. It's hard to talk about how a specific department contributes to corporate success. It's relatively easier to determine just how much a specific process costs and how much it contributes to the bottom line. Books on "activity accounting," a new approach to accounting that tracks the costs and benefits of an entire business process, have begun to appear.

Although most BPR theorists emphasize complete processes, most companies that are actually undertaking reengineering projects limit themselves to a small portion of a complete process.

7.1.2 *The Redesign Process*

Figure 7.2 provides an overview of the major steps in a large-scale BPR effort. Although IS people are normally involved at every stage of the process, the initial identification of company processes primarily involves senior managers working in conjunction with BPR consultants. The initial analysis and subsequent redesign of a specific business process usually involves departmental managers and lots of other non-IS personnel. After a process has been redesigned, some elements of the new system will usually need to be developed by human resource people. Other elements will require IS people to create new hardware or software systems. Finally, all the new elements must be brought together and implemented. The entire project requires managers who can oversee and coordinate both the human and computer sides of the development and implementation effort.

Considered in a slightly different way, Phases I, II, and part of Phase III as illustrated in Figure 7.2 normally depend on workflow analysis and the use of BPR methodologies, costing techniques, and so on. Once a process has been identified and redesigned, however, the IS department usually switches to its

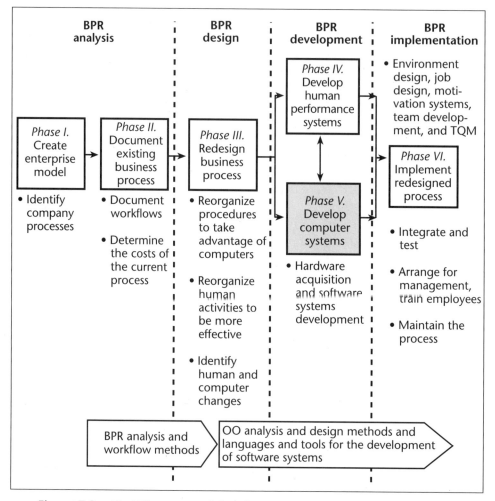

Figure 7.2   *The BPR process and the role of BPR and OO tools and techniques.*

own methodologies and techniques to analyze, design, and develop the software systems that the new process will require.

The first phase in any major BPR effort is to reconceptualize an organization in terms of its processes. Organizations that are really serious about BPR sometimes change their management structures and appoint someone to manage each specific process. This manager is then responsible for increasing the efficiency and profitability of the process.

Typically, when analysts look at a process, they find lots of duplication and lots of inefficient procedures. This is especially common when information is being passed back and forth between departments.

Once a process is identified, the next phase is to determine how that process works at the moment. A systematic analysis of a process can involve many different perspectives. Two important ways of analyzing processes emphasize (1) the use of computer systems to facilitate the process and (2) the procedures that human performers follow and the consequences that accrue to human performers. If this book were about BPR, we would pay equal attention to these two different aspects of BPR. Since we are only concerned with OO development in this book, and focusing on OO notation at that, we will ignore the human side of BPR and concentrate, instead, on how to document a business process in order to facilitate software development.

Assuming that a company is already performing a task, BPR analysts begin by documenting how the process is currently being performed. This is generally done by means of a workflow diagram. If they use a tool that supports workflow analysis, they can usually not only capture the specific flow of the activities involved in the process, but also track the times involved and then calculate the costs.

Now that they have determined how the process is currently being done, the company can consider alternatives. Generating alternatives usually involves getting a group of people together and brainstorming different ways to perform the activities. Some of the people are usually drawn from the employees who do the work now. Other members of the BPR team are drawn from the information systems group, and these individuals usually focus on what kind of computer technology could be used to support alternative ways of doing the task.

Using current computer techniques, it is usually possible to vastly improve the efficiency of business processes. For example, most companies are moving toward storing all information about customers in a single electronic file. This eliminates the need to pass paper and assures that everyone's data about a customer is current and complete. In effect, everyone within a single process stream uses a computer to access a common customer file. In many companies, a common electronic customer file requires that scanning technology be used to insert photographs, diagrams, or signed documents into the file. Similarly, if everyone is to access and update a common customer file, it often means that field sales and service people must be equipped with portable or handheld computer terminals. Some companies have extended this logic even further and used computer networks to connect suppliers and customers to some of their electronic files to automate ordering, billing, support functions, and so on. In many cases, as we have already indicated, OO and Internet techniques play a major role in the actual design of the software used to implement the new designs.

7.2 IBM's Line of Vision Enterprise Methodology Diagrams and Notation

There are several popular ways of describing workflows; most are based on some extension of what UML terms an activity diagram. The workflow diagrams we like best are IBM's LOVEM diagrams. The phrase "Line of Vision" is derived from the fact that the diagrams are arranged with the company's customer at the top. By simply moving from left to right across the top of the diagram, you can quickly see every instance in which a customer interacts with your firm. One of the major goals of most BPR programs is to improve customer satisfaction, and LOVEM diagrams are especially useful in focusing attention on this goal.

LOVEM describes workflows on a matrix. The rows of the matrix describe different departments or groups involved in the process. The horizontal axis of the matrix indicates the passage of time.

On a LOVEM diagram, the top row of the matrix is always reserved for the customer or consumer of the process. Intermediate rows are reserved for company divisions, departments, or groups within departments, depending on the nature of the business process being analyzed. If a department can be usefully divided into subgroups, these are indicated by using bold horizontal lines for the boundaries between departments and dashed lines to indicate divisions between departmental groups. The names of departments and groups are listed on the left-hand side of the matrix.

The bottom rows of the matrix are usually reserved for information systems. In fact, LOVEM diagrams have different variations, depending on the size of the process being analyzed. We will only focus on the simplest version. In a more complex version, departmental computing resources might be indicated on rows grouped with the departmental groups, and only corporate computing facilities would be shown at the bottom. Similarly, you can move from simple to complex diagrams and add a lot more information, but that would be overkill for our simple application. We'll ignore those details here and present a simple version of LOVEM that is quite adequate for small problems.

Activities are represented by round-cornered rectangles. Arrows indicate that items, information, or control flows between activities. Diamonds are used to indicate decision points when more than one outcome can occur. The outcomes are indicated within brackets by the arrows that flow from the decision diamonds. Ovals are used to represent software or hardware systems. Straight lines connect activities to computational resources used in the performance of an activity. Figure 7.3 illustrates the basic format and notation of a LOVEM diagram.

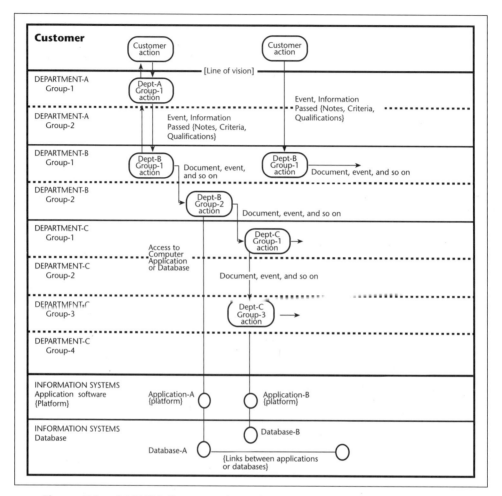

Figure 7.3   *A LOVEM diagram and notation.*

7.3 Watson's Existing Sales Process

In order to have something concrete to discuss as we consider developing an OO application, we'll use an imaginary problem. We'll assume Watson's Furniture is an established office furniture supply company that sells to companies throughout

North America. Watson's maintains a central warehouse facility, and that facility is managed by a database application that was developed many years ago. Watson's also has a general accounting and billing system that they maintain at corporate headquarters. Both applications were written in COBOL, and both rely on small IBM mainframes and DB2 relational databases. At the moment, the accounting system evaluates and approves orders, then passes them to the warehouse department to be fulfilled. When the order is actually shipped, the warehouse inventory system not only updates its own inventory, but it passes the shipping information to the accounting system so that the accounting system can initiate billing.

Until recently, the corporate sales staff, which is divided into eight regions, relied on paper, fax machines, and clerks to transmit orders from the field and to maintain records on the performance of salespeople in the regions. The larger regions had regional offices, and salespeople often maintained desks there, but in most regions the salespeople operated out of their homes. The salespeople call on office furniture companies, individuals, a few large corporate customers, and some governmental agencies.

In 1997, Watson's management group decided to conduct a BPR study of its sales process. A team of salespeople, managers, accounting people, inventory people, and information systems analysts was assembled. The team used IBM's LOVEM methodology and created the diagram shown in Figure 7.4 to describe their current situation.

The sales/order fulfillment process described in Figure 7.4 is broadly defined and includes activities that occur in the sales department, the accounting department, the manufacturing department, as well as activities that use information systems. The common thread that ties them all together is a sales process that begins when a customer places an order for new furniture and ends when the furniture is delivered and the company receives payment for the order. (Some companies refer to this process as order fulfillment.)

The workflow shown in Figure 7.4 leaves out lots of details. An entire additional workflow chart could be constructed just to show how an order is assembled or how an order is

Figure 7.4 *A LOVEM diagram of the old Watson's sales process.*

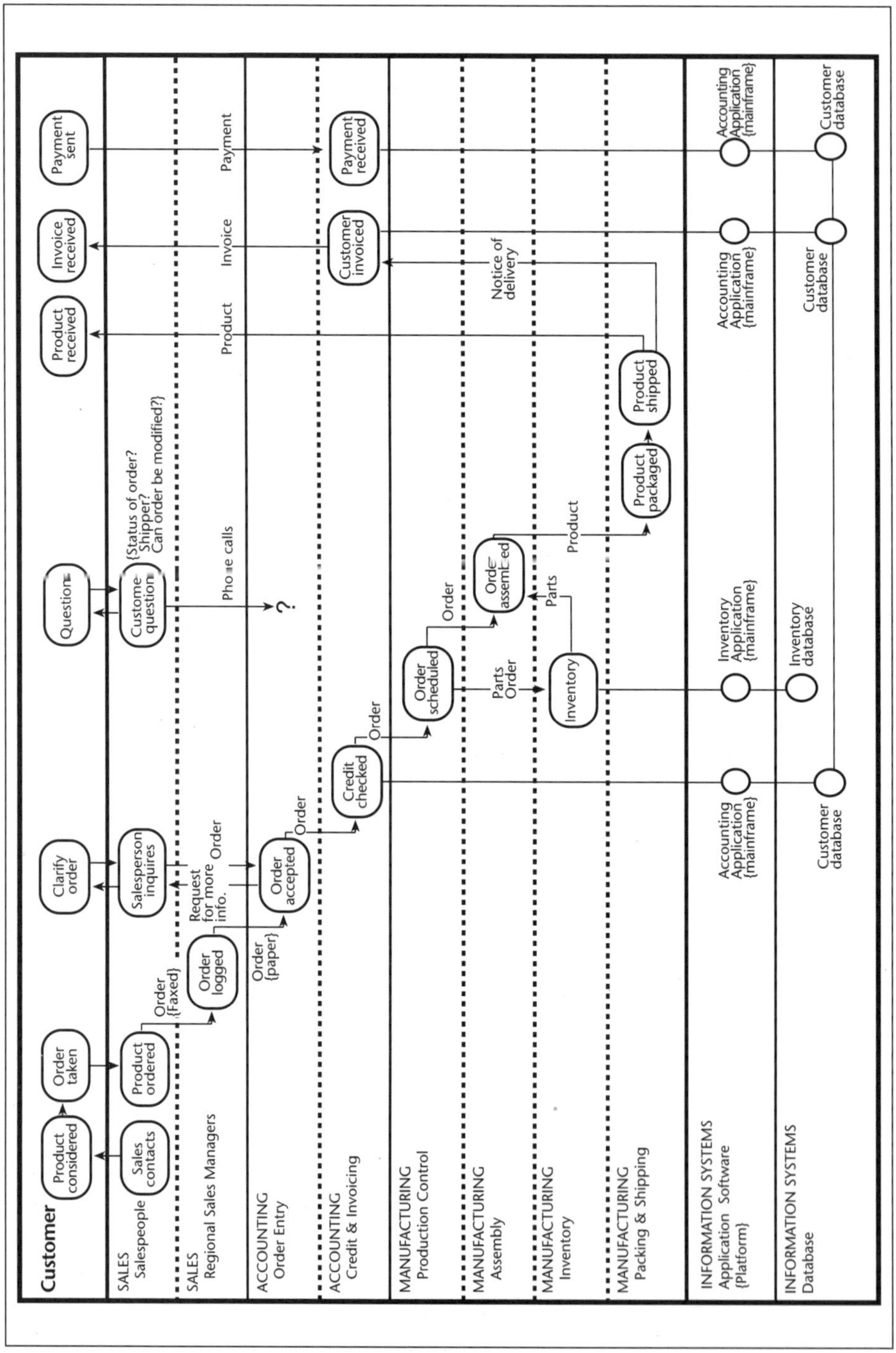

accepted. Similarly, a separate diagram could be developed to show how regional sales managers and salespeople negotiate annual and quarterly sales goals, how sales managers log orders against quotas, and how sales managers and regional managers meet to discuss how salespeople are performing.

What this high-level LOVEM diagram did show Watson's BPR team, however, was that interactions among salespeople, their managers, and accounting were all being handled by faxing paper forms back and forth. It also highlighted the fact that when customers asked salespeople questions, salespeople were often at a loss to find someone within Watson's who could answer the customers' questions. The paperwork was often in transit between one department and another, and in any case, it was impossible to identify who might have a specific order, since each department had several people working in parallel. (Several company surveys showed that this problem was a considerable source of irritation to both customers and salespeople.)

A survey of several dozen sales organizations, conducted by a BPR consulting company, indicated that as a result of their approach, Watson's employed more regional sales managers than did their competitors. Moreover, it was obvious that the regional sales offices where salespeople met to fill out forms, get the forms reviewed by sales managers, and then fax them into accounting were a major overhead cost. In addition, many argued that the time the salespeople spent traveling between their homes and the regional offices could be better spent visiting potential customers. Finally, everyone complained that the process took too long.

One key breakthrough came when the BPR team decided that salespeople should send the same order to both accounting and inventory at the same time so that order fulfillment and billing could then proceed in parallel. Accounting was a little nervous about the possibility of accepting orders from uncreditworthy customers. But they agreed that if they could check and be sure that the customers were known and were ordering within approved credit limits, parallel processing would significantly speed things up while exposing the company to only minor risks.

7.4 Watson's Reengineered Sales Process

Eventually, after several different versions had been studied, the BPR team arrived at the LOVEM diagram pictured in Figure 7.5. At first glance, the new organization might appear more complex because there are more lines going up and down the chart. In fact, the new design relies on letting salespeople, accountants, and inventory people interact directly with the existing computer systems—in effect, letting them communicate with each other via computer postings.

The new design assumes that the accounting and inventory systems will be tied together and pass information back and forth. More important, it assumes that regional sales offices will be closed and that regions will be consolidated so that fewer sales managers will manage more salespeople.

The BPR team decided that salespeople should be given laptop computers with modems. Henceforth, salespeople will be able to enter orders while they are at a customer's site, get approval and shipping dates, and then submit all the "paperwork" automatically. To facilitate this, Watson's decided to set up an Internet server that can interface with the salespeople in the field and with the existing mainframes that run the legacy accounting and inventory applications. Since the sales system could keep track of how each order was handled and when, salespeople could contact the sales system directly to find out the status of any given order.

The BPR team also assumed that a new software package would allow managers and salespeople to create sales quota agreements on-line and then allow both managers and salespeople to track their progress toward fulfilling their quotas by checking the on-line quota system.

The BPR team came up with a long list of changes they wanted to make and tasked different managers with preparing to implement different aspects of the system. The only subset of the BPR effort that we will follow from this point on is the effort involved in developing a software application that would sit on the new Internet server and on salespeople's laptops

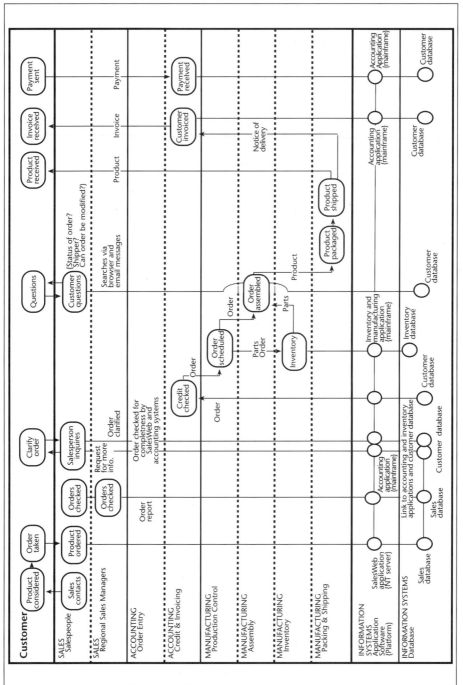

Figure 7.5   *A LOVEM diagram of the new SalesWeb Watson's sales process.*

and allow them to report sales orders and check their success in meeting their quotas. The task also included an interface to let regional managers check on the success of individual salespeople or all the salespeople within a region in meeting their sales quotas.

The BPR team that handed the assignment to a Watson's IS group didn't try to pin down lots of details. They didn't consider, for example, whether the salespeople should have an application on their laptop machines or simply have a browser. It was assumed that the sales application development team would conduct their own analysis and design effort and figure out the answers to these and other questions. The BPR team did specify that when a salesperson contacted the server, the server, in turn, would contact the accounting system and verify that the customer was placing an order within the credit limits established by the accounting system before the order was passed to the inventory system for processing.

In addition, the BPR team considered allowing some of Watson's customers to link directly with Watson's system to place their orders. In the end it was decided that neither Watson's nor their customers were ready for that change yet, but the BPR group asked the IS team to use techniques that would facilitate customer access at some point in the future. The IS group decided that this request suggested that they use Internet technology and Java, an OO programming language. A Java application would run on almost any platform a customer might have, and if the customer used a browser, it wouldn't make any difference what kind of hardware the customer had. Moreover, Java, being OO, would facilitate rapid development and reasonably rapid alteration when the time came to modify the application to support customer access.

Watson's IS department created a sales application development team to undertake the software development effort. The team accepted the assignment and decided to undertake a use case analysis as a preliminary step before beginning a more detailed OO analysis phase. Before proceeding to use case analysis, however, the IS team spent quite a bit of time trying to come up with a good name for the system they planned to develop. Someone suggested the Watson's Distributed Sales Reporting and Management System—WDSRMS—but everyone agreed that didn't have any pizazz. Finally someone suggested the Watson's SalesWeb, and everyone agreed that was a lot more exciting.

7.5 Automating the BPR Process

We have focused on the IBM LOVEM diagrams in this chapter. Popkin Software's SA/Object Architect, the OO modeling tool we will use in other chapters, has a BPR tool that is based on another popular notational system—the Department of Defense's IDEF notation. IDEF is an older notation that is, in many ways, closer to entity relationship diagrams. You could certainly represent the same information that we represented in describing Watson's problem in Popkin Software's BPR tool, but we prefer LOVEM diagrams because we think they are clearer. We especially like the fact that you can always see where the customer interacts with the system and exactly what happens after that.

There are three software tools that you can use to create LOVEM diagrams. One is IBM's Business Process Modeler, which is only available for OS/2 machines and single developers. This tool has been stabilized and will only be supported until the end of the third quarter of 1998. Meantime, IBM has entered into a deal with Holosofx, which will be incorporating LOVEM in version 4 of their Workflow*BPR Modeler product, to be available in the first quarter of 1998.

Our favorite LOVEM tool is Proforma's ProVision. In ProVision you can create Rummler-Brache diagrams (the original version of LOVEM diagrams) and then convert them to UML object diagrams. (We provide contact information on Proforma and other vendors mentioned here in Appendix D.) No matter which LOVEM tool you choose, you can create and modify LOVEM diagrams and print them as needed.

Use Case Diagrams and Ideal Object Models

Ivar Jacobson introduced use cases in *Object-Oriented Software Engineering: A Use Case Driven Approach* (Reading, MA: Addison-Wesley, 1992), a book he wrote with several coworkers. The book also introduced a general OO methodology, usually called OOSE. In OOSE, you begin with use cases and then proceed to develop a complete OO application. In the last two years, many different methodologists have embraced use cases as a way to do an initial analysis of the problem to be modeled. In 1996 Ivar Jacobson joined Rational Software and was part of the team that developed the UML notation. Thus, use cases are now a part of UML.

Many developers employ use cases as a way to do a requirements analysis, which is what we are going to do. Then we'll proceed to develop what the old OOSE methodology called ideal object models. An ideal object model is the first step in the transition from the use case model to a class diagram.

We'll rely on use cases to help us specify system requirements. We'll use the ideal object models to get an overview of the kinds of classes we are likely to need when we switch from use cases to class diagrams. Once we develop rough versions of the ideal object models, we'll switch to UML class diagrams, in Chapter 10, to refine our understanding of the classes we'll need in our final system.

A use case approach requires that you begin by creating one or more use case diagrams and then create a use case description (or scenario) for each use case–actor relationship you identify. Later, both the use case diagrams and the use case descriptions can be used to generate an ideal object model. Or you can move directly from the use case descriptions to UML class diagrams. We'll consider the steps in order.

8.1 Use Case Diagrams

A use case diagram provides a functional description of a system and its major processes and places a boundary on the problem to be solved. It also provides a graphic description of who will use the system and what kinds of interactions they can expect to have with the system. In use case modeling, entities outside the problem area that are going to use the application are called actors. Processes that occur within the application area are called use cases.

A rectangle with rounded corners represents the application or system. An application can have one or more use cases. Things inside the rectangle are to be included in the application to be developed, and those outside are to be excluded. The name of the system or application to be developed is written just inside the top left corner of the system rectangle.

An actor may be a person, another software application, or a hardware device. All are represented by a little stick figure of a person. Although it's unnecessary, most developers tend to place people who will use the system on the left of the diagram. Hardware, other applications, and systems personnel who will use the system are typically placed on the right side of the diagram.

The use case itself is represented by an oval. The name of the use case is written inside the oval (or, sometimes, below the oval). A use case is not a class or object. It is a process that satisfies some need of a user of the system.

A line connects the actors and the use cases they interact with. You can label these interaction lines. Later, a written description of the interaction between the use case and the actor will be prepared. This written scenario is called a use case description.

An initial use case diagram is an abstract model of the system. An actor describes types of users, and a use case describes a generic process that satisfies the needs of those who will use the system. (See Figure 8.1.)

Use case diagrams can go beyond simply representing isolated processes and can show relationships between processes. We won't go into these advanced use case diagramming

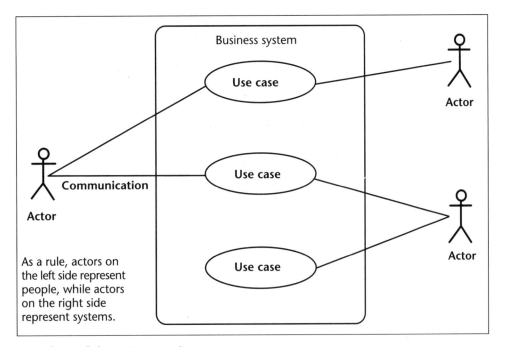

Figure 8.1   *A Use case diagram.*

techniques in any detail, since most developers simply rely on basic use case diagrams.

8.2 Use Cases and Business Process Reengineering

Some developers create use case diagrams to document BPR efforts. We find LOVEM diagrams better for BPR and prefer to rely on use cases for software systems analysis. Relative to the large–scale processes considered in BPR, most developers seem to create use case diagrams to describe relatively fine-grained software processes. In many situations, use case processes are more like software modules. Still, the scope of a use case is up to the designer, and you can create use cases that look at processes at a very high level of abstraction or at lower levels of detail.

We could create a use case diagram and label it Watson's Furniture Company and then create one use case inside: Selling Furniture. The scope of that use case would be very similar to the sales process we just considered in Chapter 7 when we used LOVEM diagrams. In this chapter, however, we'll create a use case diagram that only focuses on the sales system and identifies processes at a lower level of abstraction, similar to the way most developers do when they create use cases.

We've listed one book in the bibliography by Jacobson, Christerson, Jonsson, and Overgaard that describes how use cases can be used to drive a BPR effort and another by Tkach, Fang, and So (under the Chapter 7 listing) that includes a chapter on how LOVEM diagrams can be related to use cases.

8.3 A Use Case Diagram of the Watson's SalesWeb System

Figure 8.2 provides a high-level use case diagram of the simple sales system that Watson's BPR team assigned to the Watson's SalesWeb software development team. The large round-cornered rectangle, labeled "Watson's SalesWeb System," defines the boundary around the problem. Things outside the boundary are not going to be part of our application development effort.

In our diagram we show four actors. One is the salesperson. Another is the regional sales manager. The other two represent computer systems that the SalesWeb system will interact with. One is Watson's existing accounting system, and the other is the existing warehouse inventory system.

The use case diagram in Figure 8.2 shows three use cases: Report Sales, Review Individual's Sales, and Review Regional Sales. Each of these use cases is a process that could contain several classes. Some of the classes that will need to be modeled might occur in more than one use case. So, again, don't think

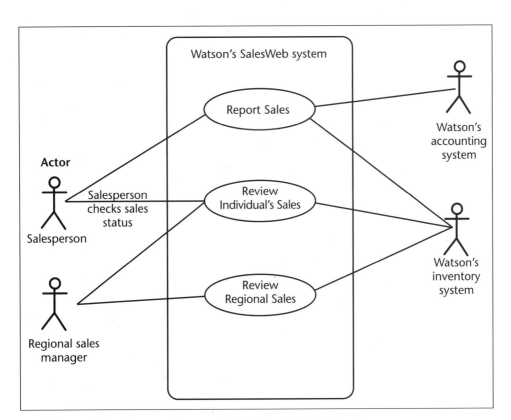

Figure 8.2   *Use case diagram of the Watson's SalesWeb system.*

of use cases as classes or objects. They are processes that occur in response to a stimulus by an actor.

The same actor can be involved in more than one use case. We sometimes speak of the relationship or communication between an actor and a specific use case as a role. In this example, one role the salesperson can perform is to submit a new order. Another role involves checking a report of his or her sales performance.

8.3.1 *Clarifying Our Vocabulary Regarding the Watson's Application*

One of the problems that any software development effort faces involves deciding what to call things. It's easy to get into a lot of confusion if things aren't clear. In the real world, the Sales-Web developers would have to work lots of these details out for themselves. To simplify things for you, however, we'll try to be a little more explicit before proceeding any further.

Figure 8.3 provides an expanded diagram that combines a use case and some icons to illustrate all of the elements that will occur as we talk about our sales system. On the left side of the diagram we can see the customer who wants to order furniture. Then there's the salesperson who will submit the order. The salesperson will use a laptop that will either have an application or a browser. In any case, the laptop will have some kind of client software.

In the middle section is the Watson's Internet server. Some kind of handler class will deal with salespeople who want to sign on and, if appropriate, create a sales order. The sales order itself will consist of at least four parts. There will be information about the salesperson placing the order. There will be information about the customer who wants to place the order. This information will include some data on the customer's credit limit, which will be obtained from the legacy accounting application/database. There will be information on each of the furniture items the customer wants to order. For each item that is ordered, there will be information on the type of item, the style, decisions about colors, fabrics or finishes, the

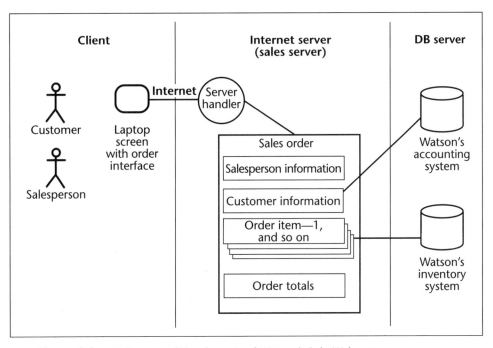

Figure 8.3   *A diagram of the elements of Watson's SalesWeb system.*

number of the item desired, the cost of a single item, and a total for the single item. There can be anywhere from one to dozens of furniture items on a single order. As the order is entered, the legacy inventory application/database will need to be checked to determine whether the items are in stock and when they can be shipped. Finally, there will be a section of the order that totals all the items, adds taxes and shipping costs, and gives total cost for the entire order.

Independent of the server, on the right side of the diagram, are the mainframe legacy applications and databases that the sales application will need to access for information, approvals, and so on.

In writing descriptions in this book, it would be easy to confuse the real customer with the information about the customer that will be listed on the sales order. We'll use "customer" to mean the actual person or company ordering furniture.

We'll use *Customer Information* to refer to the class that contains information about the customer that is included in the sales order. (In a real-world situation OO developers would never name a class *Customer Information*. They would simply call it *Customer*. After all, each of our objects will contain information, and it would be silly to attach "information" to the name of each class. We're writing an introductory book, however, and we don't want to write sentences that make it hard to tell whether we're talking about a real person or an object. So we'll allow ourselves this awkward name just to make things a little easier on the reader. We hope it won't upset OO programmers too much.)

There will be some kind of interface on the salesperson's laptop that will resemble an order form. It shouldn't be confused with the *Sales Order* object on the server. Moreover, the *Sales Order* on the server will probably be a compound object that will contain other objects, including one or more *Item Ordered* objects.

We'll use "salesperson" as a term that applies to both the actual salesperson and to the software module that sits on the salesperson's laptop machine. Thus, *Salesperson* will refer to the software module, including the sales order form, that is displayed on the salesperson's laptop. We could just as well call this module the client module, but we want to avoid terms that suggest computer architecture in favor of those that suggest how it might ordinarily be talked about. Salespeople submit sales orders. So sales orders originate from salespeople.

During the analysis phase we'll ignore the possibility of a *Sales Handler* class, since that's a software construct, and we'll simply combine its functions with the *Sales Order* class. On the other hand, we'll break the *Sales Order* class itself down into a *Customer Information* class and an *Item Ordered* class.

Initially we'll talk about *Accounting* and *Inventory* as if they were classes. When we get to the design phase, we'll get more explicit about the fact that they are really legacy applications.

Having clarified our vocabulary a bit, let's return to our use case analysis of the Watson's SalesWeb application.

8.4 Use Case Descriptions

A use case description provides a generic, step-by-step written description of the interaction between an actor and a use case. In Figure 8.2 we showed eight interactions: two between the salesperson and two use cases, two between the regional manager and two use cases, one between the Report Sales use case and Watson's *Accounting* system, and three between Watson's *Inventory* system and all three use cases.

To complete the use case analysis, you would need to write up eight descriptions. There is no correct level of granularity for use case processes, but you should try to choose processes that result in clear written descriptions. A salesperson might report a new sale and then proceed to see what her status relative to her quarterly quota was, all in a single session. To simplify things, assume that these are two independent transactions: one to report the sale and another to check performance against the quota. Also, don't consider the details of how the transaction will be implemented on computer hardware. Don't assume, for example, that the salesperson will contact the company via a browser. It could just as easily be done by an application on the salesperson's laptop that initiated a direct Internet link to the company's server. Similarly, the salesperson could create the sales order before contacting the company's server, or she could contact the server and then create the sales order while on-line. These are design details and should be ignored during analysis. If you describe the scenarios cleanly, focusing only on business classes, it will work equally well no matter how you decide to implement the application when you turn to the design phase of the effort.

A use case description is a generic scenario. It talks about salespeople, not a specific salesperson, and it talks about the generic steps in reporting a new sale, not about a scenario in which a specific salesperson starts to report a sale and then realizes that she has entered the wrong customer number, or decides to abort an entry so she can answer an incoming phone call. Later, we'll need to write lots of specific scenarios. We'll create them by working through specific variations of the generic sequences we'll describe in our use case descriptions.

Figure 8.4 illustrates a use case description for one of the interactions shown in our simple SalesWeb use case diagram—the generic scenario for any salesperson reporting a new order. Our description assumes a generic salesperson and describes a typical way in which the salesperson would report a new order. If we wanted to explore more possibilities, we would write concrete scenarios that described specific salespeople and the steps they might take to report different kinds of concrete orders.

For example, we might describe a step-by-step scenario of how Bill Jones reports the sale of 16 items of furniture to Ace Office Supplies, a long–time Watson's customer. We might also describe how Bev Smith reports a sale of 10 items to Harmon Associates, a small company with no previous credit history with Watson's. Or, we might describe an interaction in which Tina Washington signs on and reports a sale and then immediately proceeds to review her sales–to–date to see if a previous order she placed has shipped yet. In describing the steps in these concrete examples, we would, in effect, draw on our knowledge of two different use case descriptions, since Tina uses two separate processes.

Some developers are satisfied to create generic use case descriptions. Others not only write use case descriptions for each interaction, but go on to write several concrete scenarios as well. Our SalesWeb example is reasonably simple, but it would probably require several concrete scenarios to assure that we really understood all the ways the system would need to respond to support Watson's salespeople and their managers. The more complex the problem, the more scenarios we need to assure that we haven't overlooked important details.

8.5   Instances of Use Cases As Test Cases

If you develop a concrete scenario from a description of an interaction between some hypothetical salesperson and the system, in effect, you have a high–level test case that you can

Use Case Description of the Report Sales Interaction

Normal sequence:
0. Salesperson turns on laptop, brings up SalesWeb program, and chooses Report Sales Order from menu.
1. Salesperson enters name, employee number, and ID.
2. Sales Order checks to see if name, number, and ID are valid.
3. Salesperson enters customer name and address on sales order form.
4. Sales Order checks customer information to find out customer status.
5. CustInfo checks Accounting to determine customer status.
6. Accounting approves customer information and supplies customer credit limit.
7. CustInfo accepts customer entry on Sales Order.
8. Salesperson enters first item being ordered on sales order form.
9. Salesperson enters second item being ordered, etc.
10. When all items have been entered, Items Ordered are checked to determine availability and to check pricing.
11. Items Ordered checks with Inventory to determine availability and to check pricing.
12. Inventory supplies all availability dates (when it can ship), approves prices, adds shipping and taxes, and totals order.
13. Complete sales order appears on salesperson's screen.
14. Salesperson can print order, check with customer, etc.
15. Salesperson submits the approved Sales Order.
16. Sales Order is submitted to Accounting and Inventory.

Alternate sequences:
The salesperson's name, employee number, or PIN is not acceptable. SalesWeb displays a message indicating that something is wrong and asks the user to reenter name, number, and PIN. If the user reenters the wrong name, number, and PIN three times in a row, the SalesWeb system signs off and notifies the SalesWeb manager of the attempt to enter.

The salesperson enters a part of the sales order and then asks the SalesWeb system to save the document as an incomplete order. SalesWeb saves the incomplete order, setting it aside so that the salesperson can access the incomplete order from the SalesWeb menu whenever her or she signs on in the future.

The salesperson enters an order for a company, and the order exceeds the credit limit Watson's has established for that customer. SalesWeb makes an effort to increase the customer's sales limit by checking on past behavior, payment status, etc. If unsuccessful, the order is saved while the customer calls a representative at Watson's accounting department.

Figure 8.4   *Step-by-step description of use case: Report Sales.*

later use to determine whether the application you build provides the functionality that you agreed to deliver. The scenario describes a set of inputs and expected outputs you should be able to demonstrate with the final version of the new application. Thus, some developers continue working with use cases until they have a dozen specific test cases that everyone involved in the project agrees will provide a good test of the desired functionality of the system to be developed. In this sense, the use case analysis can be used later in the development cycle and isn't simply something you only use during the requirements phase of the effort.

8.6 From Use Cases to Ideal Object Models

Many developers abandon the Jacobson approach to OO development as soon as they have created a use case diagram and written up the use case descriptions of the interactions. From the use case diagram, they move to class diagrams, to begin analyzing the actual classes they will need for their application. Before doing that, however, it's often worthwhile to develop an ideal object model of each of the use cases. (In fact, in UML terms it would be a class model.) The development of ideal object models is especially useful if you are new to OO development, since it suggests some of the classes you will probably need to develop when you turn to class diagrams.

In his OOSE methodology, Jacobson suggests that you convert your use case diagram into an OOSE object model following a series of steps that we'll describe below. The first object model he suggests you develop is called an ideal object model. This model is developed during the analysis phase of the development cycle and describes an ideal system that would accomplish all of the requirements identified by the use case diagram.

Later, when you switch to design, you begin to constrain the ideal model so that it will work in the actual environment in which you will field your application. The real object model that Jacobson uses during the design phase is different from the ideal object model. It uses different icons (rectangles instead of circles) to indicate that it is a design model and reflects the constraints of the environment for which it is being developed.

We won't consider Jacobson's real object model in this book; clearly that is being superseded in UML by UML class diagrams. We will, however, take a few minutes to review Jacobson's approach to the development of an ideal object model.

An ideal object model is not an official part of UML. Instead, ideal object notation is done by means of UML stereotypes—extensions of UML for special purposes. Stereotype terms are always indicated by guillemets («»).

8.7 The OOSE Ideal Object Model

The key to Jacobson's approach to converting a use case to an ideal object model is to assume that there are three broad types of classes. Jacobson originally had slightly different names for them, but UML provides the three "stereotype" names that we will use. (Recall that UML stereotype names are more or less official extensions of UML that allow UML to provide special functionality.) In this case, the extensions are designed to allow OOSE developers to create ideal object models while still working within the general confines of the UML notation. UML provides both names and alternate icons for three special types of classes: interface classes, entity classes, and control classes.

8.7.1 *«Interface Classes»*

Interface classes interact with things outside the application. An interface class might be responsible for screens the user sees or for controlling the interaction between the application and another software application or a hardware device.

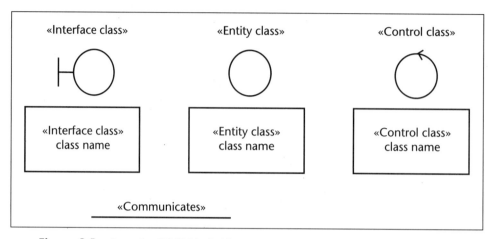

Figure 8.5   *Icons for OOSE ideal object stereotypes.*

The names of stereotype terms are always written within guillemets (or angle brackets) on UML diagrams. The UML OOSE stereotypes provide both a small icon and a way of using the stereotypes with a conventional class diagram. Figure 8.5 shows the three terms, the three small icons, and three classes, one for each type of ideal class. The small symbol for the interface class is a circle with a "T" extending to the left. (The stick figure of an actor is also a stereotype of a class, but since it is also used in the UML use case diagram, the actor is usually represented exactly as it is in a regular UML diagram.)

8.7.2 *«Entity Classes»*

Entity classes keep track of information. These classes are usually identified with the major elements of the problem as users currently describe it. They include things like forms, orders, checks, and accounts. Later, we'll see that the information stored in these classes usually needs to be stored in databases because we need them whenever we run the application. The small symbol for an entity class is a circle.

8.7.3 «Control Classes»

Control classes manage processes that transcend the various specific entity classes that are involved in the process. Control classes are commonly used to deal with transactions. These objects generally don't keep track of information that needs to be stored between uses of the application. Instances of control classes are created, they manage a transaction, and then they are discarded. (Classes that provide this type of functionality in other OO methodologies are often called handlers.)

The small symbol for a control class is a circle with an arrow inserted at the top to suggest rotation or processing.

Classes in ideal object models can be related to each other by means of association lines that are often labeled "communicates." An association line simply means that the objects of the two classes will send messages to each other. In other words, the objects will rely on each other for support in getting things done.

8.7.4 *Identifying Classes in Use Cases*

As we have already stressed, there is no one-to-one relationship between classes and use cases. Several classes are typically involved in the process that is described by a use case. Some classes are used by several different use cases.

When we start to identify the classes associated with a use case, we don't expect that we'll develop a unique set that only applies to that single use case. Nevertheless, you have to start somewhere, so one place to begin is to pick one of the use cases you have described and identify the main classes that will be involved in the process represented by that use case.

Jacobson suggests that you begin by creating an interface class to handle each of the interactions between the use case and the actors outside the system. Then, he suggests that you create at least one control class to manage the use case. If the interfaces are complex, he often creates one control object to handle each interface class. Finally, he suggests that you create entity classes for each of the major things that the process seems to involve. In other words, you create an entity class for each collection of data the use case will need to keep track of.

8.8 An Ideal Object Model for the Report Sales Use Case

Figure 8.6 illustrates a first cut at creating an ideal object model for the Report Sales use case. In this example, we've kept the oval for the Report Sales use case and placed the name for the use case near the top of the oval. We have eliminated the system rectangle since we are only looking at part of the system.

We created one interface class to represent the interface between the salesperson and the core of the application and labeled it "Browser Interface." We created a second interface object to handle interactions between our SalesWeb application and Watson's two existing applications: the accounting

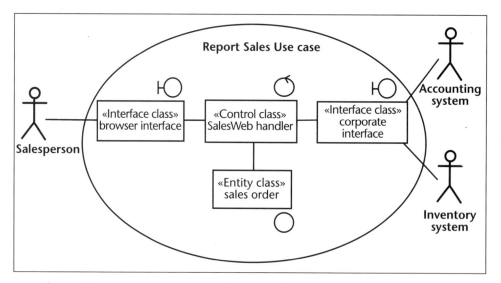

Figure 8.6   *Ideal object model for the Report Sales use case.*

system and the inventory system. We labeled that interface object "Corporate Interface."

We created one control class, *SalesHandler*, which will control the overall server process and generate sales objects as needed. And we created a *Sales Order* object to clearly maintain information on the customers who are buying products from Watson's and the items they are buying. We could have converted the Salesperson actor into a class, just as we could have converted the accounting system and the warehouse inventory system into classes, but to keep things simple we left them as they were on the original use case diagram.

All these objects are very high level objects, and we would probably break our application out a little more. Figure 8.7 represents a second cut at our ideal object model. In this case, we added two entity objects, *Customer Information*, to keep track of customer information, and *Item Ordered*, to keep track of items on the *Sales Order* (and we changed *Sales Order* into a control object to handle the *Customer Information* and *Item Ordered* objects).

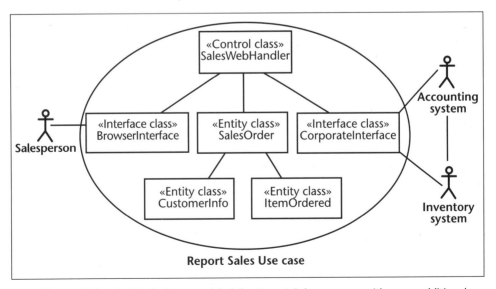

Figure 8.7 *An ideal object model of the Report Sales use case with some additional classes illustrated.*

As you can see in Figure 8.7, ideal object models can get rather complicated in short order. Imagine doing an ideal object model for a system with 25–30 objects. In our opinion, ideal object models do a nice job of suggesting the basic high-level objects a system will probably need to have. At the same time, the ideal object approach tends to focus the developer's attention on infrastructure classes (interface and control objects) more than on business objects (control and entity objects). From our perspective, you should either skip ideal modeling altogether, or, once you've developed a model like the one shown in Figure 8.7, you should switch to a UML class diagram. In the process, you should temporarily "forget" the infrastructure objects (both interface objects and the generic handler) and focus on the business objects. When we get to design, however, we'll come back to those infrastructure objects.

8.9 Creating Use Case Models with an Object-Oriented Modeling Tool

So far, we've been discussing use cases and ideal object models as if you would be drawing them on a sheet of paper with a pencil. In fact, most OO modeling tools support the creation of use cases.

We'll use Popkin's SA/Object Architect to illustrate how you could create the use case model we've described above and how you could also create an ideal model of the Report Sales use case. We've already seen how you access the SA/Object Architect tool. We'll assume that you have accessed the main menu and set the encyclopedia to *C:\saobject\salesweb*.

For our present purposes, you begin at the main menu and click on the second icon from the top left: New Diagram. Clicking on the icon brings up a box that will ask you to identify the name of the diagram you want to create and then to identify the type of diagram. We'll type SalesWeb Use Case

Diag1 in the name slot and then highlight the use case diagram type and choose OK. This will give us a screen like the one shown in Figure 8.8.

At the moment, the SalesWeb Use Case Diag1 window is blank. On the left you see a number of buttons that show the notational elements you will need in order to create a use case diagram. If you are unsure what any specific button means, you can rest the cursor-arrowhead on it, and text will appear, briefly describing the function of that button.

We'll begin by clicking on the third button from the top on the left-hand side of the palette—use case—and then use the pencil-cursor to place our first use case within the business system box. Once again, after we click on a location, a dialog box opens asking us to name the use case. We'll type Report

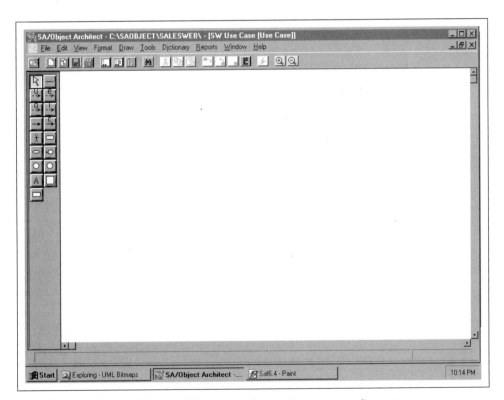

Figure 8.8   *SA/Object Architect screen for creating use case diagrams.*

Sales and then click on OK. We'll repeat this process and create two more use cases: Review Individual Sales and Review Regional Sales.

Now, we'll create some actors. We do this by clicking on the fifth button down on the left side of the menu buttons. Then we move our pencil-cursor to the left of the business system box and toward the top and click to create an actor. As soon as you click, the stick figure representing the actor will appear on your diagram, and a dialog box will open asking you to name the actor. Type in Salesperson. Next, click on the menu button on the upper right, the "communicates with" line. Using the cursor, first click on the Salesperson actor, then on the Report Sales use case. Repeat the process to link the Salesperson to the Review Individual Sales use case. Using this same approach, you'll create actors to represent the sales manager, the accounting system, and the inventory system.

Next, we'll use the fourth button down in the right-hand column: business system. Next, we'll click the cursor-pencil in the middle of our use case window. That will create a business system box, and it will also open a dialog box that will ask us to provide a name for our new use case. We'll type SalesWeb and then click on OK.

At this point, we will have a business system box on our screen with the name salesWeb under it. We now click on the arrow button and then use the cursor-arrowhead to enlarge and center the box.

Now the screen will look like the one in Figure 8.9. We've created the same use case diagram in SA/Object Architect that we created by hand as Figure 8.2.

Next we would want to create a use case description. Popkin Software's SA/Object Architect allows developers to link to Microsoft Word. Users can either build their use case description in Word or create it with the text processor of SA/Object Architect.

You can create ideal object models with SA/Object Architect in one of two ways. You can move into the class diagram and create classes, or, better, you can create ideal models within the use case environment of SA/Object Architect by changing the stereotype of the actor symbol to represent interface,

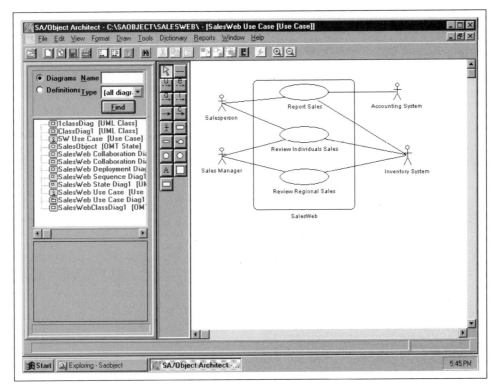

Figure 8.9   *SA/Object Architect showing the SalesWeb use case.*

control, and entity classes. In fact, if we were working in an OO modeling tool, we'd probably just draw an ideal model on a piece of paper as a thought exercise and then move on to creating a class model in the tool's class diagramming window.

CRC Cards

There are many different ways to approach OO analysis. Some developers begin by preparing BPR workflow diagrams to describe the task in a sequential manner. Many prepare detailed use case diagrams and descriptions or scenarios before they begin to develop UML class diagrams. Others prefer to create only a very general use case diagram and a minimal set of descriptions and then proceed to class diagrams. Still others rely on CRC cards as a way of analyzing the classes involved in an application. They consider CRC cards as an alternative to use case diagrams or as a supplement to use case diagrams.

Like LOVEM diagrams, CRC cards are not an official part of the UML notation. They may be recognized as a stereotype at some point, but in the meantime, they are an informal and very useful way for people to begin to develop an OO business model.

Recall that CRC stands for Classes, Responsibilities, and Collaborators. CRC cards are usually 3-inch x 5-inch lined index cards. You use cards to represent classes and write information about the classes on the cards. CRC cards are normally used by a group of five to seven people who work together to identify the classes in an application and then talk through scenarios to assure that they understand the characteristics of all the classes. In other words, developers can use the cards when they meet with end users or subject matter experts.

For those just beginning OO development, we suggest you start with a limited use case analysis like the one we described in Chapter 8. Then, we suggest you work through a CRC session like the one we describe in this chapter. Prepare your first UML class diagram only after you have first done use cases and CRC cards. Later, you may decide you would rather skip CRC cards, but on the first few tries, it will probably help.

Use cases describe processes and the actors that interact with the processes. Use cases and use case descriptions form the basis for scenarios. Ideal object models identify some of the major classes that are likely to be needed to implement a use case.

CRC cards constitute another, more informal technique for identifying and defining the characteristics of the classes that make up an application. In effect, you develop use cases to define the overall scope of the application and to generate scenarios that will describe the uses of the application. Then, you use CRC cards to actually work through scenarios and refine your understanding of the classes that will make up the application. Once you have the informal descriptions of the classes, you are ready to create your first UML class diagram.

Analyzing the classes needed for an application by means of CRC cards has some distinct advantages over simply starting with a UML class diagram. To begin with, because it's informal, it's a good technique to use with domain experts, user representatives, and other nonprogrammers who should have input during the initial definition of the system. Equally important, it's a great way to help programmers who are more familiar with procedural analysis make the transition to OO analysis. The OO approach really is different. When you are getting started, it's important to be sure everyone has the OO mind-set. CRC cards are a concrete way of understanding exactly what OO development is all about.

To use CRC cards, there are two things you need to know. First you need to know the physical layout of a CRC card. Then you need to know the steps in a CRC development session. We'll consider each in turn.

9.1 The Layout of a CRC Card

Figure 9.1 illustrates the front and back of a CRC card. Some people omit attributes or superclasses and subclasses, but we'll cover them all. At the top of each card you write the class

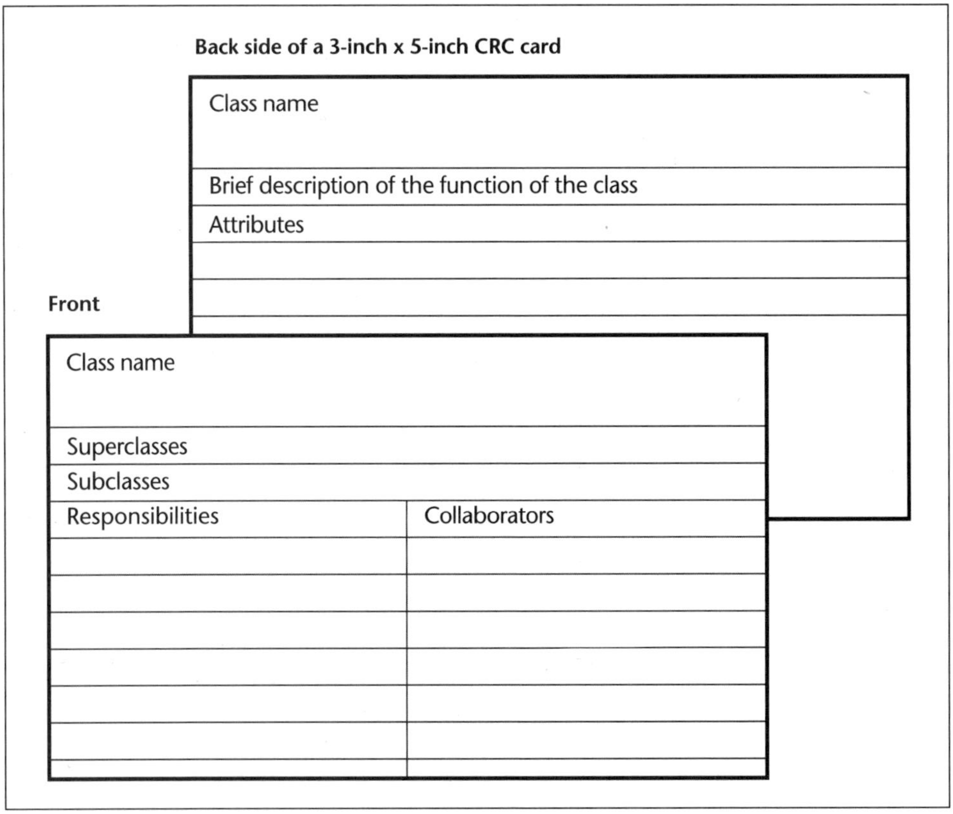

Back side of a 3-inch x 5-inch CRC card

Class name
Brief description of the function of the class
Attributes

Front

Class name	
Superclasses	
Subclasses	
Responsibilities	Collaborators

Figure 9.1   *The two sides of a CRC card.*

name for the class the card is to describe. Classes are generic descriptions of sets of objects. There is the class customer, and then there are specific objects of customers: Mary Hong, James Garcia, and Lee Smith. Class names are generally nouns. Simple, well-chosen, descriptive nouns will make the entire effort easier to understand. The class description is a simple statement about the overall function of the class.

One of the great things about 3-inch x 5-inch index cards is that they are so cheap and informal. If you try one name and decide it isn't right, you can simply tear up the card and make another. Similarly, if you find you have two cards for two different classes and subsequently find that they are really just different names for the same class, you choose one and throw the other away.

Responsibilities are operations and knowledge that the system maintains. A responsibility is usually a short phrase. It must include a verb. Thus, submitting an order, checking whether an item is in inventory, verifying a customer's credit limit, or knowing which customers have credit limits of over $10,000 are all responsibilities.

A collaborator is the name of another class that is used to perform a specific responsibility. For example, a salesperson would need to collaborate with an authorization class to verify a customer's credit limit. Each responsibility can be associated with zero to several collaborators. The same collaborators can be associated with more than one responsibility.

Attributes describe values that the object of the class will store. Thus, the *authorization* class will include the attribute customer credit limit.

When we considered class hierarchies in Chapter 2, we said that relative to any one class, the class above it in a hierarchy is its superclass, and the classes that are below it and inherit from it are its subclasses. In a multiple inheritance system, one class could have more than one superclass. If you plan to work in Java and find yourself listing more than one superclass on a CRC card, don't worry about it. Chances are you'll find that one or more of the superclasses can actually be interface classes.

In Java, as in ActiveX, you can only have a single superclass, but you can have interfaces. Interfaces have become popular since the CRC approach was first developed. In general, interface classes are infrastructure classes, and CRC doesn't focus on infrastructure classes. We suggest you ignore interface classes, and don't mention them to users or consider them yourself, if you undertake a CRC exercise. On the other hand, if you want to include interfaces, consider that they are, in fact, other classes that collaborate with a container class, and for analysis purposes, you might just as well consider them another class.

9.2 The Steps in a CRC Session

Here's a brief overview of the steps that occur in a typical CRC session:

1. Assemble a group.
2. Review requirements.
3. Brainstorm a list of classes.
4. Review the list of classes.
5. Prepare CRC cards.
6. Develop a description of each class.
7. Brainstorm responsibilities and collaborators.
8. Generate specific scenarios.
9. Talk through several scenarios.
10. Add superclasses or subclasses.
11. Repeat the process.

We'll consider each step in turn and work through our simple SalesWeb example at the same time.

9.2.1 Step 1: Assemble a Group

An ideal group has five to seven members. It should include someone familiar with object technology to act as a facilitator. It should certainly include domain experts and users who know what they want from the system, and it should include developers.

If you are working alone, you are going to have to play all the roles. If you don't have to work with groups, you'll probably give up CRC cards after a while. We suggest, however, if you are new to OO programming, that you try CRC cards once or twice when you are getting started, even if you have to do it by yourself.

9.2.2 *Step 2: Review Requirements*

The CRC session should only be scheduled after a requirements statement has been developed for the project. Similarly, use case diagrams and documentation should already have been completed before the session. The session begins by reviewing the requirements statement and the use case diagram and documentation to assure that everyone agrees on the overall goals of the project.

9.2.3 *Step 3: Brainstorm a List of Classes*

The group should develop a list of likely classes. Usually the domain experts can come up with a good list without too much prompting. You can also examine the use case descriptions, looking through the step-by-step scenarios to identify nouns that might refer to potential classes.

Don't forget that use cases refer to processes, not objects. A use case can contain several or even hundreds of classes, and the same classes can occur in many different use cases. If you created an ideal object model of your use case, that should suggest some potential classes. (Keep in mind, however, that you'll generally want to ignore the interface classes and any classes, such as handlers, that simply coordinate the work of other classes.)

Someone should write the names of the classes that the group identifies on a blackboard, chart paper, or some other media.

9.2.4 *Step 4: Review the List of Classes*

Consolidate the list of classes by eliminating names that are too abstract or too specific for the initial effort. Focus on a subset of the list if the list is too long. A group of five people is bound to disagree about what to call things. Moreover, there will be misunderstandings about the meanings of words. This is the time to talk them out. Well-chosen class names will make all future discussions more productive.

Some of the classes proposed by the group will be high-level abstractions. Some will be very specialized. Both should be avoided during the initial effort. Thus, in the case of our SalesWeb application, you will probably not want to get into the various details involved in ordering a specific item on a *Sales Order* during your first CRC session. It will be sufficient to think simply that the salesperson fills out a sales order and identifies furniture items to be purchased. You won't need to identify different types of furniture, such as desks and chairs, or consider order details such as price, number, and so on. If you can get the middle-level classes identified and sorted out, you can always go back later and identify opportunities for higher level unifications or subclasses. Similarly, as you get closer to design, you can always generate more specialized classes as they prove necessary.

Even if you limit your classes to those that fall along the middle of the potential class hierarchy, you will often find that there are lots of classes. In this case, you want to find some criteria that will allow you to focus on only a portion of the middle of the hierarchy. For example, you might only consider sales to furniture stores and ignore, for the moment, direct sales to companies. You could also ignore the possibility that sales of over a certain amount might allow stores to receive discounts.

Figure 9.2 illustrates a class hierarchy. The classes at the top are very abstract. Classes lower down in the hierarchy are more concrete. The classes at the bottom of the hierarchy are very specialized. We have circled the classes that fall along the middle, and then we have circled a subset of those in the middle.

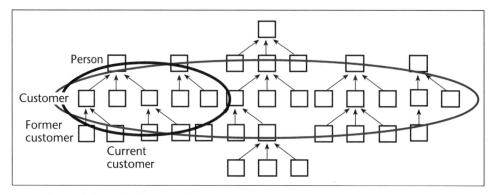

Figure 9.2 *The classes within a hierarchy on which you should initially focus.*

Of course, everyone has a slightly different idea of what constitutes middle-level classes. One rule of thumb is that you should identify all the classes you need to "process" the scenarios. So, if you're unsure, wait until you start working with the scenarios and add or subtract as appropriate.

Ideally, you would like to start with between 5 and 10 classes. If you discover a lot more (and any big application will probably involve a lot more), you need to figure out how to subdivide the middle-level classes into some groups. Focusing on just the classes involved in one specific use case is one way to subdivide a large application.

When preparing CRC cards, always ignore interface classes that are used to manage screens, databases, or classes that are, in effect, really part of a process being performed by outside software applications or hardware devices. In other words, focus on business classes.

One of the great advantages of OO development is the ability to modularize the effort and work on one part of an application at a time. Developing your initial model will offer enough challenges, and you don't want to allow yourself to be overwhelmed by trying to consider too many classes at once. Pick a subset of classes. Once you have figured out how they work together, you can easily go back and add others until you have a complete model.

9.2.5   *Step 5: Prepare CRC Cards*

Once everyone agrees on the list of classes, write the class names on 3-inch x 5-inch cards and give one or more cards to each member of the group. Each person with a card acts as the representative of that class/object as you work through scenarios.

9.2.6   *Step 6: Develop a Description of Each Class*

Before going any further, write a brief description of each class on the back of the respective CRC cards. This is a final test that everyone agrees on the meaning of each class name. If technical people are present, this can become quite complex, but it's important to be sure you understand what the class really does. People often make assumptions about class names based on the ordinary meanings of the words. Later, they find that technical people use a seemingly ordinary word in a much narrower or more specialized way.

Figure 9.3 illustrates how we might have defined some of the classes that we found in the use case description we created in Chapter 8 (Figure 8.4). Remember that we are ignoring interface and database access classes as well as handlers that simply sequence activities. We won't concern ourselves with the details of how the accounting system and the warehouse inventory systems work, but we will represent them as two classes, since they will have responsibilities in several scenarios.

9.2.7   *Step 7: Brainstorm Responsibilities and Collaborators*

Some prefer to move directly to scenario walk-throughs. Others prefer to record obvious responsibilities and collaborators on the various CRC cards before the scenarios begin. It's easy to use scenarios to learn that you must add responsibilities. It's harder to realize that you have added unnecessary responsibilities. Thus, it is better to list only those responsibilities you

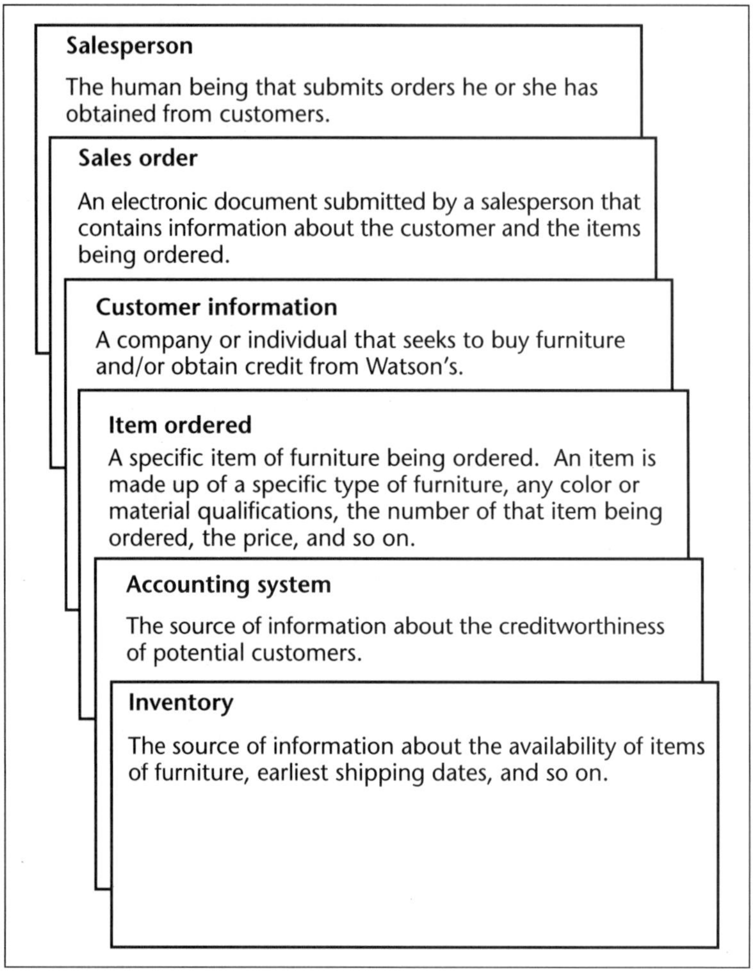

Salesperson

The human being that submits orders he or she has obtained from customers.

Sales order

An electronic document submitted by a salesperson that contains information about the customer and the items being ordered.

Customer information

A company or individual that seeks to buy furniture and/or obtain credit from Watson's.

Item ordered

A specific item of furniture being ordered. An item is made up of a specific type of furniture, any color or material qualifications, the number of that item being ordered, the price, and so on.

Accounting system

The source of information about the creditworthiness of potential customers.

Inventory

The source of information about the availability of items of furniture, earliest shipping dates, and so on.

Figure 9.3   *An initial set of CRC cards for the SalesWeb example.*

are sure of and leave doubtful responsibilities until you begin to work through scenarios.

Responsibilities are described by phrases that begin with verbs. They either involve actions (order, check) or state (approved, available). In most situations one class will call on another class to perform some task. The responsibility of the second class is to perform the task. Don't bother to add another responsibility indicating that the second class must notify the first class that it has completed the task; answering back is assumed.

There are no correct answers about which class will perform which task. In many situations, either of two classes could do the task equally well. As a general rule, you want to keep classes independent and minimize interaction. Thus, if you find two classes exchanging lots of messages to accomplish some general task, it's probably better to give more responsibility to the second class. Then, once the first class has asked the second class to do something, the second class can do lots of work and only respond when the task is done. This is just like a manager giving an assignment to an assistant. You want to delegate enough responsibility to avoid having the assistant return to ask questions every other hour.

The exception to this generalization occurs when the first class has the task of maintaining some overall control of the flow of a transaction (a handler) and needs to be able to control exactly when the second class should begin to perform step two and then step three, and so on.

9.2.8 *Step 8: Generate Specific Scenarios*

At this point, you will want to walk through several scenarios to see how the classes work in an application. The best way to get scenarios is to begin with the use case descriptions. Remember that each use case description is a generic version of a scenario. The same use case description can be used to generate a number of different specific scenarios.

Pick a use case description and then let one person talk through a specific scenario of the description. For example, in Figure 9.4 we have listed the Report Sales use case description we listed in Figure 8.4 on the left and then provided two specific scenarios on the right.

Note that in this example, since it is simple and since we assume that it's going to be done across the Web, we're inclined to assume lots of other things. We have the salespeople signing on to their laptops. We probably shouldn't. We simply did it to remind you of how the application is going to work.

Figure 9.4 *Use case description of Report Sales and two scenarios.*

Normal sequence	Scenario 1	Scenario 2
0. Salesperson turns on laptop, brings up SalesWeb program, and chooses Report Sales Order from menu.	0. Salesperson Curtis Clyde turns on his laptop and accesses the Report Sales Order form.	0. Pooks Rutherford turns on her laptop and accesses the Report Sales Order form.
1. Salesperson enters name, employee number, and PIN.	1. Curt enters his name, employee number, and ID.	1. Pooks enters her name, employee number, and ID.
2. Sales Order checks to see if name, number, and ID are valid.	2. The system recognizes Curt and lets him continue.	2. The system indicates that the entry is wrong and asks Pooks to reenter her number and PIN.
3. Salesperson enters customer name and address on sales order form.	3. Curt enters Harmon Assoc. as the customer.	3. Pooks enters her name, employee number, and PIN correctly.
4. Sales Order checks Customer Information to find out customer status.	4. The Sales Order checks with Customer Information concerning Harmon Association.	4. The system recognizes Pooks and lets her continue.
5. Customer Information checks Accounting to determine customer status.	5. The Customer Information class checks with Accounting to see about Harmon Associates.	5. Pooks enters Morrissey Office Furniture as the customer.
6. Accounting approves customer and supplies customer credit limit.	6. Accounting approves Harmon Assoc. and sets its credit limit at $5000.	6. The Customer Information class checks with Accounting to see about Morrissey Office Furniture.
7. Customer Information accepts customer entry on Sales Order.	7. Harmon Associates information is displayed on the sales order.	7. Accounting approves Morrissey and sets its credit limit at $50,000.
8. Salesperson enters first item being ordered on sales order form.	8. Curt enters the type of desk that Harmon Associates wants to buy and indicates that that's the only item on this order.	8. The Morrissey information is displayed on Pooks' screen.
9. Salesperson enters second item being ordered, and so on.	9. Sales Order checks with Item Ordered to determine availability, and so on.	9. Pooks enters several desks and chairs that Morrissey wants to buy and then indicates that the order is complete.

Normal sequence

10. When all items have been entered, Sales Order checks Item Ordered to determine availability and to check pricing.

11. Item Ordered checks with Inventory to determine availability and to check pricing.

12. Inventory supplies all availability dates (when it can ship), approves prices, adds shipping and taxes, and totals order.

13. Complete order appears on salesperson's screen.

14. Salesperson can print order, check with customer, and so on.

15. Salesperson submits the approved Sales Order.

16. Sales Order is submitted to Accounting and Inventory.

Scenario 1

10. Item Ordered checks with inventory.

11. Inventory provides the availability (immediate) and price ($1500), adds shipping and taxes, provides a total, and estimates when the order will arrive at the customer's site.

12. Curt prints the order, shows the complete order to the purchase order manager and Harmon Associates (Paul Harmon), and gets his approval.

13. Curt approves the order.

14. The Sales Order is forwarded to both Accounting and Inventory.

Scenario 2

10. Sales Order checks with Item Ordered to determine availability, and so on.

11. Inventory provides availability and price, and so on.

12. Pooks prints the order and shows it to Mr. Morrissey.

13. Mr. Morrissey insists he needs the desks sooner.

14. Pooks queries about rush ordering the desks.

15. Item Ordered/Inventory indicate that they can't be rush ordered.

16. Mr. Morrissey says he'll have to get the desks elsewhere.

17. Pooks modifies the order to eliminate the desks, gets approval for the chairs, and submits the order.

Figure 9.4   *Use case description of Report Sales and two scenarios.*
(continued)

In an ideal world, analysis ought to focus on the logical organization of a system without regard to how it will be arranged when it is actually developed. It would be better to imagine a salesperson, an order form, someone who would approve customers, and so on, all in a single room. Once you have the classes worked out, you can figure out where they will be physically located when an actual order is processed.

Since we went halfway and talked about the salesperson signing on with a laptop, it seems awkward to have the laptop talking with *Sales Order*. In fact, as we'll see when we get to design, we'll have a Sales Handler that will always be active on the server. The laptop will access the *Sales Handler*, which will approve access and then cause the *Sales Order* to create an instance of itself, and so forth. None of this makes too much difference with a simple system like this because you can maintain a good overview of what's happening. When you start analyzing much larger systems, however, and have to deal with dozens or hundreds of classes, then it's very important to be more precise about these things.

9.2.9   *Step 9: Talk Through Several Scenarios*

Each person takes the card(s) they are responsible for and makes entries on it as their class card becomes involved in a scenario. One person begins by describing a scenario. For example, suppose the group begins by walking through Scenario 1 from Figure 9.4. The walk-through begins with the person with the *Salesperson* CRC card beginning the dialog, which then runs as follows:

> *Salesperson:* I'm Curtis Clyde. I want to enter an order from Harmon Associates for an executive desk. I turn on my laptop and access the Report Sales Order program and choose the Report Sales option. I now have a sales order form on my computer screen. I enter my name, employee number, and PIN. My laptop sends information over the telephone to the SalesWeb system.
>
> *Sales Order:* I need to determine whether the name, employee number, and PIN match those of someone I

can work with. I check my table of salespeople and identify Curtis Clyde. I tell Curt to go ahead.

Salesperson: I enter the name Harmon Associates on the order form on my screen.

Sales Order: I can see anything that the *Salesperson* enters on the order form. When I see that Curt has entered a customer's name, I ask *Customer Information* to verify the customer and to find out what the customer's credit limit is.

Customer Information: I check with *Accounting* to see if Harmon Associates is OK and to find out what their credit limit is.

Accounting: I check my tables when asked and then tell *Customer Information* that Harmon Associates is an established customer and that we've approved them for a credit limit of $5000, all of which is currently available.

Customer Information: Once *Accounting* tells me Harmon Associates is OK, I pass the information on to *Sales Order*.

Sales Order: I highlight the name Harmon Associates on the order form and show the current credit limit.

Salesperson: Once I see the customer's name highlighted and see the credit amount, I enter the first (and only) item that Harmon Associates wants to buy—an executive desk.

Sales Order: As soon as I see that the *Salesperson* has entered an item, I ask *Item Ordered* to check on its availability, price, delivery date, and so on.

Item Ordered: I check with *Inventory* to find out about availability, and so on.

Inventory: I check my database tables and determine that we have an executive desk like the one Harmon Associates wants, and it is available to ship. Using zip codes, I determine when it could arrive at the Harmon Associates site. I also provide information on the current price of the desk, shipping costs, taxes, and so on.

Item Ordered: I pass the information from *Inventory* on to *Sales Order*. If there had been more than one item ordered, I would have done the math to figure out the total cost of the order.

Sales Order: I display the information about the executive desk on the order form.

Salesperson: Once I have the information about availability, I check with the guy at Harmon Associates to be sure it's OK, then I press SUBMIT.

Sales Order: Once the *Salesperson* tells me to submit the order, I send copies of the order to *Accounting* and *Inventory*.

We can stop now, since *Accounting* and *Inventory* are legacy systems that are outside the scope of this development effort. They already know how to process orders once they are received. They ship and bill.

In considering this dialogue, remember that we are using CRC "class" cards, but we are talking as if they are passing messages to each other. In other words, we are acting as if each class is an object. The class *Customer Information*, for example, is, for the purposes of this dialogue, the object Harmon Associates.

Also keep in mind that we are talking about objects sending messages to each other. An actual system creates objects at run time and only maintains them as long as they are needed. Try to avoid falling into procedural terms and beginning to think of "calling an object" as if objects were a block of procedural code that always exists. It might be easy to think this way about a *Sales Handler*, if we were including one in our example, since it will have some kind of permanence. But even the "permanent" *Sales Handler* will in fact be a class that will create an object of itself to handle each specific call from each Salesperson. Indeed, the *Sales Handler* might easily have a dozen objects of itself in existence at one time if the server it is on is equipped to handle several salespeople calling at the same time.

The *Sales Order* is a better example of an object. An object of the *Sales Order* class is created when a new order is entered. It accumulates information, updates the accounting and inventory systems, and then ceases to exist.

Next, consider that we have already experienced some problems as a result of assuming we know about the architecture of the system. We might decide to store the *Sales Order* class on each salesperson's laptop and have it send to get authorizations as needed. We could even make it an applet, have the salesperson use a generic Web browser, and then download the *Sales Order* applet whenever a salesperson contacted the server. As it is, we're assuming that an application on the laptop machine initiates the link between the laptop and the server. But whether you know this or not, you should ignore architectural issues at this point. Assume that everything is taking place on a single computer and that all of the classes are available to each other. This is an ideal system that we are analyzing at this point. We'll take design issues into account later. For now, you simply want to know what the key objects are and what each one will be responsible for accomplishing.

Now consider the actual events that occurred. *Salesperson* sent a message to *Sales Order* containing his name, number, and ID. *Sales Order* returned a message approving it. *Sales Order* must have a table listing the salespeople and their numbers and IDs. *Sales Order* might store this information in a database and access it as needed (largely depending on how many salespeople there are), but we don't need to concern ourselves with that. At a minimum, the object derived from *Sales Order* will need attributes to store the values for *Salesperson*'s name, *Salesperson*'s number, and *Salesperson*'s PIN.

Salesperson sent another message giving the customer's name. Thus, the *Sales Order* object will also need an attribute to store the customer's name. The *Sales Order* object then sent a message to the *Customer Information* object, to check on the status of the customer. The *Customer Information* object will also need a slot to store the customer's name, and it will generate a message to the accounting system to determine the creditworthiness of Harmon Associates and their credit limit. Thus, the *Customer Information* object will also need an attribute for credit limit, and so on.

By working your way through the dialogue, you can begin to see which classes need to be able to send messages to which other classes. You can also see which classes need to have attributes that will allow them to access or to store data (names, numbers, etc.).

The individuals responsible for each CRC card should write these things down as they take part in the dialogues. When people holding CRC cards have to ask someone else for help, that is a trigger for writing down a responsibility on their cards. Similarly, if they ask for or receive a data item, they need to enter an attribute name to remind them that they will have to be able to store that data item.

9.2.10 *Step 10: Add Superclasses and Subclasses*

To keep this example simple, we haven't begun to consider the possibility of creating new classes or subclasses yet, but this will probably arise if the participants make the dialogues a little more detailed than we have so far. For example, the address to which a bill is shipped is not always the same as the address to which the furniture will be shipped. It might be in the case of an individual but probably won't be in the case of a large company. Hence, we'll need to have one attribute for billing address and another for shipping address. Accounting will be interested in the first, and inventory will be interested in the second. In addition, an address isn't a simple data type. It usually involves several fields. In fact, in most OO systems, address would be an object in its own right. In effect, *Sales Order* or *Customer Information* will be compound objects and include within them another object, *Address*. (Or, since we are using Java, this may be handled via interfaces. In other words, *Sales Order* or *Customer Information* would support an address interface.)

Since a billing address and a shipping address are very much alike, we might create one class for address and then create two subclasses: one for customers whose billing address and shipping address are the same and another for customers with two or more addresses. We might, for example, get an order from a company that wanted office furniture delivered to all six of its regional offices.

We won't go further into this issue at the moment. We are primarily using this superclass/subclass relationship to give us an opportunity to show inheritance. In reality, there are several ways this could be solved, and we'll certainly consider it further

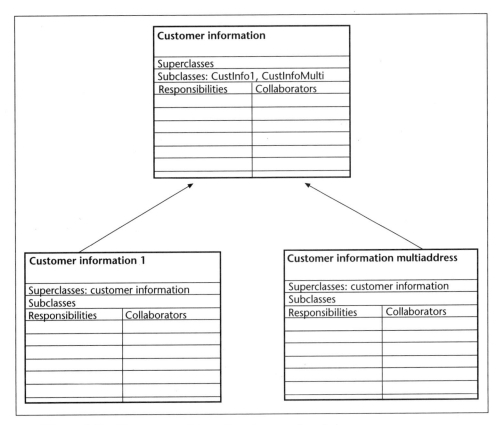

Figure 9.5   *The customer information class and its subclasses.*

when we get to the design phase of our effort. Meanwhile, we'll assume that our team has decided to subdivide the *Customer Information (CustInfo)* class into two subclasses: *CustInfo1*, which supports a single address, and *CustInfoMulti*, which will support two or more addresses. (See Figure 9.5.)

Using a similar kind of logic, we might decide to subclass the *Item Ordered* class into subclasses that describe more specific groups of furniture. Consider that some furniture items are simple, while others come in a variety of woods, paints, and coverings. Desk chairs, for example, can be ordered in a wide range of fabrics or leathers, and the finish on chairs can be various colors. It's easy to imagine that it would make sense to subclass *Item Ordered* into a number of subclasses, one for each major type of furniture. They might all inherit some general characteristics (as, for example, the shipping address) but might diverge as we began to consider the different types of decisions the customer would have to make before we could provide information on availability or price. Standard oak desk chairs might be in stock, but desk chairs in rare woods might be a special order. These are issues that will come up if you are working with users who know about furniture. The smart *Inventory* system card holder will ask lots of questions of the *Sales Order* CRC card holder before he or she is willing to speak about availability or provide a firm price.

At this stage, if possible, put off worrying about possible subclasses. Assume we are only going to develop a small prototype system to establish that the overall design of the Sales-Web system will work. Ask everyone to agree to limit the furniture available to two items for now. The point is that you will have to deal with all these issues, but at the moment you are only trying to decide on the main classes you will need and the most important attributes and responsibilities each class will need to accommodate. Keep things as simple as you can.

Assuming you stick with the initial set of classes, each member should now have a reasonably good idea of the responsibilities, attributes, and collaborators for his or her class. We show the set of CRC cards we came up with below.

Class: *Salesperson*

Responsibilities	Collaborators
Initiate sales order report	*Sales Order*
Enter customer name	*Customer Information*
Enter customer address	*Customer Information*
Enter items to be ordered	*Item Ordered*
Indicate that order is complete and acceptable	*Sales Order*

Attributes

Customer name

Customer address

Item-1 (type, style, size, wood/fabric, number)

Class: *Sales Order*

Responsibilities	Collaborators
Recognize/authorize salespeople	*Salesperson*
Ask *Customer Information* to check customer credit	*Customer Information*
Update salesperson's screen with credit limit	*Salesperson*
Ask *Item* to check item availability	*Item Ordered*
Pass item information to *Salesperson*	*Salesperson*
Pass final approval on to *Customer Information*	*Customer Information*
Pass final approval on to *Item Ordered*	*Item Ordered*

Class: *Customer Information*
Subclasses: *Customer Information1,*
Customer Information Multi

Responsibilities	Collaborators
Obtain customer credit approval	*Accounting*
Pass credit approval to *Sales Order*	*Sales Order*
Pass final approval to *Accounting*	*Accounting*

Attributes

Customer name

Customer billing address

Customer credit limit

Class: *Customer Information1*
Superclass: *Customer Information*

Responsibilities

Set shipping address equal to billing address

Class: *Customer Information Multi*
Superclass: *Customer Information*

Responsibilities

Establish shipping address

Attributes

Customer shipping address

Class: *Item Ordered*

Responsibilities	Collaborators
Determine availability of item	*Inventory*
Pass availability to *Sales Order*	*Sales Order*
Pass final approval to *Inventory*	*Inventory*

Attributes

Type of item

Style of item

Characteristic-1

Characteristic-2

Number needed

Price per unit

Shipping cost

Applicable taxes

Total price

Class: *Accounting*

Responsibilities	**Collaborators**
Know customers	*Customer Information*
Know credit limit of customers	*Customer Information*
Determine whether limit can be raised	*Customer Information*
Process order	*Customer Information*

Attributes

Customer

Credit limit

New order

Class: *Inventory*

Responsibilities	**Collaborators**
Know items in inventory, price	*Item Ordered*
Calculate shipping charges	*Item Ordered*
Calculate arrival date	*Item Ordered*
Estimate time if item is ordered	*Item Ordered*
Arrange to ship items once approved	*Item Ordered*

Attributes

Item number

Type of item

Style of item

Characteristic-1

Characteristic-2

Number needed

Price per unit

Shipping cost

Applicable taxes

Total price

Of course, a real CRC group would have come up with different names, and you could probably add a few more. In any case, if the group runs through a half dozen additional scenarios, they will surely add several more and modify some of these.

For example, someone might argue that the *Sales Order* class would need to keep track of the time and date. It would be an additional responsibility and another pair of attributes. You probably wouldn't want the *Sales Order* class to actually calculate the time or date. Instead, you'd probably create a separate class to provide time and date information upon demand. Hence, the *Sales Order* class would simply have the responsibility to record the time and date of the transaction. It would do this by asking the *Time-and-Date* class for that information. We've ignored this detail in our analysis effort, but eventually it will need to be added.

9.2.11 *Step 11: Repeat the Process*

So far we have only been considering scenarios generated by a single use case, Report Sales. Once the CRC group is satisfied that they have exhausted all the possibilities of this use case, they should proceed to the other two use cases.

In dealing with the review of individual sales and the review of group sales, for example, we would probably find we needed to add a class to handle sales quota information and another to handle keeping track of which salespeople belong to which region. This wouldn't expand the number of classes too greatly, but it would undoubtedly lead to the discovery of some additional classes and to additional responsibilities for the classes we have already identified.

9.3 CRC Cards and Object-Oriented Thinking

We hope this brief exercise has been sufficient to give you an overview of how to use CRC cards and to convince you that it's a good way to start learning to think like an OO analyst.

By letting cards be objects and having them ask each other to take responsibility for knowing and doing things, you are already a long way toward the mind-set of someone who routinely thinks in an OO way. Moreover, once you have completed your set of CRC cards, it will be easy to create your first UML class diagram.

We have described CRC cards and CRC sessions as a technique that can be used by a group to learn about objects while developing a list of classes that will occur in a specific application. It won't be as effective as an individual exercise, but if you are new to OO development, and are working alone, it will probably still be worth working through one or two personal CRC sessions just to familiarize yourself with this popular way of identifying classes and their characteristics.

9.4 CRC Terms versus UML Terms

We have not yet introduced the UML vocabulary for class modeling, but suffice it to say that it's somewhat different from the vocabulary used in developing CRC cards. CRC is not an official part of the UML notation, so its terms vary slightly. Figure 9.6 illustrates which terms are associated with which. Later, when you consider creating a UML class diagram, if you are uncertain of the correct analogies, check this figure.

CRC cards, since they require that you enter both attributes and operations (or responsibilities), are like UML classes. On the other hand, you develop CRC cards in the context of specific scenarios in which you pretend that actual people pass actual data from one card to another. In that sense, during a scenario, you are acting as if the cards were objects. Classes never really interact with each other. They are templates that are used to generate objects. When an application is run, objects are generated as needed from classes, and data is stored in objects. Hence, CRC cards have some of the characteristics of UML classes and some of the characteristics of objects.

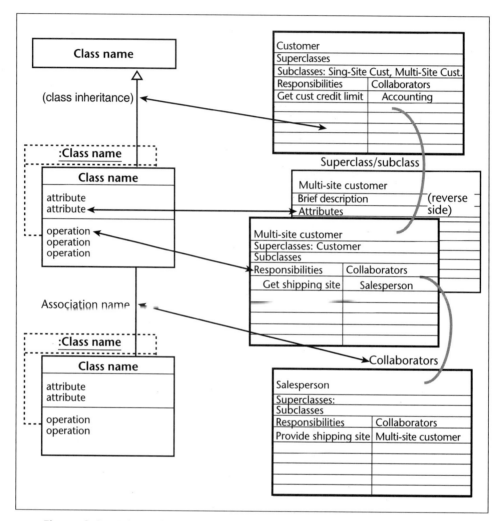

Figure 9.6 *Relationships between UML and CRC names.*

The other relationships are straightforward. Attributes mean the same thing in both systems. UML operations are CRC responsibilities. Superclass and subclass relationships in CRC describe class inheritance relationships in UML. And collaborators in CRC are simply classes that have associations in UML. In effect, collaborators pass messages to one another, and that's exactly what associations indicate in UML.

9.5 **Automating the CRC Process**

Up to this point, we've described the CRC process as if it were always done by hand using real 3-inch x 5-inch cards. In fact, Popkin Software sells a product especially designed to facilitate CRC sessions. It's called SA/CRC Cards. It isn't part of their SA/Object Architect OO modeling tool, but it is compatible with it. If you create a "set of CRC cards" in SA/CRC Cards, you can then use the set to generate a class diagram in SA/Object Architect.

In SA/CRC Cards, the format for the cards on the screen is just as it would be if you were preparing cards as we have shown earlier. To create a card, you simply click on a new card and a dialog box opens, asking you to enter the name, super- and subclasses, responsibilities, and collaborators. (See Figure 9.7.)

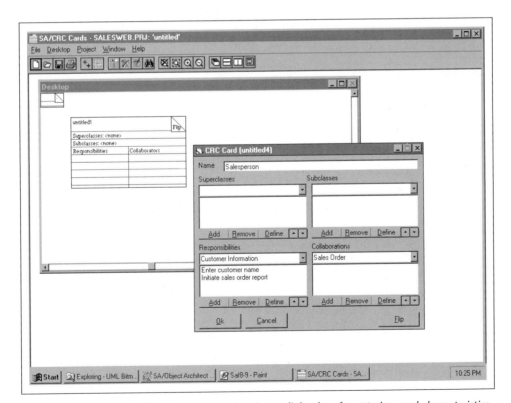

Figure 9.7   *SA/CRC Cards screen showing a dialog box for entering card characteristics.*

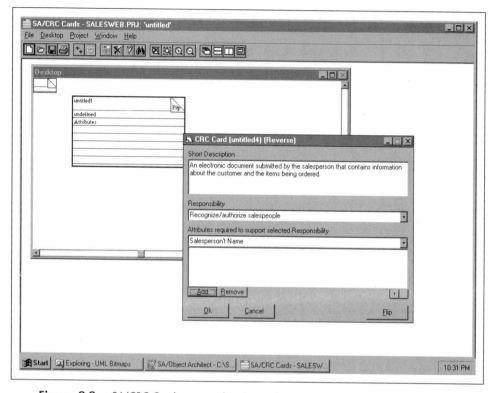

Figure 9.8   *SA/CRC Cards screen showing a dialog box for entering information on the reverse side of the card.*

When you have finished the "front" of the dialog box, you "flip it over" and add a short description and attributes. (See Figure 9.8).

This approach makes it easier for an individual to conduct a personal CRC session. If you are working with a group, it's probably still best to use actual cards, so individuals can hold a card and make notes on it when they have to ask for help or want to keep track of something. In a group setting, the main use of a product like SA/CRC Cards is to quickly record the results of a session after it is over, so everyone can have a copy of the results. Equally important, if you use SA/CRC Cards, you can use the results to help generate your first UML class diagram.

Once you are done with your CRC sessions and are satisfied that your deck of CRC cards is reasonably complete, you can use your cards to generate an object model in SA/Object Architect. This is as simple as pulling down the File menu and selecting Export to System Architect. Once you choose the option, you are asked to name the new class diagram and to indicate what notation you want to use. If we were going to do this, we would name our model SalesWeb and choose UML. In fact, however, we don't want to go directly from the CRC cards to a UML model, so we'll simply use the CRC program to print out a neat set of CRC cards.

UML Class and Object Diagrams

A complete set of hand-drawn UML static structure diagrams is made up of anywhere from one to hundreds of specific class and object diagrams. Most of the diagrams will be class diagrams. Some will be very high level views of the system, while others will describe specific subsections of the overall model. Some will be very detailed. A few might show how specific objects would interact. If the system is large, you might decide to partition it into packages and then develop different class diagrams for each package.

In general, dividing an application into packages is something you leave for the design phase of a project. If you are doing a relatively simple application, like the SalesWeb application we are focusing on in this book, you would probably develop an overall object model of the entire application and worry about subdividing the classes into packages at a later time. If the application is very large, however, you might decide to focus initially on a small part of the overall application. In that case, you might begin by creating a diagram of the possible packages in the system and then select one package and create class and object diagrams for that package first. Whatever you do, you will probably go through several iterations, and any decisions you make at the beginning can be modified as you learn more about the system you are developing. (UML package diagrams are discussed in Chapter 14.)

However you begin, keep in mind that class diagrams and object diagrams are both static diagrams. They picture classes and their relationships with other classes and, in some cases, relationships between objects. They are fundamental because you need to define what you are dealing with before you can describe when or how those things might change.

You begin the analysis effort by creating a simple class diagram that shows the core classes that you anticipate will be in your first prototype system. You then enhance and expand that initial class diagram throughout the first analysis phase. Later, you continue to expand the class diagram throughout the design phase, constantly adding more details to the class diagrams until they are ready to serve as the primary source of information when you begin to write code (or use an OO modeling tool to generate code) during the prototype phase.

After testing your first prototype, you return to the analysis phase again, when you begin the second prototype cycle. You begin the second round by modifying your high-level class diagram to incorporate things you learned during your first prototyping cycle. Then, if you are going to focus on new classes during the second prototyping cycle, you start by expanding your class diagrams to describe them. And, as before, you then proceed to expand and fill in details on those new class diagrams throughout the analysis and design phases of the second prototype cycle, which ends when you implement and test your second prototype. You keep repeating this process through one prototyping cycle after another until you complete your entire application.

Thus, to begin any UML development effort, you must first learn to create and then enhance class diagrams. To keep things from getting too complex, we'll begin by introducing a few basic class diagramming terms. Then we'll develop a simple class diagram. After that, we'll develop a simple object diagram.

10.1 Class Diagramming Basics

The UML class diagram shows classes and the relationships between classes. The simplest way to represent a class is to draw a rectangle and place the name of the class inside the rectangle. UML suggests that class names begin with capital letters.

Later, when you want to add more details, you draw a larger rectangle and divide it into three horizontal compartments. In the top section you indicate the name of the class. In the second section you list the attributes of the class, and in the lower section you list the operations that the class can perform. Attribute and operation names usually begin with lowercase letters.

10.1.1 Attributes (Variables)

Each attribute must have a name. Descriptive names are best. Because the attributes of one class are usually hidden from the attributes of other classes, you can use the same attribute name in more than one class. If you do this, we recommend you do it in a consistent way so you'll be able to remember what the attribute stands for, no matter what class it occurs in. If an attribute name is made up of more than one word, most OO languages require that you link them with hyphens or underscores so they form a single unit. (Java, for example, allows underscores.) Some developers prefer to combine two words and capitalize the first letter in the second name. Thus, part_number and partNumber are examples of attribute names.

When you create your first class diagrams you will probably start by listing the names of a few attributes—just those that are needed for the prototype you are working on. As you learn more about the application, you may specify the data type of the value that can be associated with various attributes. Similarly, if there are default values associated with the attribute (e.g., an initial value that the attribute is always set at), you may want to list them. For example:

```
attributeName : data_type = default_value
```

UML provides a whole collection of symbols that you can use to indicate different characteristics of an attribute, but we'll ignore them for the moment. In fact, you won't need them for most small to midsized development efforts.

10.1.2 *Operations (Methods)*

Operations are modules of procedural code that respond to messages by providing information or by causing something to happen. Initially, you only specify the names of the operations. By the time you get to design, you may want to create some pseudocode to document what each operation will do. You don't usually get around to writing Java code for the operations until the prototyping phase of the cycle.

Operation names, like attribute names, should be descriptive. If they involve more than one word, they should be linked into a single unit by an underscore or by capitalizing the first letter in the second word.

As you refine your model, you may decide to identify operations that have associated arguments or parameters, or you may want to list the arguments that are associated with specific operations. If you simply want to indicate that an operation can have one or more parameters associated with it, you put opening and closing parentheses after the name of the operation. If you want to go further and specify the argument or arguments associated with the operation, you can list it (or them) within the parentheses.

You may also want to specify the data type of any results you expect the operation to return. If you indicate a result type, you do it after the argument list, for example:

```
operationName (argument1, argument2) : result_type
```

As with attributes, there are additional UML symbols you can use to indicate specific characteristics of an operation, but we'll ignore them for the moment. Figure 10.1 illustrates the generic form for the class notations we have just discussed.

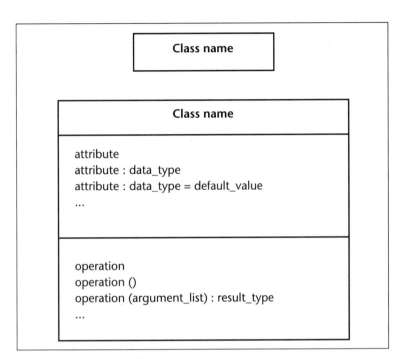

Figure 10.1   *Basic UML notation for classes.*

10.1.3   *More on Attributes and Operations*

Earlier, we mentioned that attributes were generally private but could be public (although this would be very bad Java programming). When you see an attribute listed within a class box with no special symbol in front of it, you assume the attribute is private.

If you want some attributes to be public and others private, UML suggests that you put a – in front of the names of private attributes and a +$ in front of public attributes.

More useful is the distinction between public, protected, and private operations. Again, recall that the default is always public operations. If you need to discriminate, you should place a + in front of public operations, a # in front of protected operations, and a – in front of private operations, for example:

```
+performOperationX (argument1, argument2) : result_type
-performStep1OfOperationX  [a private operation]
```

10.1.4 *Associations*

An association documents a physical or conceptual connection between two or more classes. If one class has the responsibility of telling a second class that a social security number is valid or invalid, for example, the two classes have an association. The most generic association is represented as a line between two classes. An association is naturally bidirectional. In other words, an association implies that the objects of one class will send messages to operations associated with the objects of the second class and that the second class's objects will respond when appropriate.

The line representing the association can be given a name. The association name is written just above or below the line connecting the two classes. (Association names begin with uppercase letters.) The association name may be omitted if the association represents a single, obvious relationship between the two classes.

In some cases you will want to provide names for the roles played by the individual classes making up the relationship. In UML, these are referred to as roles, and they are written just under or just over the association line. The role name on the side closest to each class describes the role that class plays relative to the class at the other end of the line, and vice versa. Role names are written in all lowercase letters. (See Figure 10.2.)

In the example shown in Figure 10.2, you can see that the role of the *Sales Order* is that of being made up of parts being ordered. The part, in turn, is included in a *Sales Order*. In effect, made_up_of and included_in are the two roles involved in the Contains association.

Indicating roles is especially critical when an association exists between two objects of the same class. In this case the association line begins and ends on the same class rectangle,

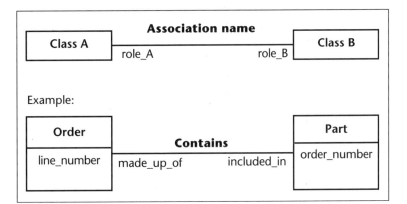

Figure 10.2 *Basic notation for an association.*

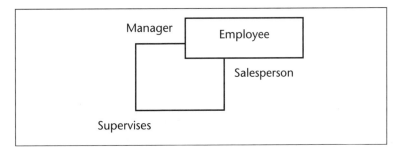

Figure 10.3 *Notation for a self-referencing association.*

as we've illustrated in Figure 10.3. The association illustrated by this "loop" is between various objects of the *Employee* class and involves supervision. Some objects of *Employee* are managers, while other objects of employee are salespeople who are supervised by sales managers. Role names are usually necessary to clarify this kind of relationship.

The Multiplicity of an Association

UML also provides a way to indicate the multiplicity of an association. Multiplicity refers to how many objects of one class can relate to each object of another class. Multiplicity isn't something you worry about when you are first creating a class diagram. As you expand the diagram, however, it's important to discriminate, at a minimum, between associations that only involve one object and those that involve many objects.

Figure 10.4 provides an overview of the symbols available in UML to indicate multiplicity. An unadorned line between two classes, as we showed in Figure 10.2, indicates one and only one object on each end of the association. An asterisk above one end of a relationship line indicates that zero or more objects of that class can be linked to objects of the class at the other end of the line. Obviously, there should be an asterisk on the end of the association line in Figure 10.2 where it touches the part class. Several objects of the part class can belong to a single order object. A single order, on the other hand, can own many different parts. Similarly, an asterisk should be added at the "salesperson" end of the association line shown in Figure 10.3. One manager can supervise many salespeople, but each salesperson has only one manager.

To indicate more precise relationships, you can place numbers over the line. For example, 0..1 indicates that zero or one object can be involved, 0.. * indicates that zero to many objects can be involved, and 1–3, 5 indicates that one, two, three, or five objects can be involved.

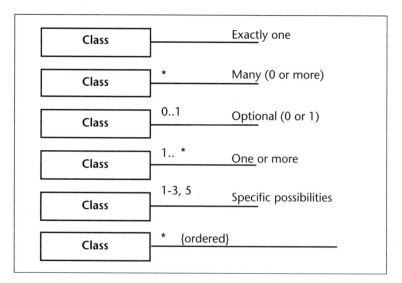

Figure 10.4 *Notation for multiplicity of associations.*

In some cases the class that will be represented by many objects will order those objects in some particular way. If it is important to indicate this, UML suggests you place the word "ordered" within braces (squiggly brackets) above or below the association line, close to the asterisk, as shown in Figure 10.4. (This is a specific example of the use of braces to include information about constraints on a diagram. Information within braces can be included on any diagram to indicate that constraints apply. We'll consider constraints in more detail a little later in the chapter.)

In most cases you will either have a plain line or a line with an asterisk at the end—these are the two most common multiplicities to note.

Association Classes

At times you may want to think of an association as an object in its own right and to imagine it has its own attributes. This is especially useful when there is an association between many objects and many other objects, and the attribute (or attributes) that describes the relationship is not a characteristic of either of the classes being linked but, rather, a characteristic of the linkage itself.

You can include a single attribute or multiple attributes and operations within an association class, as shown in the lower example in Figure 10.5.

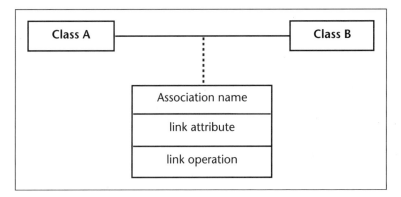

Figure 10.5   *An association class.*

Consider our earlier example where the association defined a relationship between objects of employee who were managers and those who were salespeople. Now imagine we wanted to add the attribute supervisorsTitle. It wouldn't properly be an attribute of employee, so it would be better to simply attach it to the association itself. We might also decide we wanted to add an attribute, numberSupervised. And we might decide to add an operation that would determine which employees were supervised by which managers.

Dependency Relationship

In Figure 10.5 we linked our association class to the regular association line with a dotted line. A dotted line denotes a dependency. A dependency indicates that one of the elements will change when the other changes. This can occur as a result of the fact that a message is sent, but it can also involve more abstract relationships. As we examine other diagrams, we'll see that dependency relationships are used to suggest a relationship without getting too specific about it.

Qualified Associations

In some cases you may want to qualify a specific association. This occurs when one class is linked to another in a one-to-many relationship and you want to specify the nature of the association more precisely. Thus, the *SalesManager* class is linked to many objects of the *Salesperson* class. Sometimes a manager will want to see how all of the salespeople reporting to him or her are performing. At other times a manager might only want to examine how one salesperson is doing. In that case the association could be qualified by the specific salesperson's name or employee number. You could show that specific or qualified association as we have in Figure 10.6.

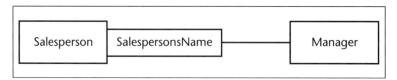

Figure 10.6 *Notation for a qualified association.*

Note that once you have qualified an association you no longer need to use an asterisk to indicate that there is a multiple relationship. The qualification says that this association is going to function as a relationship between a single object of the *Sales Manager* class and a single object of the *Salesperson* class. The single object of the *Salesperson* class will be governed by a specific salesperson's name.

10.1.5   *Class Inheritance*

Class inheritance refers to a situation in which one class inherits the code of another class. The class the code is inherited from is usually referred to as the parent class or the superclass, and the class that inherits the code is referred to as the child class or the subclass.

Class inheritance is good for two things. In some cases you find that you want to create a number of classes that are similar in all but a few characteristics. In other cases you will find that someone has already developed a class that you can use, and all you need to do is modify that class. We'll consider both possibilities.

Imagine that we decided to create a class for each of the furniture items that Watson's sells. All of the furniture items would have certain things in common—a stock or item number, a price, an availability number or date, and so on. In fact, whole groups of items would have things in common. For example, all desk chairs would either have wheels or not, would either have padded seats or not. Whole lines of chairs would have common fabric or leather options. In developing our first prototype we might very well just use a generic class called *FurnitureItem,* or *Item,* but when we began to refine our application, we would probably take some time to create classes for the different furniture items. The most effective way to do that would be to create a class hierarchy. The top class would be *FurnitureItem* or *Item.* That class would have subclasses that divided the actual furniture items into groups. And each of those groups would probably have classes that represented the specific furniture items stocked by Watson's. When it came time to identify the attributes and operations, we would begin with the superclass and work down. If an attribute or operation is identified in the top item, it wouldn't have to be identified again in a lower class, since lower classes always inherit all of the attributes and operations of their parent classes.

In creating a UML class diagram, you usually begin by showing only a top-level class, like *FurnitureItem,* and how that class relates to other classes, for example, *Sales Order* and *Inventory.* Later, if you subclass furniture, you still tend to leave the links between the high-level *FurnitureItem* and *Inventory* as they were; otherwise, you would need to show links between each of the subclasses and the *Inventory* class. Thus, associations are, in effect, inherited, just like attributes and operations are inherited.

Once you have subclassed a class, as a rule, the actual objects used in an application are instantiated from the subclasses. In that case, the only function of the superclass is to serve as a template for the subclasses. Developers sometimes refer to the high-level class, which is only used as a template for other classes, as an abstract class.

If you have been doing OO development for any period of time, you will usually have some classes that can be reused when you create a new application. In most cases, however, the older class will need to be modified in some way before it's ready to use in the new application. To keep things neat, the best way to do this is to leave the older class as it was and simply create a subclass of the older class. Then, make whatever modifications you need to make in the subclass. You can modify a subclass by adding new attributes or operations that don't exist in the superclass. Or you can use the name of an attribute or operation in the subclass and define it differently from the way it's defined in the superclass. Since objects always use the attributes and operations in their parent class, if you overwrite an attribute or operation in the subclass, it is the attribute or operation that will be used by the object. If you don't overwrite attributes or operations, the object will inherit them from the superclass via the subclass.

You can easily develop small OO applications without using class inheritance. Once you become involved in reuse, or you find yourself considering writing a new class that will have operations or attributes just like or very similar to those in another class, you should consider using inheritance.

Creating classes that can be reused in other applications can get very complex, because you need to keep the super-classes' attributes and operations generic. It's too complex to consider in this book, but it is important if you intend to develop a lot of OO applications. If you do, you should certainly study some books on developing code for reuse.

UML indicates superclass relationships by using an open arrowhead or pyramid, as illustrated in Figure 10.7.

10.1.6 *Interfaces*

UML indicates that a class uses an interface by attaching a "lollypop" to the side of the class, as we saw earlier. A lollypop indicates that the class is a composite class and that an interface is contained within the class.

10.1.7 *Identifying Aggregations*

An aggregation refers to part–whole relationships. In effect, aggregation suggests that some classes are contained within another class, and indeed, some notations allow you to literally place the part classes inside the class that represents the whole. This can get messy fast, however, and in reality, the

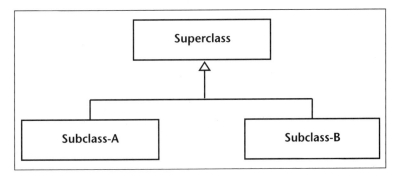

Figure 10.7 *Notation for an inheritance relationship.*

classes usually aren't contained but are simply organized by the fact that messages go to the class representing the whole, which then passes them on to classes representing parts, and vice versa.

An aggregation relationship is indicated by placing a small diamond at the end of the association line that runs between part classes and the whole class, pointing at the whole class. Figure 10.8 illustrates two ways to diagram a whole–part relationship. UML refers to the type of aggregation represented by placing one class inside another as a composite class.

10.1.8 *Constraints and Notes*

Constraints are functional relationships between elements of a class or object model. A constraint sets limits on the values that one of the elements can take. A constraint can limit the value an attribute can take, or it can limit the value that an operation can accept. It might limit the number of objects of the class that can exist at any point in time. For example, it may be a matter of policy that no corporate sales order can exceed $200,000 without the explicit approval of the vice president of accounting, or that salespeople may not enter sales orders for individuals or companies outside their sales region. If you identify a constraint that you want to remember, you can write it in braces below the class involved. (Constraints can also be noted on the various other OMT diagrams in a similar way, between braces.)

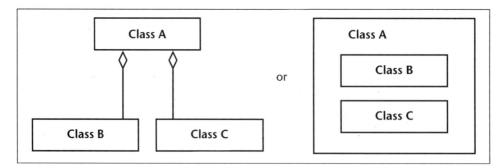

Figure 10.8   *Notation for an aggregation (whole-part) relationship.*

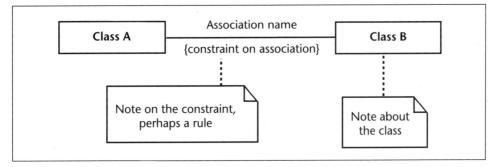

Figure 10.9 *Notation for a constraint and for notes.*

UML also allows developers to write notes on diagrams by putting them in rectangles with a dog-eared right corner. Thus, if you discover something that is more complex than a constraint—perhaps an explanation of why you handled a specific aspect of the problem in a particular way—and you want to be sure to remember it, you can simply write it in a box off to one side of the diagram. Figure 10.9 illustrates both the use of a note and the specification of a constraint.

10.2 Diagramming Objects

Occasionally you will want to diagram objects of classes to clarify some particular situation. Some developers create an object diagram for each sequence diagram that they create. In this case they probably use collaboration diagrams. Object diagrams are used for more informal analysis.

UML indicates an object as a rectangle—the same way it indicates a class. You can tell the difference, however, by noticing the way the name is written inside the rectangle. UML offers you three ways to name an object:

1. You can simply write the class name, preceded by a colon and underlined:

    <u>:Class Name</u>

This can be used to refer to "generic" examples of an object—in other words, any object of the class.

2. You can write the name of the specific object, underlined and followed by a colon:

`object name:`

3. You can write the specific object name followed by the class name, thus:

`object name:Class Name`

You can also expand the size of the rectangle and include attributes and values associated with the object, as shown in Figure 10.10. This is useful if you are creating a diagram and want to show how messages will result in changes in attributes.

There is never an occasion in which you would enter the name of an operation inside an object rectangle. Operations are always associated with classes and accessed by objects when needed.

If you want to show that an object has been instantiated from a class, you use a dashed line with an arrow pointing to the class from which the object derived. This is also shown in Figure 10.10.

Notice that the instantiation line is a dotted line. This is an example of a dependency relationship. Solid lines show associations or links—relationships that based on semantic relationships. Dependencies are relationships that aren't based on message passing but on some other relationship. In this case, the object is an instance of the class.

Just as classes are related by associations, objects are related by links. In effect, a link is an instantiation of an association. Or, conversely, an association represents all of the links that could occur between objects of the two related classes. Links are also represented by lines. There is no need to indicate multiplicity when you are diagramming objects. If one object relates to several objects of another class, you can actually show the existence of multiple objects relating to single objects. Indeed, whenever you are trying to figure out the multiplicity of a particular association between classes, you can usually draw an object diagram to clarify it. Figure 10.11 illustrates an object diagram and the related class diagram.

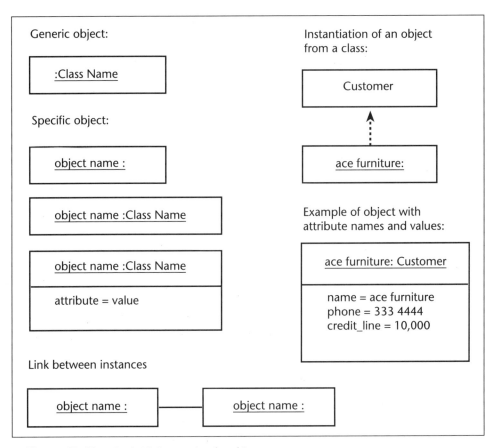

Figure 10.10   *Basis UML notation for objects.*

10.3 Creating a Class Diagram

Your first class diagram should be a very simple affair that shows the major classes in your application and the obvious associations between them. Later, you can redraw it, adding attributes to the classes, indicating multiplicity for the associations, and adding new classes as you identify them.

When you develop BPR workflow charts, high-level use case diagrams, or CRC cards, you tend to look at the whole system. You need to do this simply to know what the whole system will have to include. Once you get an overview, however, in

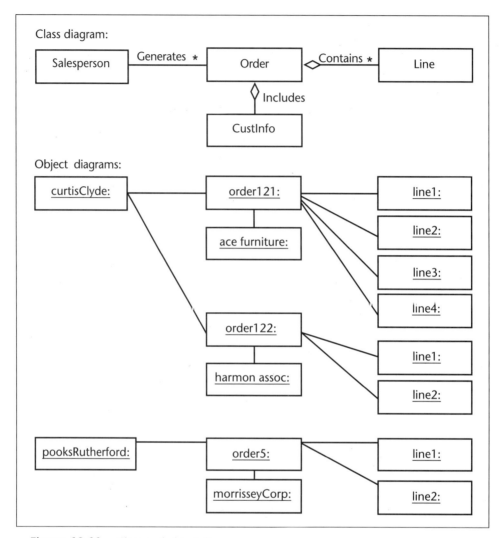

Figure 10.11   *Class and object diagrams.*

most cases you'll want to focus on a subset of the entire application and develop a prototype of that before moving on to other subsets of the application. Earlier we said that we would focus our first prototype on the Report Sales use case. Thus, we're ignoring other potential classes, such as *Regional Sales Manager*, *Quota*, and *Regions*. During the second prototype phase, our SalesWeb development team can go back and add classes, attributes, and relationships to handle the two other use cases. For the moment, we're only working with scenarios that involve reporting sales, and our first class diagram will only be a model of the sales-reporting portion of our application.

Since we've developed a use case analysis of our SalesWeb system and created use case descriptions and an ideal object model, we already have an idea of the classes that should appear in our first OMT object diagram. We also worked with CRC cards, so we have another version of the classes that might be in our application. We've listed the results of the two separate approaches below.

Ideal Object Model Classes	CRC Classes
Salesperson	*Salesperson*
Browser Order Interface	
SalesWeb Handler	
Sales Order	*Sales Order*
	Address
Customer Information	*Customer Information*
	CustInfo1
	CustInfoMulti
Item Ordered	*Item Ordered*
	(subclasses for different types of items)
Corporate Interface	
Accounting System	*Accounting* System
Inventory System	*Inventory* System

There is quite a bit of overlap between the two approaches and some differences that we'll need to resolve. In a real CRC effort, the participants would probably have come up with different names than what we chose during our use case analysis, and this would be the time to decide which names to use from now on.

The ideal object model, by emphasizing interface objects and objects to handle coordination tasks, creates classes that we will need when we get to design but which we can ignore during analysis, when we are primarily concerned with business objects such as *Salesperson*, *Sales Order*, and *Item Ordered*.

The CRC approach, which tends to include end users and subject matter experts in the process and which emphasizes business classes, messages sent (responsibilities), and attributes, is more likely to generate more superclass/subclass relationships. It's also likely to lead to people suggesting more practical new classes, such as address and time-stamp.

All of these issues would come up at some point during analysis and design. If we were working with a larger project, we might want to be more systematic about putting off certain considerations until design. Since we are working with a small problem, we are ignoring side issues until they occur.

Let's review both lists and focus only on the major business objects, ignoring all the subclasses for the moment, except the distinction between customers with a single address and those with multiple addresses. We're keeping this one inheritance relationship at this point only so we can show the UML notation. Thus, we arrive at this list: *Salesperson*, *Sales Order*, *Customer Information*, *CustInfo1*, *CustInfoMulti*, *Item Ordered*, *Accounting*, and *Inventory*—eight classes to represent on our first UML class diagram. Since we're going to be constructing a UML diagram, we might as well convert these names into UML style. From here through the remainder of the book we'll place all class and object names in italics in the text to make them more obvious. We'll also combine multi-word names into a single name and eliminate some letters, as shown below.

Salesperson	*Salesperson*
Sales Order	*SalesOrder*
Customer Information	*CustInfo*
Customer Information1	*CustInfo1*
Customer Information Multi	*CustInfoMulti*
Item Ordered	*ItemOrdered*

Accounting   *Accounting*

Inventory   *Inventory*

Initially, we could just use a large sheet of paper and put the classes on one at a time as we begin identifying the associations between them. As a general rule, with a simple diagram, we think of events as flowing from left to right, so we'll put the *Salesperson* class, which provides the initial stimulus, at the top left of the page and go from there. We have one inheritance relationship, so wherever we put *CustInfo* we'll want to leave enough room near it for the two *CustInfo* subclasses.

Associations indicate high-level relationships between classes, which will be implemented, at lower levels, as messages that will flow between the objects of the various classes. At this point, assuming you've done a CRC card exercise, you can consult your cards to see who was collaborating with whom. Or you can review the use case description and any scenarios you developed for the Report Sales use case to see what relationships will need to exist between classes. It's not important that you find them all at this point; you can continue to add associations as you go.

Most of the input to the system will enter via the *Salesperson* class. It will need to interact with the *SalesOrder* class to get signed on, and then it will provide all the customer and item information that will drive the other classes in the application. The input that doesn't come from the *Salesperson* class will come from the accounting and inventory databases that will provide information on creditworthiness and item availability.

Figure 10.12 shows our initial UML class diagram of our simple SalesWeb system for inputs from the field sales staff of Watson's Furniture. In thinking about this diagram, try not to think of it as a procedural diagram; it describes the logical relationships between the various items, not flow. (We chose an example that's easy to think of in procedural terms because we wanted an example that was easy to understand. On the other hand, if you have an application that involves changing a Web browser page around as the user clicks on one thing or another, that will be a lot harder to think of in procedural terms, since you'll never know where the user is likely to click next. Class

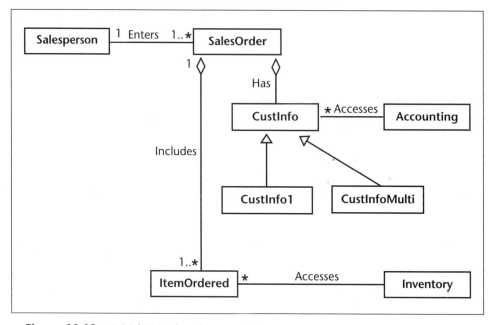

Figure 10.12   *Initial UML class diagram of the SalesWeb application.*

diagrams are designed to show logical relationships, and they only incidentally suggest a procedural flow in some cases.)

In Figure 10.12 we've connected our classes with lines to show associations. The associations should largely match the responsibilities and collaborators we identified in the earlier CRC exercise. We've given names to the associations, although other people might prefer different names. We've also included numbers and asterisks to show where relationships could involve one or more objects. And we've used diamonds to show whole–part relationships (aggregations). The figure in the next section will help clarify this.

10.3.1   *An Object Diagram*

Rational Software's UML documentation does not have an object diagram, as such. Perhaps UML purists prefer to think of object diagrams as collaboration diagrams that show the objects and links but no messages or events. Whatever they are called, there will be occasions when you will want to draw diagrams that show objects and their relationships.

Figure 10.13 is a UML object diagram of the same set of classes we've been discussing. Of course, being an object diagram, it deals with objects of classes and shows the multiple relationships more clearly. We also substituted a slightly different type of UML notation for an aggregation. We've shown the objects that are parts of an aggregation inside the bolder rectangle, which represents the whole class. (UML calls this particular way of representing an aggregation a composite object.) Notice that although we show the superclass *CustInfo*

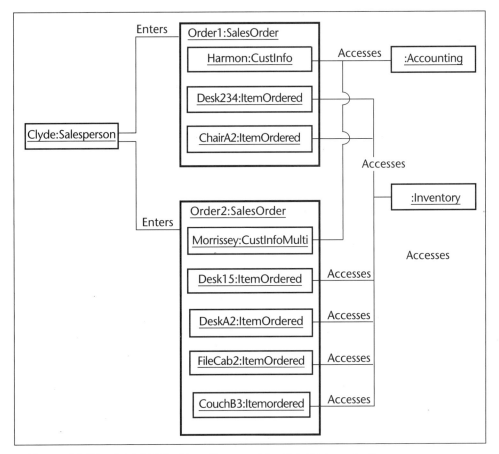

Figure 10.13   *Initial UML object diagram of the SalesWeb application.*

accessing *Accounting* in Figure 10.13, in fact, it will be an object of one of the two subclasses of *CustInfo* that actually accesses *Accounting*.

Using this object diagram, we can talk our way through the problem. Once a single salesperson, Curtis Clyde, initiates a transaction, he can submit one or more sales orders. In Figure 10.13 we show Curt submitting two sales orders. The orders might be given numbers so Curt can keep track of them, in which case there will be an attribute of each *SalesOrder* called number. Otherwise, the system will simply assign a system-designated number to each instance of *SalesOrder* that it creates. A single *SalesOrder* object is made up of one *Customer* object and can have from one to many *ItemOrdered* objects. The number of *ItemOrdered* objects depends on how many different types of furniture the customer is ordering. *Accounting* can receive information requests from different *CustInfo* objects. Similarly, *Inventory* can receive availability and pricing requests from many different *ItemOrdered* objects.

10.3.2 *A More Elaborate Class Diagram*

In Figure 10.14 we have expanded the initial class diagram and included some of the attributes of several of the classes. We've taken these from the attributes we identified via our CRC card exercise. Assuming some knowledge of design, we know that *Accounting* and *Inventory* are legacy systems, and we will not have to create them but only interface with what already exists. Thus, to simplify our task, we've left them on the diagram but haven't bothered to generate attributes and operations for them.

So far we've been using a phrase to explain what a method would do. At some point, however, you will need to determine specific names for the attributes and methods and use those names on your class diagrams. Following are some we've decided on.

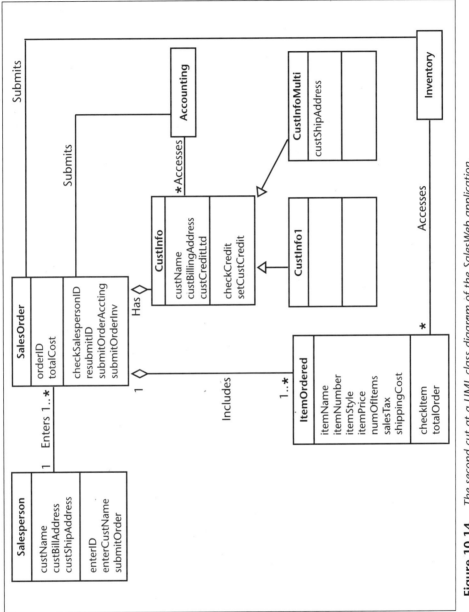

Figure 10.14 *The second cut at a UML class diagram of the SalesWeb application.*

Attributes:

orderID	The unique number of each order submitted
custName	The name of the customer ordering items
custBillAddress	The billing address of the customer
custShipAddress	The address to which the items are to be shipped
custCreditLmt	The maximum amount the customer can order on credit
itemName	The catalog name of the item
itemNumber	The catalog number of the item
itemStyle	The catalog style of the item
itemPrice	The price of one unit of the item
numOfItems	The number of units of an item being ordered
salesTax	The sales tax on the item
shippingCost	The shipping cost of the item
totalCost	The total cost of the order

Operations:

enterID	Enters salesperson's name and ID
checkSalespersonID	Checks to see if salesperson and number is acceptable to the system
resubmitID	Asks the salesperson to reenter name and ID
enterCustName	Enters customer name
checkCredit	Checks customer credit
setCustCredit	Sets customer credit
enterItem	Enters item number 1
checkItem	Checks item availability and price

enterItem	Enters item number 2
checkItem	Checks item availability and price
totalOrder	Totals items and adds shipping and tax
submitOrder	Submits completed/approved order
submitOrderAcct	Order information sent to *Accounting*
submitOrderInv	Order information sent to *Inventory*

In the process of entering the attributes and operations listed above, we were forced to think again about which object would do what and decided that while the *CustInfo* and *ItemOrdered* objects would contact the *Accounting* and *Inventory* systems for specific information, the *SalesOrder* itself would actually submit the final order. No individual item class will know the total of all the item classes. Clearly, that attribute and the operation to do it should reside on the *SalesOrder* class. Hence, *submitOrderAcct* and *submitOrderInv* required that we establish associations between the *SalesOrder* class and both the *Accounting* and *Inventory* systems.

At this point, you could think about adding more attributes, more operations, and perhaps a couple of additional classes. Similarly, you could begin to consider inheritance issues and think about breaking out subclasses for the *ItemOrdered* class. Given the small size of our application, however, we probably have a pretty good first approximation. So it's about time to switch and use some dynamic models to refine our understanding of the relationships between the classes we've identified. Before doing that, let's pause to consider how we would have created the class diagram shown in Figure 10.14 in an OO modeling tool.

At various points we've mentioned other things you could do to the SalesWeb application. We've suggested creating a class for addresses and for date and time stamps. We've also talked about breaking the *ItemOrdered* class into a hierarchy that would classify the various types of furniture that Watson's stocked. If you were to do these things during the first cycle of your application development effort, you would need to add the items onto your class and sequence diagrams and perhaps generate other diagrams, besides, to be sure you understood each addition. To keep our application simple, we'll assume that all of those additions are to be put off until the next cycle. Thus, we'll assume that the class diagrams we have developed so far are the ones we will carry forward into the design phase of the first cycle.

10.4 Creating UML Class Diagrams with an Object-Oriented Modeling Tool

Up to this point we've described the development of class and object diagrams as if we were simply drawing our diagrams on paper. And, of course, our example is so simple that we could easily do that. However, as we considered more complex problems, the diagramming would become more tedious. An OO modeling tool provides a way to automate the diagramming process and, subsequently, reduces the effort involved in generating other diagrams.

Let's consider how we would have generated our initial class diagram in Popkin Software's SA/Object Architect. Figure 10.15 shows the screen that a developer would use to create UML class diagrams in SA/Object Architect. To get to the screen we show in Figure 10.15, we had to provide a name for the diagram—ClassDiag1—which appears at the top of the window. Notice that the symbols along the left side of the drawing area are the UML class diagramming elements we have been discussing in this chapter.

Since we want to create a diagram that is like the one in Figure 10.12, we begin by clicking on the class rectangle and placing a rectangle on the screen. Once we click on the rectangle, the cursor will change into a pencil. We'll place the pencil in the middle of the screen and double-click the mouse. This will cause a new window to appear. In effect, the window

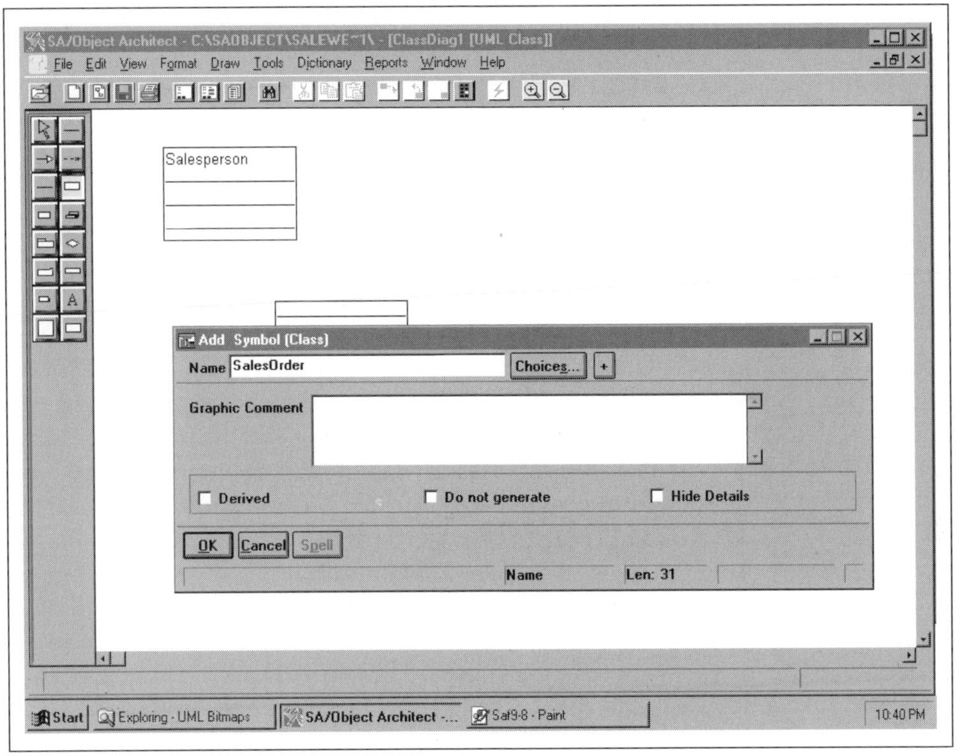

Figure 10.15   *SA/Object Architect screen for creating class diagrams.*

will ask us what we want to name the new class. We started by entering "Salesperson" and pressing RETURN. Next we clicked on the class button again and a second dialog box appeared. In the second box we have entered SalesOrder.

Now let's look more carefully at Figure 10.15. First, SA/Object Architect doesn't normally support the simple rectangles we used in Figure 10.12. (In fact, a developer can modify SA/Object Architect diagrams so they would show only class names, for example, but we'll simply use the defaults.) SA/Object Architect puts a "complete" class diagram on the screen when you click on the class rectangle and then click on the screen. Second, SA/Object Architect uses a modified UML class box. Instead of having only three rows, it has four. The top three are for the same things that the regular UML diagram uses: the class name, attributes, and operations. The bottom box allows the developer to indicate whether the class is persistent or transitory.

If you say that the class is persistent, it means that the objects created from that class will be saved. In other words, the objects will be persistent. That means the application will store the objects in a database and save them even when they are not being used. If you say that the class is transitory, that means the objects will be transitory. They will be eliminated by Java's garbage collection mechanism whenever they are no longer referenced by some other object. In Java and most other OO systems, the default is transitory. SA/Object Architect allows you to avoid making this decision, and we will ignore it during the analysis phase of our initial cycle. Later, during the design phase, we'll return to it. In passing, it's worth noting that SA/Object Architect allows the user to develop entity diagrams and to structure relational databases. This information is needed when it comes time for SA/Object Architect to generate entity diagrams for database tables. But, as we already said, that's a design issue.

Using SA/Object Architect, our first class diagram will necessarily look like a cross between Figures 10.12 and 10.14. If we just place the class boxes on and arrange them more or less as in Figure 10.12, we get Figure 10.16.

Assuming that once we have placed all the class boxes in place, we clicked on the association button and then drew a line between the *Salesperson* class and the *SalesOrder* class, we would get another dialog box asking us to name the association. (See Figure 10.17.) Once we have drawn the association line, we could then choose the Association item on the Edit pull-down menu, and we would get the dialog box shown in Figure 10.17. Using this dialog box, we can indicate the multiplicity of the association. We click on the down arrow in the slot by *Salesperson* and select "exactly one" and then choose "one or more" for *SalesOrder*. Once we click OK, SA/Object Architect will add numbers and asterisks to our association line.

Note that there is a box by each class that you can check if the class is an aggregation of other classes. If you look at the menu of buttons, you won't see an aggregation symbol. You create an aggregation by drawing an association line between two classes and then using the association definition dialog

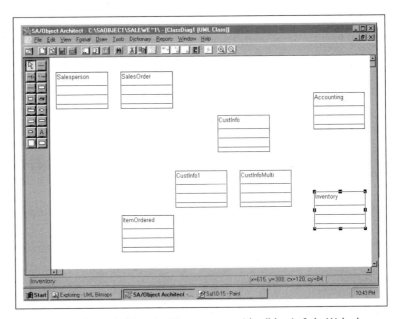

Figure 10.16   *SA/Object Architect screen with all basic SalesWeb classes.*

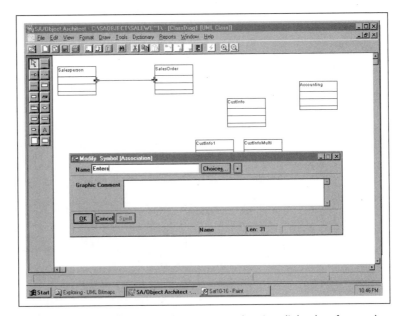

Figure 10.17   *SA/Object Architect screen showing dialog box for naming associations between classes.*

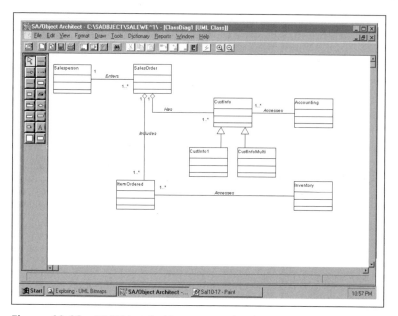

Figure 10.18 *SA/Object Architect screen showing initial SalesWeb class diagram.*

box to indicate that the relationship is an association. Assuming we now work through the diagram and define all the associations, we end up with the diagram shown in Figure 10.18, which is reasonably close to Figure 10.12.

Now, assuming we're prepared to move on and add attributes and operations to enhance Figure 10.18 and, in effect, convert it into Figure 10.14, we start providing more information on each class. Let's begin with *Salesperson*. We highlight *Salesperson* and then click on the Edit pull-down menu and select Definition. This brings up a dialog box that allows us to enter information about the class. In Figure 10.19 we have entered the names of the attributes and operations in a dialog box that allows us to further define the *Salesperson* class, as identified in Figure 10.14.

In Figure 10.19 you'll see a button under attributes and operations marked Definition. By clicking on this you can add information about the nature of the attribute or operation (public, private), about the data type involved, whether the

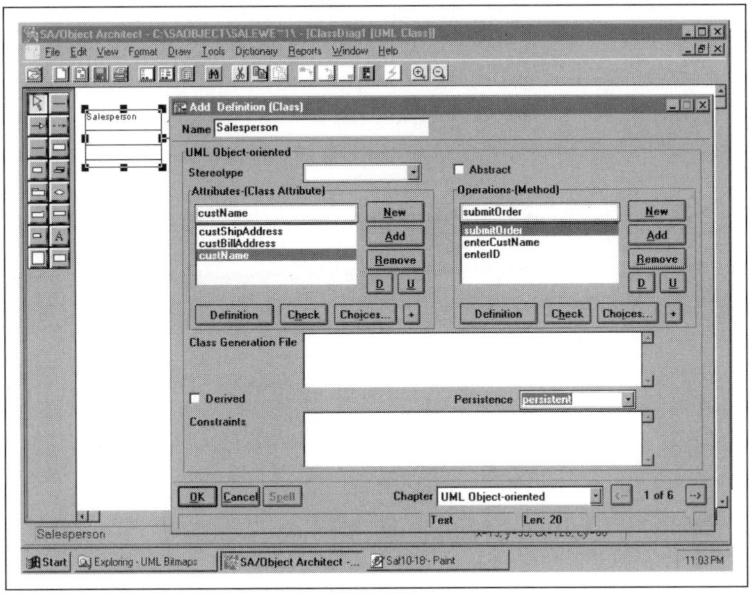

Figure 10.19   *SA/Object Architect screen showing the dialog box in which the properties of a class are defined.*

operation involves passing parameters, and so on. We won't do it at this time, but we could. Indeed, the great thing about developing diagrams with an OO modeling tool is that it prompts you for all the details you might want to add, and you can add them whenever you want, confident that once you specify something it will be saved to the encyclopedia and then become available to any other diagram that involves that class, attribute, or operation.

Similarly, if you notice the bottom of the class definition dialog box, you see buttons that allow you to move to six other definition boxes. By clicking on the right-hand button, you move to dialog boxes that let you define a variety of things: arguments and responsibilities, Java properties, OMG CORBA IDL definitions, SQL data values, distributed computing information, and development information about who created the class, when it was modified, and so on. Once again, most of these decisions will wait till we get to design, but they suggest things we will have to determine in order to complete our application. Moreover, once we have created any class, the encyclopedia sets aside space to keep track of these characteristics for us. (By the way, you can print out the encyclopedia and obtain an extensive report on all the information you have on any element in your application.)

Figure 10.20 is an SA/Object Architect diagram with all the information that we had on our earlier Figure 10.14. Once we've saved the diagram in SA/Object Architect, we can recall it whenever we want. Similarly, we can print out a copy whenever we need to. Moreover, unlike hand-drawn diagrams that must be redrawn when you want to enhance them or change them, you can modify the SA/Object Architect class diagram by simply going to the encyclopedia and changing the definition of the class. Moreover, when you change the definition of the class in the encyclopedia (say you change the name of an operation), you modify the information on every other diagram that uses that item. Whereas a project that depended on hand-drawn UML diagrams might easily produce a dozen

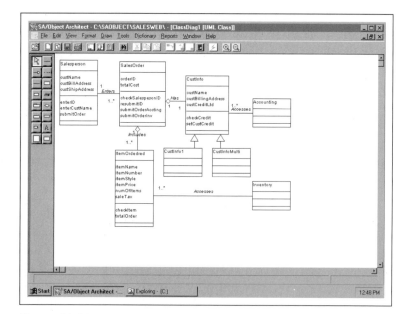

Figure 10.20 *SA/Object Architect screen showing SalesWeb class diagram with some attributes and operations.*

class diagrams in the course of even a simple application like SalesWeb, when we develop the application with SA/Object Architect, we really only have one class diagram that we simply keep enhancing as we refine our definitions of the classes, relationships, attributes, operations, and other characteristics of the application.

If we created one class diagram and wanted to save it, while creating another slightly different version of that class diagram, we would need to start using the version control feature of SA/Object Architect and indicate which version which diagram was associated with. We won't worry about that sort of thing as we develop our simple application, but it would prove valuable to a team working on an application.

To create an object diagram in SA/Object Architect, you simply create a class diagram but use object names and object symbols, such as link instead of association, to show relationships between objects.

If you would like to examine the diagrams we created in Popkin Software's SA/Object Architect, you can do so by using the Internet and connecting to Popkin Software's Web site. There, you can access a version of SA/Object Architect with the diagrams that we have created to illustrate the SalesWeb application, and you can load and examine the SWCD1 diagram. See Appendix A for specific instructions about how to do this.

UML Sequence and Collaboration Diagrams

The UML class and object diagrams provide a static view of a system. Using the class diagram you systematically identify the classes in the system, define their attributes and operations, and describe their relationships with one another. When you look at a class diagram, however, there is no sense of starting at one point and working through the system in any order.

Often it's useful to diagram a system in a way that indicates the order in which things occur. UML offers two sets of diagrams that can be used to show the dynamics of a system. The first set, the sequence and collaboration diagrams, show how the objects in a system send messages to one another. These diagrams provide a macro-level analysis of the dynamics of a system. The second set, the state and activity diagrams, which we'll consider in the next chapter, focus on workflow processes on a specific class and show how that single class changes as it receives and sends messages.

11.1 Approaches to Diagramming

Sequence diagrams (sometimes called event trace or interaction diagrams) provide a more detailed view of the interaction between the objects of the major classes in the system or between the objects of some subset of classes. They provide specific information about the order in which events occur and can provide information about the time required for each activity. Collaboration diagrams combine object diagrams, numbers, and arrows to show the sequence of events traveling over the links connecting the objects. A collaboration diagram is similar to a Booch object diagram.

In developing an OO application, you always need to develop class diagrams. You will probably also always need to prepare one or more sequence diagrams. You may not always need to develop state or collaboration diagrams; it depends on the complexity of the system you are developing.

Most developers begin their analysis effort by preparing use case descriptions and scenarios. Then they move on to either class diagrams or sequence diagrams. As a general rule, subject matter experts—people who are already familiar with the problem to be automated—prefer to do class diagrams first. They usually find it easy to identify all the major business classes that will be needed in the application.

Programmers who aren't subject matter experts, on the other hand, normally find it easier to start with a sequence diagram. To develop a sequence diagram you also need to specify classes, but since you specify the classes in the process of spelling out the activities that will occur, programmers often find that this more "procedural" approach is an easier way to begin to understand a new system.

Popkin Software refers to the series that goes from a use case diagram to a sequence diagram to a class diagram as a *problem-centric* approach and recommends that approach. They refer to the alternative that goes from a class diagram to a sequence diagram as a *data-centric* approach. Historically, OO developers have usually preferred a data-centric approach, although programmers moving to OO methodologies from more procedural methodologies may very well find the problem-centric approach an easier way to begin.

There's no correct order in which to proceed; it depends on the system being developed and the inclination of the developer. The simple SalesWeb system we are considering could be modeled equally well either way. We've rather arbitrarily begun by developing class diagrams, but we could just as well have started by developing sequence diagrams.

SA/Object Architect tool can create the initial sequence diagrams from use cases. Popkin Software, in fact, recommends you begin by moving from use case diagrams to sequence diagrams. Either way, you'll soon discover whether the classes you identified in the class diagram are really workable when you consider them in a dynamic context.

We'll consider sequence diagrams before collaboration, since we generally find them the most useful. We'll start developing our sequence diagram by using the classes we identified when we created class diagrams in the previous chapter. Before converting our SalesWeb class diagram into a sequence diagram, however, we'll need to define the basic sequence diagram conventions used in UML.

11.2 Sequence Diagrams

A sequence diagram is a graphical way to illustrate a scenario. Sequence diagrams are among the most popular UML diagrams and are used in conjunction with class diagrams to capture most of the information about a system. They show the sequence in which objects pass messages to each other. Sometimes they also show how long an object takes to process a message. Some other uses are to show when objects are created and destroyed and to note when messages are synchronous or asynchronous.

11.2.1 Sequence Notation

To create a sequence diagram, you begin by identifying a set of classes that will probably be involved in a scenario. The diagram itself can be concerned with either generic objects

(*:CustInfo*) or specific objects (*Chou Furniture: CustInfo*); you can use either.

Once you have identified the objects involved in the scenario to be described in your sequence diagram, you list the objects in a line along the top of a page and drop a dotted line beneath each object. (See Figure 11.1.) The dotted lines are referred to as lifelines. You should list the objects more or less in the order they are used in the scenario. The leftmost object should be the one that provides the stimulus that starts the scenario. If you can figure it out in advance, go ahead and list the objects in order. If you aren't sure, begin at the top left and list the first object, and then ask what object comes next. In other words, work your way through the scenario, listing each new object, in turn, as it enters the scenario.

Figure 11.1 illustrates the minimum notation needed to create a sequence diagram. The line on the left often represents

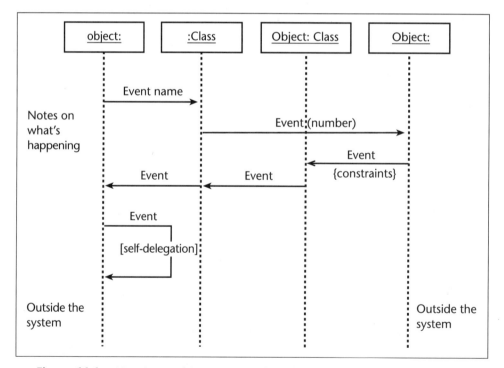

Figure 11.1   *Notation used in a sequence diagram—1.*

an actor or event that is outside the system boundary. In other words, it might be an individual or an input from some other system. Something represented by the left-hand line provides the initial stimulus that leads to events. Similarly, the right-hand line often represents the outside boundary of the system. If it does, it is understood that events reaching the right-hand line pass to systems that lie outside the focus of the current effort.

A sequence diagram can depict many different event sequences. In each case, events within a sequence that occur lower on the chart are understood to occur later in time than those that occur higher on the chart. Some developers are very informal about this and simply move the event arrows all down by a small set amount. Others try to capture information about how long things take to occur and space the arrows to show the difference between long and short time durations. In some cases, developers will actually note the interval of time between an incoming and an outgoing arrow.

An event arrow connects objects. In effect, the event arrow suggests that a message is moving between those two objects. An event line can pass over an object without stopping at that object. The event stops at an arrowhead.

Events are given names, which can be a phrase or an operation or message name. Some developers record additional information after the event name. For example, if the message is sent three and only three times, you might record a 3 in parentheses after the event name. This could be used in an application that asks a salesperson for his or her identification number three times before the session is terminated by the sales server.

Constraints are listed within braces. Information—for example, a rule or condition that determines when an event fires or succeeds—is indicated by the event line within square brackets.

Sometimes an event is a message passed between two different objects of the same class (i.e., self-delegation). This can be represented by an event arrow that begins and ends on the same object as the last arrow on the leftmost object in Figure 11.1.

Some developers place notes on the left-hand side of a sequence diagram to remind themselves or others of what's happening at different points in the sequence diagram. For most purposes the notation shown in Figure 11.1 will be adequate to show the initial sequences you will want to diagram.

Figure 11.2 is a slightly more complex version of Figure 11.1. In this case we have added tall, thin rectangles that lie on top of the dotted lines below the object rectangles. These rectangles indicate when the object is active. They are called activation lines. We have also added times to indicate how long each object is active.

In some cases several objects are active simultaneously, even if they are only waiting for another object to return information to them. In other cases an object becomes active when it receives a message and then becomes inactive as soon as it responds.

In Figure 11.2 the two objects on the left side of the diagram are active throughout. The object on the right side,

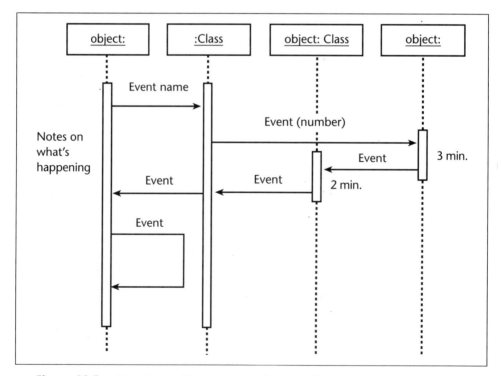

Figure 11.2   *Notation used in a sequence diagram—2.*

however, becomes active only when it receives a message and then becomes inactive soon after it responds.

Figure 11.3 shows a still more complex version of a sequence diagram. In Figure 11.3 the third object in the diagram was created by the second. The event arrow leading to the third object rectangle rather than to the tall rectangle below it indicates the creation of that object. Similarly, the bold "X" at the bottom of the lifeline of the third object indicates that the object is terminated at that point.

Most developers don't bother to show when objects are created or destroyed, especially during the analysis phase, but it's sometimes useful to do this if the system is complex and it's important to keep track of exactly which objects exist at any specific point in time.

In Figure 11.3 the left-hand object isn't a software object. It could be a customer who is entering information via a computer screen. In this case, you can leave the rectangle off the

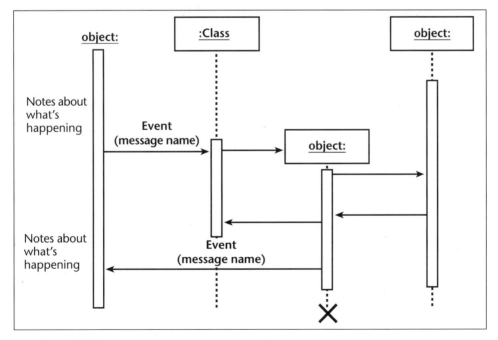

Figure 11.3   *Notation used in a sequence diagram—3.*

name, leave out the dotted line, and have a continuous tall activation rectangle instead to indicate that the source of the stimuli isn't a real software object.

11.2.2 *Creating a Sequence Diagram*

Let's consider how we would prepare a sequence diagram for a scenario we considered when we did the CRC exercise. We'll diagram Scenario 1 from Figure 8.4. In this scenario, Curtis Clyde, one of Watson's salespeople, wants to report an order that he received from Harmon Associates for a new desk.

Figure 11.4 shows how we would diagram that scenario. You wouldn't normally enter both the class name and the object name at the top, but we did it in some places to make things a little clearer. The object names would probably be best, but the "class names" would be acceptable, as long as you understand that you are using the class name to stand for a generic object in this diagram.

If we were going to continue to work on this example, we would probably do several more sequence diagrams as we added classes (e.g., additional objects of item or an address class) or break some of the events out into more detail. And, of course, as we embark on subsequent cycles and keep enhancing our prototype, we'll keep doing new sequence diagrams to capture new functionality.

11.3 Collaboration Diagrams

The collaboration diagram provides a second way of showing the sequence in which events occur. In effect, a collaboration is a cross between an object diagram and a sequence diagram. As in an object diagram, objects are shown in rectangles, connected by lines that indicate links between them. (Recall that lines connecting classes are called associations, while lines connecting objects are called links. In both cases they represent the fact that messages will flow between objects.) Unlike object diagrams, however, numbers, operation names, and arrows are placed over the links to indicate the flow of specific

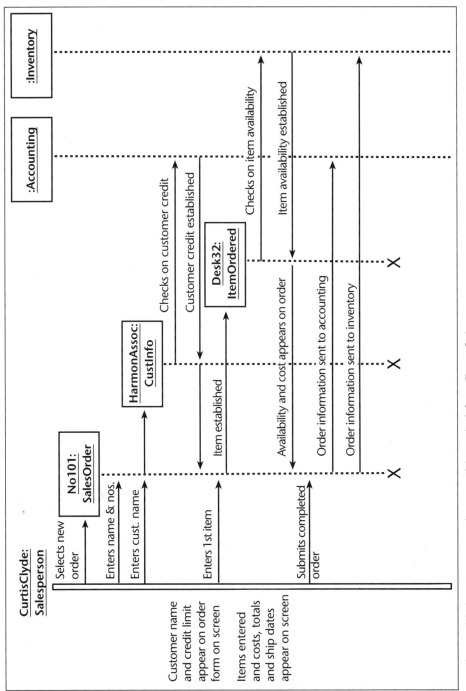

Figure 11.4   *A sequence diagram of Scenario 1 from Figure 8.4.*

messages. Thus, although there is no axis to indicate time, as there is in a sequence diagram, the numbers assure that we can actually follow the events or messages in sequence as they move from object to object. In a complex diagram several messages could pass back and forth across the same link.

Some developers may prefer to use the collaboration diagram in place of a simple object diagram and hence capture not only the objects involved in a scenario, but also the use of specific operations and some of the data flow. As with all the diagrams, different types of applications will favor different diagrams. The collaboration can get awfully complex and messy rather quickly, but it may be ideal for developers who want to analyze a narrowly focused scenario in a great deal of detail.

11.3.1 *Collaboration Notation*

Figure 11.5 illustrates the basic notation used in collaboration diagrams. Objects are represented as rectangles with either object or object:class names. If appropriate, you can also show the attributes associated with an object.

The lines between the objects are links. Each link can be labeled with one or more operation names. Each operation name is preceded by a number to indicate the order in which

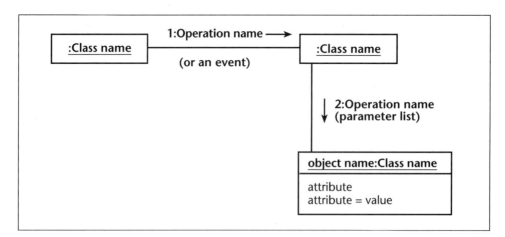

Figure 11.5   *UML collaboration notation.*

the operation is executed. An arrow, either after or beside the operation name, indicates the direction of the flow. (The operation being executed always resides on the object the arrow is pointing away from.) The reason we don't show returns is that, in most cases, this is an automatic response and not the result of a new operation being executed in the target object.

You don't need to show numbers or asterisks on a collaboration diagram, because it's an object diagram, and you can actually show multiple objects if you wish.

11.3.2 *Creating a Collaboration Diagram*

Now let's consider how we might apply the collaboration notation to our SalesWeb problem. We'll start by looking again at our first class diagram of our SalesWeb application (Figure 10.12). That gives us an overview of the classes and their relationships. Next we might look at Figure 10.13, which is an object diagram of Figure 10.12. That suggests one specific scenario we might want to consider in more detail. In fact, we'll develop a collaboration diagram to illustrate the top sequence, involving a sales order for Harmon Associates.

Finally, we might look at Figure 11.4, which is a sequence diagram of a series of events that rely on the structures described in Figures 10.12 and 10.13. By combining all of the insights we got from each of these three diagrams, we arrive at the collaboration diagram of Scenario 1, which we've illustrated in Figure 11.6. Here, as with our second class diagram, we use the attribute and operation names that we decided on in Chapter 9.

This collaboration shows a generic *SalesOrder* entry scenario, much like the one we discussed earlier as Scenario 1. We've eliminated numbers and asterisks, since this is really an object diagram and doesn't need them. If we wanted, we could show more than one object of any class involved in this sequence. And, as we already noted, we didn't bother to make the legacy applications, *Accounting* or *Inventory*, into objects. Similarly, we didn't bother to trace the return of values, although in most cases the object on the receiving end of the arrow would, sooner or later, obtain a value that it would pass back, ultimately to the *:SalesOrder* object, which would display it on the salesperson's computer screen.

The key things shown in Figure 11.6 are the operations that are invoked to pass information and the order in which the operations are used. You could capture this same information on the sequence diagram by simply using the operation names, rather than the phrases we used there.

If we had created several different scenarios, and felt the need, we could do one of these diagrams for each scenario, just as we could do a different sequence diagram for each scenario. We could also have gone into a lot more depth with this diagram. We could, for example, have shown the attributes and the values that were being changed when specific methods were executed.

One important thing to keep in mind is that all these diagrams are just tools to help you understand the system you are developing. There is no value in doing diagrams for their own

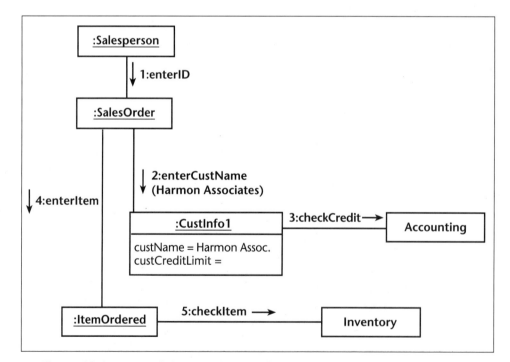

Figure 11.6   *UML collaboration diagram of the SalesWeb application.*

sake. You should do them when you have a specific purpose and a specific audience in mind. They document information or communicate it to others. You will probably use some, such as the sequence diagram, every time you develop an application. Others, such as the collaboration diagram, are only useful occasionally, when you encounter a special problem that can best be clarified by means of a collaboration diagram.

11.3.3 *Collaboration Diagrams and Patterns*

Patterns describe ways of solving recurring problems. Thus, many different OO applications require that developers use a time/date stamp. A pattern describes an especially good way to accomplish this. There are books on OO patterns that every OO developer should acquire and study in order to assure that he or she is acquainted with proven ways of solving common, recurring problems. We'll go into the use of patterns in more detail, in Chapter 15, when we consider design and coding, which is where the topic is more appropriate. We only mention it here to point out that most books that describe patterns rely on something like collaboration diagrams to illustrate the patterns in their catalogs.

11.4 Creating Sequence and Collaboration Diagrams with an Object-Oriented Modeling Tool

We looked at the general workings of Popkin Software's SA/Object Architect modeling tool in Chapter 6. Since then, we have seen how SA/Object Architect diagrams can be created for use cases and class diagrams. In a similar way, if we wanted, we could start from scratch and create sequence diagrams and then collaboration diagrams. SA/Object Architect has New Diagram entries for both sequence diagrams and collaboration diagrams. If we highlighted Sequence Diagram and then provided a name like "SalesWeb Sequence Diag1," we would be given a blank screen, and the various icons for a sequence diagram would appear on a palette on the left side of the screen. By clicking on the object icon, we could begin to lay out the lines for objects and then type in names to identify the objects, proceeding to create a diagram similar to the one we drew by hand in Figure 11.4. (See Figure 11.7.)

Whenever you create a sequence diagram (or a collaboration diagram), you are also creating the other diagram and only need to switch between them to see the alternative representation. Thus, if we switch from the sequence diagram to a collaboration diagram, we get Figure 11.8.

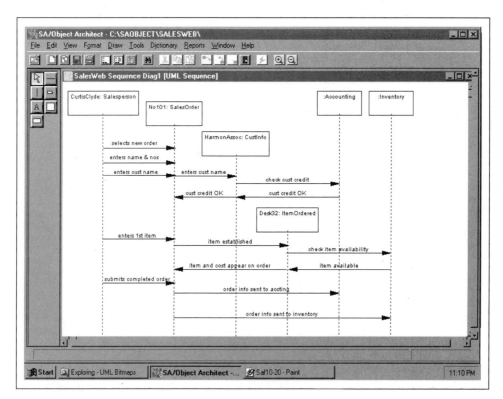

Figure 11.7   *SA/Object Architect screen showing SalesWeb sequence diagram.*

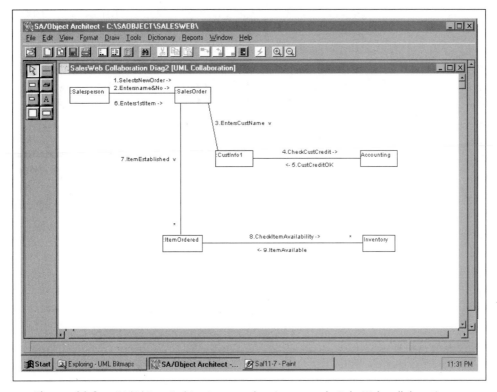

Figure 11.8   *SA/Object Architect screen showing an early SalesWeb collaboration diagram.*

As with class diagrams, SA/Object Architect gives you a large "drawing space" so that you can create very large drawings. In addition, since SA/Object Architect maintains dynamic links once they are established, you can move objects around, and the lines connecting them will remain attached. If you were drawing these diagrams by hand, you would make mistakes and find yourself starting over to put in a new object between two others. With SA/Object Architect, you can easily insert a new object without having to start a new diagram. When you work by hand, you usually end up with lots of different sequence diagrams, representing different options or different stages in your analysis of the problem. Since you can keep modifying and enhancing diagrams so easily in

SA/Object Architect, you tend to end up with only one diagram of each type—the final diagram with all the details.

Indeed, if there's a problem with SA/Object Architect, it's the reverse of having too many versions of the sequence diagram. If you keep adding details you will soon end up with a sequence diagram that's useful for developers but too complex to show users. Sometimes you have to remember to save early versions of diagrams just to document how you started or to remind yourself of an alternative you considered and rejected. This is easy enough. It's simply a matter of using a function key to copy everything on one diagram, starting a new diagram with a different name, and pasting all the objects from the first diagram onto the second diagram.

UML State and Activity Diagrams

So far, we have considered use case, class, and object diagrams which provide us with an understanding of the static, logical relationships in our application. We have also looked at interaction diagrams, including sequence and collaboration diagrams, which provide us with a dynamic view of how objects interact with one another. Now we'll turn to a third group of diagrams, collectively called state diagrams. State diagrams are designed to show us how one specific object changes state as it receives and processes messages. Compared with the earlier diagrams that provide us with overviews of our entire application, or at least views of a number of different classes or objects, state diagrams are narrowly focused, fine-grained diagrams that are good only for analyzing very specific situations.

As we commented earlier, Rational's documentation treats activity diagrams as a special type of state diagram. This may be logically correct, but in reality, activity diagrams are just the opposite of state diagrams. A state diagram focuses on activity within a specific class. An activity diagram, on the other hand, describes activities and flows of data or decisions between activities. In effect, activity diagrams are the diagrams used in most workflow analysis tools. They provide very broad views of business processes. Or they can be used to break out the activities that occur within a use case. Activity diagrams commonly show lots of different activities that will be handled by lots of different objects.

We'll consider both state and activity diagrams in this chapter, but keep in mind that they are very different diagrams used for very different purposes. Activity diagrams provide overviews of procedural flows. State diagrams provide precise information on changes in the values associated with a specific class.

12.1 State Diagrams

State refers to the set of values that describe an object at a specific moment in time. In other words, the state of an object is determined by the values associated with its attributes. As messages are received, the operations associated with the object's parent class are invoked to deal with the messages. As these operations are executed, they often change the values of attributes contained by an object.

Imagine we had a *:CustInfo* object that contained the name of a company. If the *:CustInfo* object received a message (*getCustName*) asking for the name of the company, an operation contained in the *CustInfo* class (e.g., *returnCustName*) would be invoked. That operation would check the attribute *custName* and then pass the value associated with that attribute back to the object that sent the message in the first place. In this case the state of the *:CustInfo* object would not have been changed.

Now assume that the same *:CustInfo* object received a message (*updateCustName*) that included a parameter (Harmon Corp.):

```
updateCustName (Harmon Corp.)
```

In this case, the object would invoke an operation from its class that would modify the value associated with the attribute *custName*, changing it from Harmon Assoc. to Harmon Corp. In the process, the state of the *:CustInfo* object would have been changed.

State diagrams are sometimes called state-transition or Harel diagrams. (The diagrams are derived from the statecharts that David Harel originated. They were originally developed for modeling process control systems.) These diagrams provide a detailed look at one specific class. In effect, by showing successive state changes, they illustrate the life cycle of a class, showing every state the class passes through as events occur.

Sequence diagrams need not be too complex and are useful to assure that you have a good overview of the messages passed between a number of different objects. State diagrams must be more precise and provide a narrow but exact view of what happens to one object as it receives successive messages. Many development efforts avoid state diagrams. Most complex applications, however, will probably have a few classes worth analyzing in this kind of detail. And almost any process control application will require that you prepare several state diagrams.

Some developers use a single state diagram to describe the state changes in several closely related classes simultaneously, but such a diagram can become very complex, very quickly. At least initially, you should probably stick with modeling a single class in a single state diagram.

There is certainly no reason to prepare a state diagram for each class in your system. Indeed, many developers create rather large systems without bothering to create any state diagrams at all. State diagrams are useful when you have a class that is very dynamic. In that situation, it is often helpful to prepare a state diagram to be sure you understand each of the possible states an object of the class could take and what event (message) would trigger each transition from one state to another. In effect, state diagrams emphasize the use of events and states to determine the overall activity of the system.

12.1.1 *State Diagram Notation*

States are represented as rectangles with rounded corners. The name of the state is placed inside the box. Events are shown connecting states with an arrow to indicate the new state that results from the transition in a value.

An event occurs at an instant in time when a value is changed. A message is data passed from one object to another. At a minimum, a message is a name that will trigger an operation associated with the target object. The message name may also be accompanied with values. For most practical purposes, you can think of the message and the event that the message causes as the same thing and use the terms as synonyms. This is convenient, since you have already created names for operations, and those names are generally used to describe the messages they send. Those names are generally also used to describe the events that result when the messages are received by target objects.

For example, a message might look like this:

```
CustInfo.setCustName (Harmon Assoc.)
```

or:

```
CustInfo.getCustName : string
```

In the first case, the operation *setCustName* (which is part of the *Salesperson* class) has generated a message (which is also called *setCustName*) for an object of the class *CustInfo*. The message, which includes the parameter Harmon Assoc., will trigger an operation associated with the *:CustInfo* object to set "Harmon Assoc." as the value of its *custName* attribute.

The second message *getCustName* is a message sent by some object to an object of the *CustInfo* class to determine the value associated with the target object's *custName* attribute. The return_type linked to the message name requires that the data returned by the target object be a string data type.

Unlike a message, which seeks to determine the value associated with an attribute, the name of a state often refers to the name of an attribute and the value associated with it. Thus, at one point, the name of a state of *:CustInfo* is *custName* = Harmon

Assoc. Then, after receiving a message telling the object to change the name to Harmon Corp., the name of the state of :*CustInfo* becomes *custName* = Harmon Corp.

You can be very precise about the names of events in state diagrams, but most developers aren't. Instead, they simply use a short phrase to remind them of the nature of the message, state, or state change indicated by a single event arrow.

A state is a box with rounded corners that describes an object and one or more of its attribute value tuples at one instance in time. The name of the state is placed in the top compartment of the round-cornered box. The state variables (or the state variables of substates if the box represents a high-level view) are listed in the second compartment of the box. The operations associated with the state are listed in the lower section of the box. In some cases the operations are described by a phrase. In other cases, one or more of four reserved words are used to identify the nature of the actions stimulated by the operations.

The following are four reserved action descriptions:

entry	a specific action performed on the entry to the state
do	an ongoing action performed while in the state
on	a specific action performed as a result of a specific event
exit	a specific action performed on exiting the state

For example, Figure 12.1 illustrates a state of the object :*CustInfo1*.

In most cases state diagrams, like initial class diagrams, don't show the attributes and actions within a state and focus more on the overall changes in states and the changes in substates. Figure 12.2 illustrates the basic high-level state notation and the notation of states and substates. Notice that it shows several state boxes. In the top case, two states are connected by an event arrow.

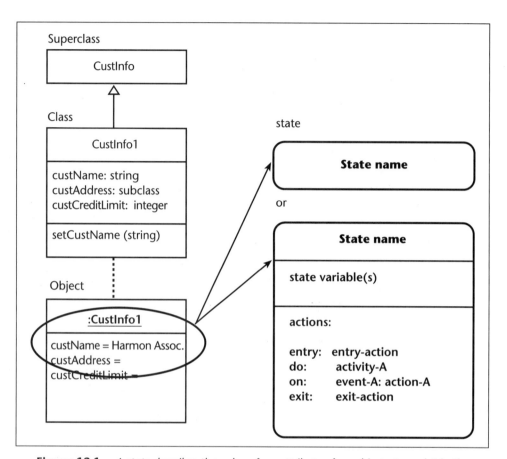

Figure 12.1   *A state describes the value of an attribute of an object at a point in time and the actions that occur while the object's attribute maintains that value, or when it changes the value.*

In some cases, a black dot is used to indicate where the system starts. If a starting point is indicated, the first state that occurs is sometimes called the initial state. A black dot inside a circle is used to signify when the state transitions end. Some systems, such as software programs, do not normally have a start and finish (in the sense that these terms are often used with physical systems). The program code resides on a hard disk and simply transitions back and forth between on and off. (A state description of a lightbulb would be the same. A

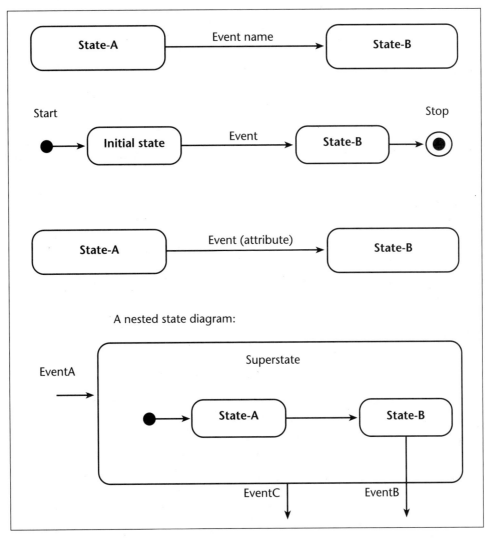

Figure 12.2   *Basic notation for state diagrams.*

lightbulb has two states: on and off, and it simply transitions between them until the lightbulb is worn out.)

It is sometimes useful to include additional information in state diagrams. You can expand the state box and include information on actions that are stimulated by the state change (as in Figure 12.1), or you can include additional information with the event name by placing the information in parentheses after the event name.

When things become more complex, it's often useful to do layered state diagrams with one group of states placed within another, as illustrated in the lower example in Figure 12.2. In this case the superstate (one object) is triggered, which in turn triggers a series of state changes in another object. Imagine a state diagram that showed an object of our *SalesOrder* class, with an object of the customer class contained within it. The object of the *SalesOrder* class would be the superstate, and the object of the company class would be shown inside.

Even more complex nesting structures are possible, especially when you have systems that may be doing things in parallel. In effect, you show one superstate, then subdivide the superstate box into two or more compartments. Within each compartment of the superstate diagram, you draw a state diagram that shows one of the series of state transitions that are going on simultaneously. Imagine that our object of the *Sales-Order* contained three objects of the *ItemOrdered* class and that each object was simultaneously sending a message to the inventory application to determine the availability and price of the item.

12.1.2 *Creating a State Diagram*

To clarify all this before going on to a more elaborate example, consider a class designed to model a light switch. The class itself might be modeled as we show in Figure 12.3. In addition, we could draw a simple sequence diagram of an object of the light switch class. In effect, the inputs come from a user class, and the results of changing the light switch are communicated to a light class. (Notice in this case that the user is a person who physically moves a switch, and thus the initial stimulus for a state change is an event that the object registers and not a message, as such.)

Figure 12.4 shows how we could represent the states of a generic instance of the *LightSwitch* class by using a state diagram. Notice that our system is so simple that the diagram doesn't show a start or stop condition. In effect, the light

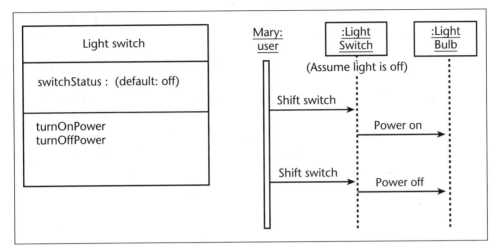

Figure 12.3   *Overview of the light switch class and an event trace.*

switch is always running and always in one of its two states. The key here is to realize that both the states represent the same instance of the *LightSwitch* class, and the only thing that is changing is the value associated with the attribute switch status. The events that connect the two states of the *:LightSwitch* object come from an outside class, but here they are only used to show that an event has triggered a state change. The operation that would allow electricity to flow is

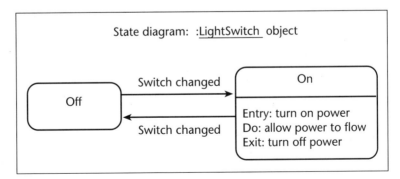

Figure 12.4   *State diagram of the :LightSwitch object.*

captured by placing the "do" comment under the value of the right-hand state of the instance.

Having looked at a very simple situation, let's turn to our SalesWeb application. Most of the classes in this application are not worth the kind of analysis that goes into a state diagram. As you continue to develop the system, the one class that might merit a state diagram is the *SalesOrder* class. In Figure 12.5 we've drawn a very high level state diagram for an object of the *SalesOrder* class.

To create this, we began by going down the sequence diagram for Scenario 1 (Figure 11.4) and examining all the inputs to the :*SalesOrder* object. Some came from the :*Salesperson* object, and others came from objects to the right of the *Sales-Order* line. Some were repeating events that had already occurred. Taken together, they gave us a good start. Next we would have examined Scenario 2, and so on. In other words, we would keep reviewing scenarios and looking for changes in the attributes of the :*SalesOrder* objects that were stimulated

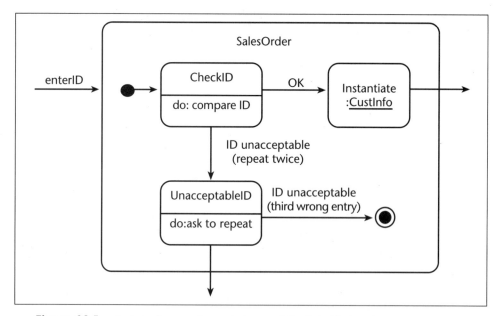

Figure 12.5   *A state diagram for an instance of the* SalesOrder *class.*

by outside events or which caused outside events, and then work out what must be going on inside the object.

By using the sequence diagram and supplementing it with state diagrams, and the activity diagrams we'll consider next, you can gradually capture all of the dynamics contained in the scenarios and, in effect, determine each of the operations you will need to create when you move to the prototyping phase.

12.2 Activity Diagrams

Activity diagrams are used to model the flow of activities in a procedure. In UML, activities are called states, and thus, activity diagrams are associated with state diagrams. A good example of an activity diagram is the LOVEM diagrams we used in Chapter 7 when we discussed BPR. (In a LOVEM diagram, the state rectangles are called actions and the lines showing flows are called events.)

In an activity diagram, the states are usually termed activities. Events are generally referred to as transitions. Diamonds are introduced to allow the developer to show what happens when a transition can have more than one consequence. Activity diagrams tend to be drawn without placing them inside some larger frame. Bars are used to show when several streams of events must come together before the next activity can occur. You can use the state symbols for beginning points and end points, but they usually aren't necessary.

Unlike state diagrams that focus on the events occurring within a single object as it responds to messages, an activity diagram can be used to model an entire business process or to provide a high-level view of what's going on inside a use case. Thus, activities could easily represent a module of several different classes. More to the point, an activity describes the performance of a task and isn't directly related to objects. In that sense, the activity diagram is much more like the BPR workflow diagram or the use case diagram, neither of which describes objects, as such. This is probably why activity diagrams were left out of the Booch and OMT methodologies. Many OO developers use activity diagrams, however, to get an overview of how some process works, and thus they have been included in the UML documentation. As far as we are concerned, the best example of an activity diagram is the LOVEM diagram we used in Chapter 7. For completeness, however, we'll consider how UML formally defines an activity diagram in this chapter.

Figure 12.6 illustrates the basic symbols used in a UML activity diagram. Since we've already considered a large-scale activity diagram in Chapter 7, we'll focus on a small-scale activity diagram at this point. Specifically, we'll consider an activity diagram that focuses on the activity within a specific object.

Figure 12.7 shows how we would represent an object of the *CustInfo* class as an activity diagram.

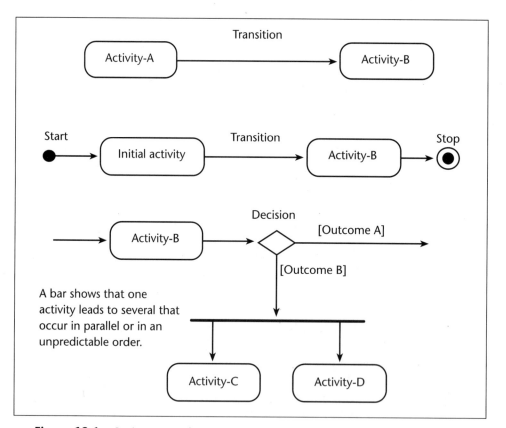

Figure 12.6   *Basic notation for an activity diagram.*

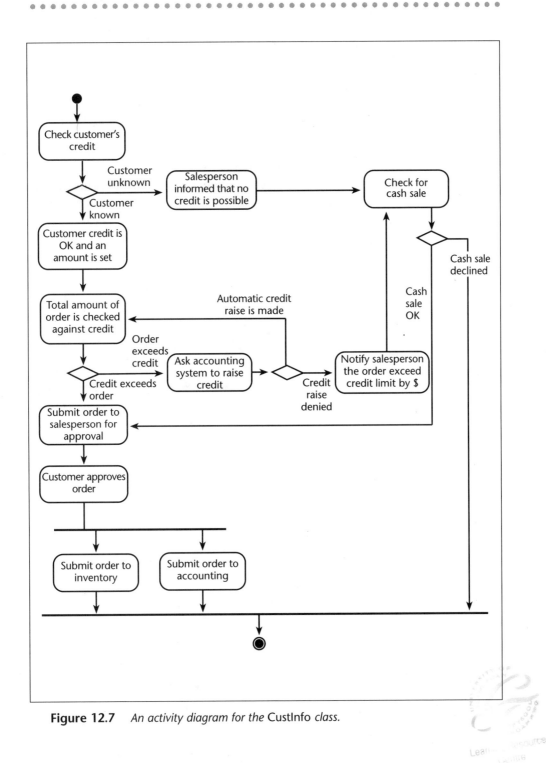

Figure 12.7   *An activity diagram for the* CustInfo *class.*

12.3 Creating State and Activity Diagrams with an Object-Oriented Modeling Tool

Having now considered how we could describe an object's states in terms of either a state diagram or an activity diagram, let's consider how we could create a state diagram using Popkin Software's SA/Object Architect. We simply select New Diagram, select a UML state diagram, and name it SalesWeb State Diag1. Then, using tools available on the palette that SA/Object Architect displays, we quickly create the diagram shown in Figure 12.8.

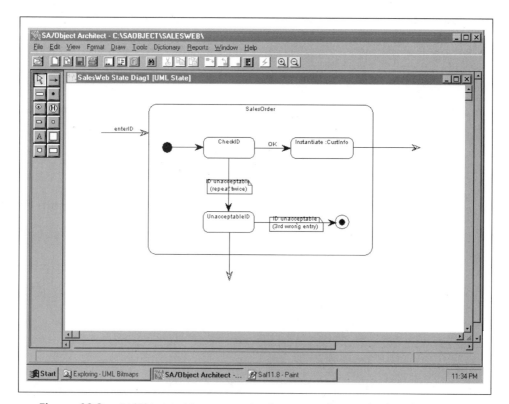

Figure 12.8   *SA/Object Architect screen showing a state diagram for the* SalesOrder *object.*

In a similar way, we could create an activity diagram in SA/Object Architect. If we wanted to create workflow diagrams, we could also use Popkin Software's SA/BPR tool.

Designing an Object-Oriented System

Thus far, we have tried to talk in abstract, logical terms about analyzing a problem. We've been trying to find a clean, ideal solution to the problem that was described in the requirements statement and the use case diagrams. Now it's time to shift from creating a model for an ideal system to creating a design that can be implemented in the environment in which you will run the application.

UML doesn't make a sharp distinction between analysis and design notation. Indeed, one of the best features of the OO approach is the lack of any difference between the diagrams and constructs you use during analysis and those you use during design. The same UML diagrams that you used during analysis will continue to be used and enhanced as you proceed to make the more concrete decisions typical of the design process. There are, however, three Implementation Diagrams that primarily capture information about the architecture of an application that we will discuss in the next chapter.

Keep in mind that if you are developing your application using a cyclical, iterative methodology, once you have created the diagrams to describe your prototype at the end of the first iteration, you will have all those diagrams to consider when you begin to enhance your system during the second iteration. Thus, any distinction between analysis and design that we have maintained up until now will have vanished when you begin your second analysis phase.

In this chapter, we want to pull together some general ideas about how to proceed to develop your system. We assume that once you get to design, you will continue to use your existing UML diagrams. Thus, our concern here is not so much to teach you new UML notation, although there will be some, but to provide you with practical suggestions about how to complete the effort that you began with the diagrams created during the first analysis phase of your development effort. Moreover, since the emphasis in design is on tailoring an abstract design to a specific environment, and since that's hard to do in an abstract way, we will organize our discussion around the problems of moving our SalesWeb application from an abstract model to a concrete application.

13.1 Moving from Analysis to Design

We suggested that during at least the first analysis phase you start by developing an object model that describes the entire application. Then, once you have that overview, we suggested you choose a portion of the entire application to develop in more detail. In the case of our SalesWeb application, for example, we chose only one of the use cases, Report Sales, and created diagrams for just that portion of the application.

Different prototypes will suggest very different designs. In some cases you will be working on a prototype that will require that you develop an elaborate infrastructure to support its implementation. In other cases you will have avoided the necessity for an elaborate infrastructure effort on the first cycle. Whatever you do, when you consider design for the first time, you should develop at least a general view of the overall architecture you will need to implement the final system, even if you then proceed to implement only a part of the final infrastructure during the first phase.

During the first design phase you will need to elaborate the portion of the overall application you have selected to develop first. Even then, however, you will need to decide how complete you want to make your first prototype. For example, you may decide to create flat files to simulate links to a mainframe database, rather than actually linking with the mainframe during the first development phase. In one sense, this is design. In another sense, it is merely deciding on tactics to guide your iterative development process.

Figure 13.1 is another version of our general cyclical development model. It reminds you where you are in the overall process, and it suggests some of the things you must accomplish during any design phase.

We have listed some of the tasks that must be accomplished during the design phase of an OO development project on the right side of Figure 13.1. We used bullets, rather than numbers, because we didn't want to suggest that these were steps that should be followed in a specific order. Depending on the nature of the application, the experience of the developer, or the size of the development team, these tasks would be handled in a different order, or even in parallel. We will work our way through them in more or less the order we have suggested in Figure 13.1, beginning with a consideration of application architectures and the introduction of two new UML diagrams—the deployment and the package diagrams—in Chapter 14. Then we'll proceed to a discussion of elaborating the business model in Chapter 15.

Before getting into any details, however, it is useful to consider how much time you might spend in the design phase. Most methodologists who have studied OO development have concluded that OO development is different from more conventional development. OO development rewards the effort spent on analysis and design and leads to a reduction of the time spent on coding. This occurs in large part because

Figure 13.1 *An iterative approach to OO development.*

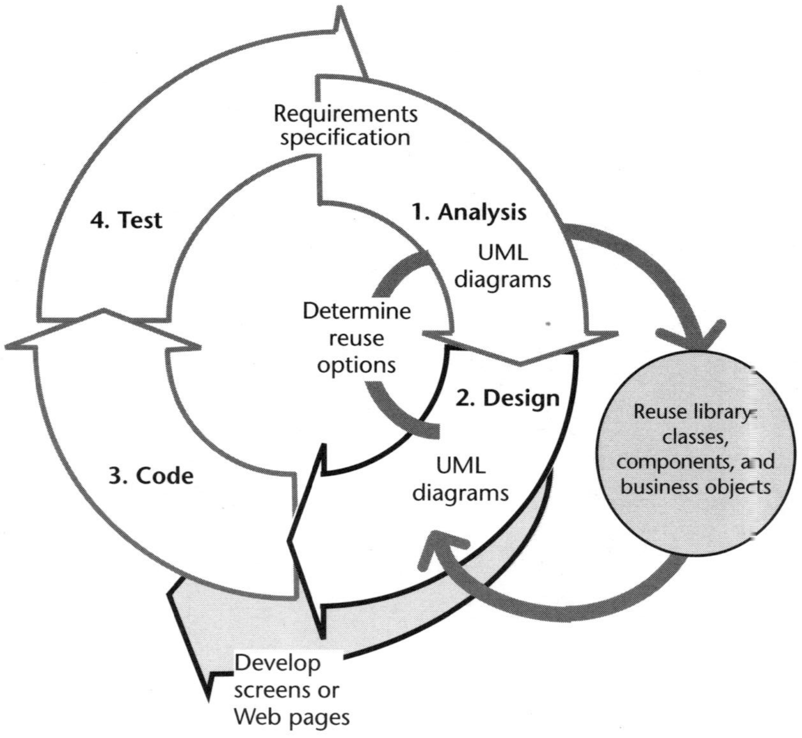

Key activities for the design phase:

- Settle on the overall architecture of the application.
  1, 2 or 3 tier
  location of major modules
  inter-tier communications

- Create UML deployment and package diagrams.

- Elaborate the business object model to incorporate infrastructure classes. Extend all classes to include needed operations.

- Extend UML class, sequence, state, activity, and collaboration diagrams.

- Consider opportunities for reuse of class libraries and components.

- Create UML component diagrams as needed.

- Design interface screens.

- Design database, or linkages, as needed.

- Elaborate UML deployment diagrams, etc.

- Consider problems associated with threads of control.

Reuse library classes, components, and business objects

1. Analysis
UML diagrams

2. Design
UML diagrams

Requirements specification

Determine reuse options

Develop screens or Web pages

4. Test

3. Code

lots of problems are solved in analysis and design that would otherwise be solved during coding—and, of course, because of reuse. If you spend time during the design phase and locate several components that will provide 30% of the functionality you need, you won't have to write that code later.

Figure 13.2 suggests the balance of time spent in different phases in an OO development effort. These times are approximate and will vary depending on the nature of the application. Still, they emphasize that lots of time is typically spent in analysis. And, more to the point for this chapter, they emphasize that most of your time should be spent in design.

In the analysis phase you consider the object model in the abstract. You work out the logical relationships between the business objects. In the design phase you determine the physical architecture of the system. This in turn suggests the infrastructure objects you will need. And the infrastructure objects

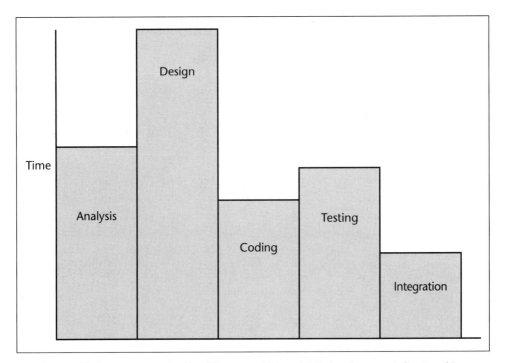

Figure 13.2   *Time required in different activities of OO development (after Booch).*

suggest lots of different operations that will be needed to handle the communications between all the new objects. By the same token, during design you decide what classes and components you can reuse, and they also suggest changes in your object model. And, of course, you design the user interfaces during this phase, and that also takes time.

If you did a good job of analyzing the business model during the analysis phase, you probably won't need to change too many of the classes you have already developed. You will, however, need to develop several new classes and lots of new operations to create a complete application. Then, finally, you will need to worry about lots of really detailed issues involved in obtaining the performance you will require.

Since this book is intended to introduce you to the UML notation, we do not provide a detailed prescription for designing OO applications. More important, our goal is to give you an overview and assure that you don't get lost in the details. Hence, we won't go into great depth about the various different design issues. We do, however, want to make some general comments and suggestions in the next two chapters.

Choosing an Object-Oriented Architecture

What hardware will your application run on? Will the application run on one machine or be distributed across many platforms? How will your application software be modularized? Does the system have to perform within certain time limits? Are existing applications going to be incorporated into or used by the system? What databases will be used by the system? These are the kinds of questions you must ask when you begin to think about how to create a concrete design for an application.

Some of these questions may already have been answered. Your company may own equipment or have adopted standards that determine or constrain the answers to some of these questions. Similarly, your BPR team may have answered some of these questions when they designed the new business process your application will support. You may even have spelled out some of the design characteristics of the system when you created your initial requirements specification or when you made presentations to users before the project began. Whatever has gone before, when you begin the first design phase, you must reconsider the issues raised by these questions and come up with a firm design.

Of course, the conclusions you reach are not irreversible. The whole point of developing an application by means of successive approximations is to allow you to test alternatives before you finalize the entire system's design. Most developers start with an idea of how to develop their system, complete a few classes and test a portion of the idea, and then modify the idea as necessary. Similarly, if your first approximate or subapplication is intended to test the infrastructure and your plan for integration, and something doesn't work as well as anticipated, then during your next cycle you will revise the design and test an alternative. Given all those qualifications, when you end your initial design phase, you should have a good approximation of your final design—if only in order to test it to see if it really works.

This book is not a comprehensive or detailed treatment of system design, so we won't go into many of the points that apply equally to conventional and OO development and are treated in many other books. (We recommend some of the best of these books in the bibliography.) We will comment on a few of the considerations that you will face during development in order to clarify how these issues might affect the way you develop and extend the diagrams you are creating to document your system design. And we'll discuss how we might modularize our simple SalesWeb system.

14.1 Dividing an Application into Tiers

Let's start with a basic consideration: will our application run on a single machine or on multiple machines? And, if on multiple machines, will it use a two- or three-tiered architecture?

Many small applications are designed to run on a single machine. The user loads the entire application onto his or her computer, including data in flat files or a local database, and then runs it. It's the simplest possible design because you don't need to worry about interfaces between one platform and another.

Increasingly, however, systems are designed to run on multiple machines. If you are creating a multiplatform system, your primary choice is likely to be between a two- and three-tiered architecture. Some developers call a two-tiered system a simple client/server system, and they call a three-tiered system a complex client/server, or distributed, system.

14.1.1 *A Two-Tiered Design*

A two-tiered system places a portion of the application on user platforms and the rest of the system on a server. Usually, three basic modules are assigned: (1) the user interface screens and associated logic, (2) the business logic of the application, and (3) the database and associated logic. A typical simple client/server system puts the user interface and the business logic on the client platform and puts the database and associated logic on the server portion of the system, which is usually a database server.

Many simple Internet systems use a two-tiered approach. In some cases the Internet client/server systems arrange things just as we described above. In other cases, the two-tiered Internet application assumes that the user has a Web browser. The server has the user screens, the business logic, and the database. The user signs on via the Internet, and the screens and some or all of the business logic are downloaded over the Internet. (Interestingly, that's just the way mainframe systems used to work with dumb terminals. Everything was on the mainframe, and the user screens and some logic were downloaded to the user's terminal, as needed.) Figure 14.1 illustrates a simple two-tiered Internet-based system.

In considering Figure 14.1, bear in mind that the tiers are, in fact, the platforms. The network hardware and software that links the client and server platforms are middleware. We'll consider connections between tiers in a moment.

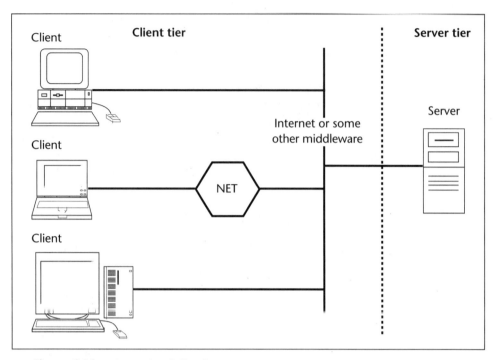

Figure 14.1   *A two-tiered client/server system.*

14.1.2 *A Three-Tiered Design*

More complex applications typically rely on a three-tiered design. A three-tiered design divides the business objects and their operations or business rules from both the user interface and from the database(s) and from any other legacy applications that might be used. A typical three-tiered design puts the screen interface on the user's machine, the business logic on an intermediate server, and keeps legacy applications and databases on whatever machines they currently reside on.

Larger Internet applications tend to be three-tiered systems. This usually means that a new Internet application must be designed to connect to both browsers and existing company databases or legacy applications. Three-tiered Internet systems may keep the user screens on the Internet server and download them when the user connects to the server. In this case, we assume that the user has a Web browser on his or her machine. Or there may be small applications that reside on the user machines and that initiate the contact with the Internet server. Figure 14.2 illustrates a three-tiered system. Again, the tiers are platforms, and the wiring and software in between the platforms constitute middleware.

If you develop a two-tiered system, you only have to develop an interface between the two tiers. Moreover, if you are going to rely on the Internet, you might also rely on the user having a browser, in which case you might only have to develop an applet and a server application, and ignore concerns about what kinds of machines the users have.

A two-tiered system tends to be a new system. It's easier to develop, but it's harder to maintain. If you know that your system is going to grow, or if your system will need to interact with existing databases or other applications, a three-tiered design is cleaner and easier to enhance and maintain.

A three-tiered system will require at least two interfaces: one between the user and the Internet server and another between the Internet server and a database server or another application on another platform. Most large distributed systems, in fact, require several "backend" interfaces, since they typically link to multiple legacy applications and multiple databases. In any case, client/server or distributed systems bring up the possibility that different parts of the application will be written in different languages or that they will be running on different kinds of platforms. Either or both will make application interfaces more complex.

You might initially design and implement a two-tiered system that later evolves into a three-tiered system. This typically occurs when additional business logic is added to the server tier, for security reasons, or to better distribute the processing load.

14.2 Assigning Packages to Tiers and Platforms

If your entire application is going to run on a single platform, you don't need to worry about dividing your application into packages and assigning the packages of your application to different platforms. Indeed, if your application is small

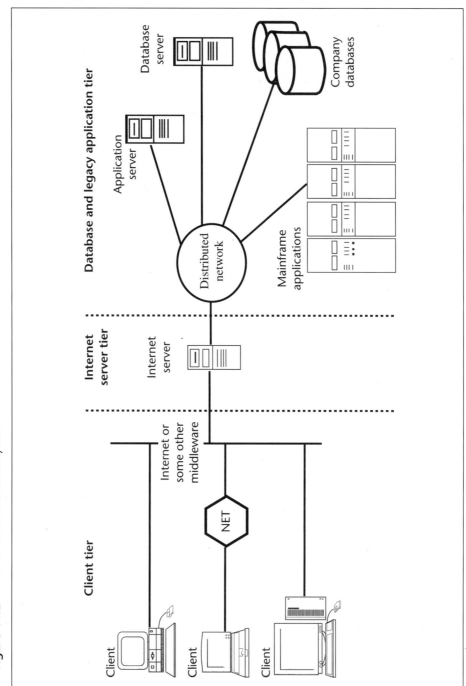

Figure 14.2   *A three-tiered distributed system.*

enough, you can leave all the objects together in a single package and be done with it.

Most Internet applications, however, as well as nearly all midsized to large applications need to run on multiple platforms. In this case you will usually want to subdivide your code into packages and assign it to different platforms. The simplest Internet application, for example, typically has a Java application on a server and one or more applets that are designed to be downloaded and executed within a client browser environment.

The SalesWeb code that we include in Appendix A is implemented as a two-tiered system. We provide a client and have both the logic and data on the server. We did this so you wouldn't have to own any specific database software to examine the code, which can be downloaded from Web sites identified in Appendix A.

At a minimum, you will want to isolate the parts of the application that will be on different tiers. If you are building a simple, two-tiered Internet system, you will need at least two packages: one for the server and another for the client. Of course, the portion of the application that you set up for the client may not be an application package in the traditional sense. It may be an applet that is downloaded along with an HTML Web page, or it may be a JavaBean that is incorporated in another application.

By the same token, if you have a three-tiered system, you may not actually have any part of your application that will reside on the mainframe server. You may simply have one or more database objects that sit on the server and manage the communication with the mainframe server. In all but the simplest systems, however, it would be useful to isolate the database interface portion of the application in a separate package.

14.2.1   *Two- and Three-Tiered Class Diagrams*

Before considering adding infrastructure classes to your class diagram, you might want to modify your class diagram by dividing it into two or three sections to indicate which tier each class will reside in.

Although a three-tiered class diagram is not an official part of the UML notation, we notice that Rational Software, when they brought out the new version of their OO modeling tool, Rational Rose for Visual Basic, introduced the idea of dividing the class diagram into three columns so that developers can locate classes in one tier or another. We think it's an excellent idea. If you did it during analysis (as Rational Rose does), it would be just another example of how it's hard to separate analysis and design when you create OO applications.

At the very least, we suggest you use the idea when you are working on the design of your application. If you are doing a two-tiered client/server application, divide your class diagrams into a client and a server side. If you are doing a three-tiered application, divide your class diagram into thirds, with the left third for the client, the middle third for the server, and the right third for the database server or for legacy applications. In Figure 14.3, we've placed a three-tiered grid over the initial SalesWeb class diagram we did in Chapter 10 (Figure 10.12).

14.3 UML Implementation Diagrams

The UML notational system provides three diagrams called implementation diagrams:

- Package diagrams allow developers to show how classes could be divided into modules. Package diagrams are logical diagrams and do not necessarily imply a physical division of the classes.

- Component diagrams are used to show the physical modules that a developer might use.

- Deployment diagrams allow developers to model the physical platforms and network connections that will be used in their applications.

All three diagrams are relatively simple, high-level diagrams compared with the diagrams we have considered earlier. We'll

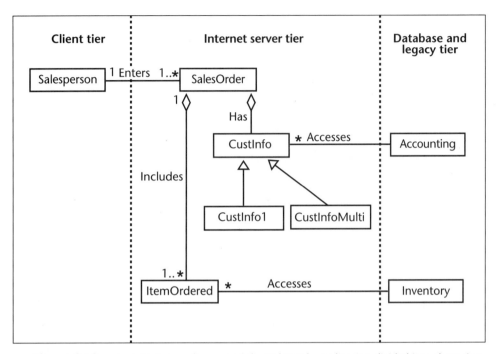

Figure 14.3   *An initial class diagram of the SalesWeb application divided into three tiers.*

introduce all three types of implementation diagrams in this chapter and then apply them to our SalesWeb system in this chapter and the next, as appropriate.

14.3.1 *The UML Package Diagram*

UML provides a package diagram that allows the developer to indicate how classes might be divided up. A file folder-shaped icon is used to represent a logical software module, which UML calls a package. Links between packages are indicated by dashed arrows. The arrows can be labeled to indicate dependency names, if desired. If necessary, you can show packages within packages to any desired depth. The name of the package is usually written inside the package, although if packages are placed within packages, the superpackage name may be written on the tab of the largest folder.

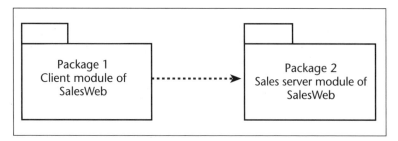

Figure 14.4 *A UML package diagram showing the SalesWeb application divided into two packages.*

You can show packages to show high-level logical groupings, as we did when we first described the way the frameworks were divided in the Java Virtual Machine (Figure 5.1), or you can show the classes inside the package, as we did in Figure 5.2, when we showed the classes inside the Java RMI package.

Figure 14.4 illustrates how SalesWeb could be subdivided into two packages. The dotted arrow indicates dependencies between the packages. (If, in drawing the classes, there were association lines running between classes that are now in separate packages, you should show that there are dependencies between the two packages.) Package diagrams are often used to show that you intend to modularize your object model. If you do this, you would show the major classes within each package.

14.3.2 *The UML Component Diagram*

We've already discussed components at several points. Component diagrams refer to physical components in your design. These high-level physical components may or may not be equivalent to the many smaller components you use in the creation of your application. For example, a single physical user interface component might contain dozens of JavaBeans or ActiveX components that are used to put graphical features on the user interface.

As far as most developers are concerned, a physical component will usually turn out to be the equivalent of a package. A package is used to show how you might group classes (and smaller scale components). In some cases the package will only be used to indicate a logical grouping to help highlight some particular perspective. In most cases, however, the package will be a first approximation of what will eventually turn into a physical grouping. In that case, the package will become a component.

In some cases a component is composed of classes. In other cases a component may simply be a wrapper for a legacy application. In a few cases, as when you are involved in development for Windows applications, you may actually want to package an application, or part of an application, as an OLE or ActiveX component so it can be integrated with other components in the Windows environment. And, of course, a Java applet can easily be conceptualized as a kind of component. For example, in Figure 14.4, package 1 could be an applet. In that case, it could just as well be represented as a component. Similarly, package 2 could easily be a JavaBean, or an ActiveX component, and so forth. The use of components will undoubtedly play an ever increasing role in the design and development of OO applications in the near future as more ActiveX and JavaBeans components become available. We're not sure the UML component diagrams will be useful in representing the components that most developers will use. Keep in mind when you use UML component diagrams that you are describing physical modules of code.

UML also provides a notation for components, and you can create diagrams in which you show several components interacting with each other. A component is represented by the icon shown in Figure 14.5. The names of the components are written on the surface of the icon, and dependencies between components are indicated by dotted arrows.

In most cases you will use component diagrams in conjunction with deployment diagrams to show how physical modules of code are distributed on various hardware platforms. In fact, they might as well be the same diagram: a component/deployment diagram.

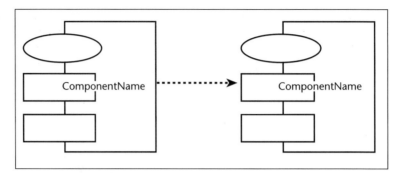

Figure 14.5 *UML component diagram notation.*

14.3.3 *The UML Deployment Diagram*

In UML deployment diagrams, each node or processing element in the system is represented by a three-dimensional box. Links between the nodes or platforms are shown by solid lines. Figure 14.6 provides the basic UML notation for a deployment diagram.

You can describe a class-level configuration by writing the names of each node as you would the names of the classes, in which case you would only have one node for each type of element in the system. In this case, our SalesWeb application would only show one salesperson's laptop computer. Or, you can label the nodes with names that refer to specific instances of the node and label them as you would objects, underlined with a colon after the "object" portion of the name. If you chose this approach, our SalesWeb application would show several salespeople, each with his or her own laptop, all linked to the common sales department's Internet server.

You can go further and place components inside nodes to show how the actual code will be distributed. You could also show packages or even classes inside the cubes to show which platform specific elements of the system will be placed on, but that can get rather complex. In any case, it involves mixing a physical and logical description of your application and is probably best avoided, except to demonstrate a very specific or narrowly focused aspect of a distributed solution.

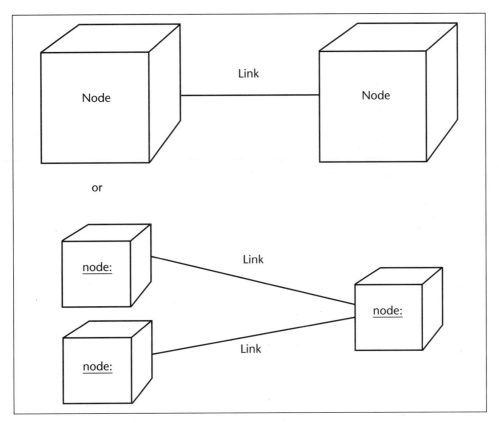

Figure 14.6   *UML deployment diagram notation.*

14.4 **Linking the Tiers**

In a distributed system, you might want to do either of two things. First, you might want to pass data from one object to another object or to a database. Or, you might want to have one object ask another object to perform some task. We'll consider how you might deal with data in Chapter 15. At this point, we want to discuss how an object on one platform might send a message to an object on another platform.

If you were building a simple Internet application, you could make the client portion of the system an applet. In order to use the client applet, you would then need to create a Web page in HTML. You rely on the client using HTTP to access the server and download the HTML code, which would then call the applet. You could also rely on the applet to pass the information back to the server.

14.4.1 *Object Request Brokers*

The minute you encounter more complex problems, you should begin to think about using an object request broker (ORB). An ORB is a communication system that allows one object to send a message to another object without regard to where the other object is located. The objects might be located on the same platform, but ORBs are most valuable when the objects are located on separate platforms. In effect, an ORB keeps track of where objects are (or has a mechanism for finding out where they are) and provides mechanisms for routing a message from the sender to the target without the developer having to worry how it's done. An ORB allows us to locate useful remote objects and make remote procedure calls (RPC) on those objects.

Sun's Remote Method Invocation

Figure 14.7 illustrates a simplified version of Sun's Remote Method Invocation (RMI) ORB. In this case, a class on a client platform, *Salesperson*, wants to send messages to a class on an Internet server platform, *SalesHandler*. To accomplish this, the ORB either arranges to preplace a stub for *SalesHandler* on the client platform, or moves one there when *Salesperson* indicates that it wants to send a message to *SalesHandler*. The stub is a surrogate object that accepts messages directed to *SalesHandler*. When the stub receives a message, it encodes the parameters of the message into a format suitable for transporting them across the Internet (often called parameter marshalling). Then the stub launches the parameters across the network. They are received on the server platform by a second interface object, called a skeleton. The skeleton unmarshals the parameters and passes the message to the *SalesHandler* object.

If the data sent to the *SalesHandler* object was intended to update a database, *SalesHandler* might then initiate a message

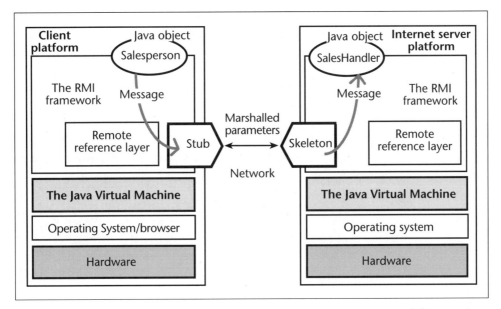

Figure 14.7   *Java's RMI ORB locates and passes messages over a network from one Java object to another.*

to a database object, but we'll ignore that aspect for the moment. *SalesHandler* passes any information back to the *Salesperson* object by reversing the process. It passes parameters to the skeleton object, which marshalls the parameters and passes them back to the stub object, which unmarshals them and returns them to *Salesperson*. This sounds complex, but most of it is hidden from the developer. The developer relies on the Java RMI package to generate the stub and skeleton objects and to handle the transfer operations.

Several ORBs are available, but there are three that you should know about:

- Sun's Remote Method Invocation (RMI) is appropriate for communicating between Java objects on one machine and Java objects on another machine. The classes needed to implement RMI are included in Sun's JDK. In the near future RMI will be linked to CORBA.

- Microsoft's Distributed COM (DCOM) is appropriate for communicating between Java objects on one Windows platform and Java objects or ActiveX components on another Windows platform. The code needed to implement DCOM is included in the Windows 95 and NT operating systems. DCOM will eventually become available on other operating systems. Bridges are being built to link DCOM to CORBA.

■ The Object Management Group has developed a standard for an ORB that will allow any object on any platform to send messages to any other object on any other platform. The OMG's Common Request Broker Architecture (CORBA) is the high-end option for serious distributed applications. This is the only approach that will let a Java object transparently send messages to a Smalltalk object on a server or to a COBOL object on a mainframe. The OMG does not sell CORBA; it only provides the standard. Individual vendors sell implementations of CORBA. Different implementations of CORBA can talk with each other, although many companies prefer to use the same implementation of CORBA on all their platforms. (We list a few of the better known CORBA implementations in Appendix D.)

We have already discussed RMI. Let's briefly consider the two alternatives.

Microsoft's Distributed COM

Distributed COM (Component Object Model), Microsoft's ORB entry, isn't fully OO, and it is primarily designed to pass information between ActiveX components. DCOM comes built into Windows 95 and NT operating systems, but it isn't yet available on other platforms. Microsoft has deals with Software AG, Digital, and Hewlett-Packard to put DCOM on their machines and on other platforms, though that will take some time.

If you are building a Java application that will run entirely on Windows 95 and NT and you plan on using ActiveX components, you will probably want to consider DCOM. Unfortunately, DCOM, like ActiveX, will limit your application to Microsoft environments. Microsoft is making a major effort to promote ActiveX and DCOM. If they succeed and developers use this approach, it will destroy Java's greatest feature—its ability to run on any platform without changes. We recommend that developers consider this matter very carefully. If you'll want your Java application to run on any non-Microsoft platform, now, or in the future, we recommend you avoid both ActiveX and DCOM.

We've already mentioned that you can encapsulate ActiveX components as JavaBeans. Microsoft and several CORBA vendors are working on bridges between DCOM and CORBA, and at some point in the future, you will be able to send messages via CORBA to DCOM, but it will always be a hassle. If DCOM were easy to use, it might be different, but it isn't, and we suggest you avoid it if you program in cross-platform environments. For simple Java applications, use RMI. For complex applications and for any applications that will mix Java and any other language, use a CORBA implementation.

The Object Management Group's Common Request Broker Architecture

CORBA solves the problem Java's RMI avoids and allows a message from a Java object to reach a Smalltalk or COBOL object on a different platform. It does so, unfortunately, at the expense of quite a bit of overhead.

Consider Figure 14.8. Like RMI, CORBA relies on stubs and skeleton objects. Unlike RMI, the stubs and skeletons won't always be interfacing with Java objects. To deal with this, CORBA uses a special language, OMG's Interface Definition Language (IDL) to represent the operations that objects can interact with. If you are going to create a CORBA system, you need to define all the signatures of all the objects that will be involved in the system. These are placed in an interface repository so that a message from one object can determine which platform the target object might reside on. Thus, messages are changed from the language of the sending object to IDL, are marshalled, sent, unmarshalled, then converted to the language of the target object. In effect, each platform is equipped with a CORBA object that can deal with sending and receiving IDL and marshalling parameters. The CORBA client and

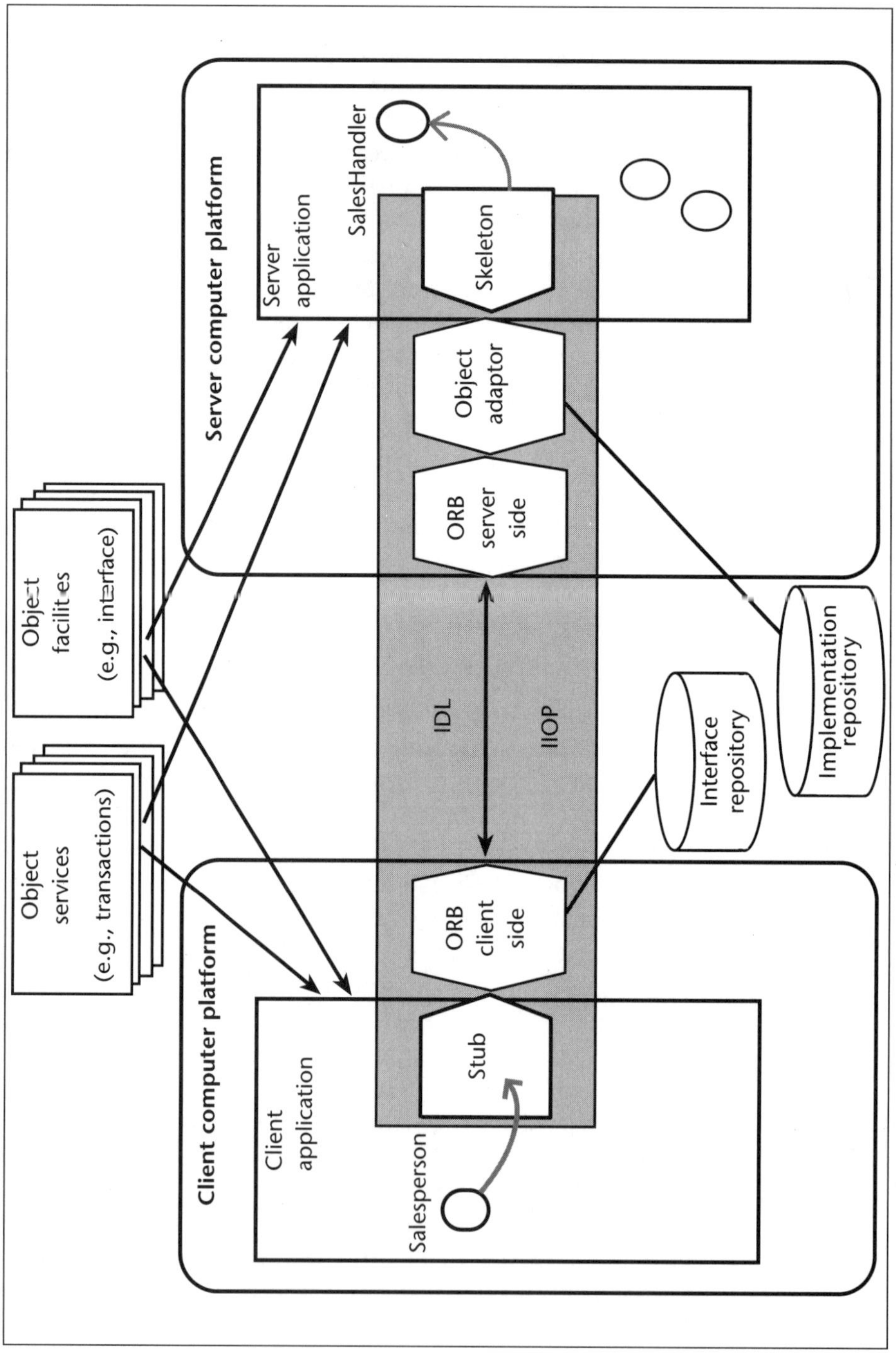

Figure 14.8 *An implementation of the OMG's CORBA architecture.*

server objects can access the interface repository and an implementation repository as needed.

CORBA uses an OO version of TCP/IP, called Internet InterORB Protocol (IIOP), when it transmits IDL. Several companies, led by Netscape, have proposed IIOP as a standard Internet protocol. Netscape has also incorporated CORBA into their browser and server tools, so any Java applet running on a Netscape browser can send a message, via CORBA, to any object on a server. (Netscape's approach to CORBA is more efficient than Sun's CORBA implementations, NEO and JOE. Sun requires that the stub be downloaded as an applet. Netscape simply makes the stubs available in the browser.

Again, this sounds complex, but much of it is transparent. Still, compared with RMI, there's quite a bit more to CORBA, and it takes more work to set up a CORBA system. This is to be expected, since CORBA can work with multiple servers and can move messages transparently between any of the major OO languages.

CORBA has been around longer than either RMI or DCOM, and the OMG has standardized a wide variety of classes and frameworks for handling the complex problems involved in dealing with finding objects, handling security, dealing with transaction processing, and so on. The latest CORBA implementations are combining CORBA with Message Oriented Middleware (MOM) to handle large-scale asynchronous applications.

Clearly, CORBA isn't appropriate for systems written entirely in Java, or for small systems. It is, however, the emerging standard for large systems that have to route messages in a heterogeneous environment. Indeed, Sun recognizes this fact and sells NEO and JOE, CORBA implementations for Java. Moreover, Sun is embedding support for CORBA in its Java environment. Sun's new Enterprise JavaBeans initiative, for example, has produced an extended version of JavaBeans for enterprise development. This advanced component model is especially designed to encapsulate business objects or legacy applications and to work in heterogeneous environments. Moreover, it is specifically designed to work with CORBA. (See Figure 14.9.)

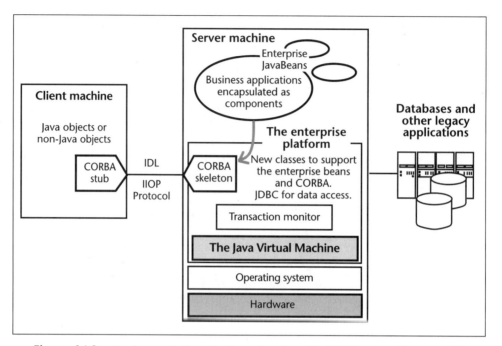

Figure 14.9   *Sun's new platform for the enterprise with CORBA networking capabilities,
a transaction monitor, and enhanced enterprise JavaBeans model.*

14.5 Summing Up

The three major steps in designing an architecture for an
application are (1) identify the platforms, (2) break your application into packages and assign the packages to platforms,
and (3) decide how to link your platforms together. You document these decisions with UML's implementation diagrams.
In the process you have to modify all of your earlier diagrams
to incorporate infrastructure classes and new JDK classes, and
write lots of attributes and operations to make it all work.

14.6   The Architecture of the SalesWeb System

Our SalesWeb application could take several forms, but we have assumed from the beginning that we were developing a three-tiered application. Salespeople use laptops and modems. The salespeople could have different types of laptops. Let's assume that some have Intel machines running Microsoft Windows and others have Apple Powerbook laptops running the Macintosh OS. They will contact the Watson's sales Internet server via the Internet. Let's assume that the server will be a Sun workstation running Sun's version of UNIX. We have already assumed that the legacy applications owned by accounting and inventory are mainframe applications supported by DB2 databases. Let's assume they are running on midsized IBM mainframes.

We could diagram the physical layout of our SalesWeb application as shown in Figure 14.10. We have shown the SalesWeb system at the class level and thus only have one generic laptop node.

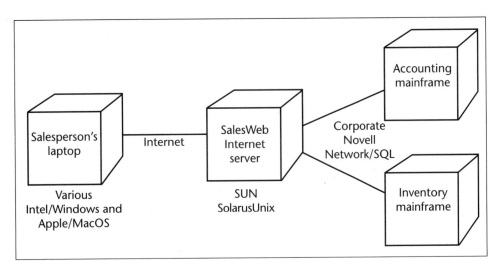

Figure 14.10   *A UML deployment diagram of SalesWeb.*

We developed our SalesWeb application on a single machine. To field it, however, we will need to divide those classes that will go on the salespeople's laptops from those classes that will reside on the sales server. Thus, in effect, we have two SalesWeb packages. Package 1 includes the client classes and Package 2 includes the sales server application. In addition, we would subdivide Package 2 on the Internet server into two subpackages: 2.1, the core business classes, and 2.2, the classes that deal with the database. (See Figure 14.11.) Obviously, this is simply a logical overview. We might find it convenient to subdivide any of these packages into smaller modules. Similarly, we might want to show the actual classes that we placed in each package.

Figure 14.12 indicates how we plan on modularizing and distributing our final application code. In effect, we will simply change each logical package into a physical component. Again, we might have subcomponents inside the components and might show them if it were useful—though it isn't in our simple SalesWeb application.

In the case of the SalesWeb system, we wanted the linkage to be as simple as possible while still allowing the Java client applications to pass the appropriate arguments from the client GUI screens to the remote *SalesHandler* object. Since both client and

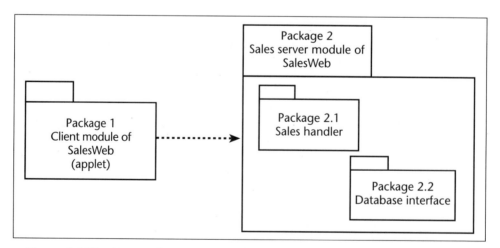

Figure 14.11   *UML package diagram showing the SalesWeb application.*

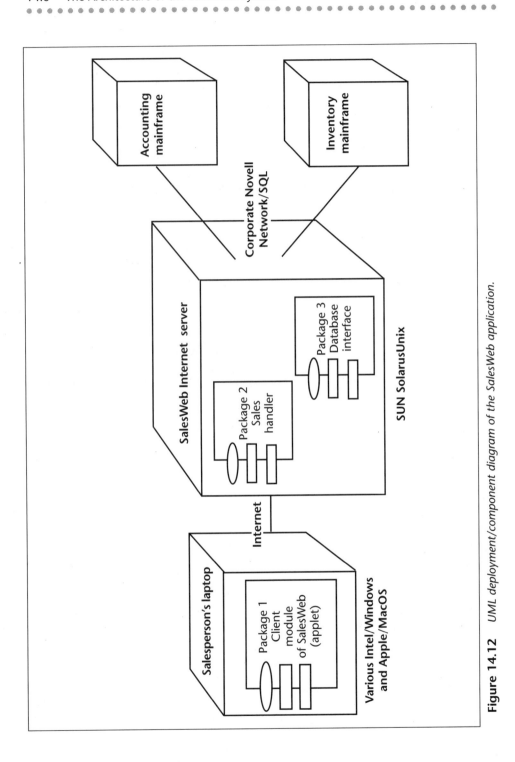

Figure 14.12 *UML deployment/component diagram of the SalesWeb application.*

server programs are implemented in Java, the Java RMI interface is the simplest way to link local client objects to the remote server object. We chose RMI for ease of implementation.

14.7 Capturing a Design in an Object-Oriented Modeling Tool

Popkin Software's SA/Object Architect supports UML deployment diagrams. Thus, we could easily create the diagram illustrated in Figure 14.13 by opening SA/Object Architect to its

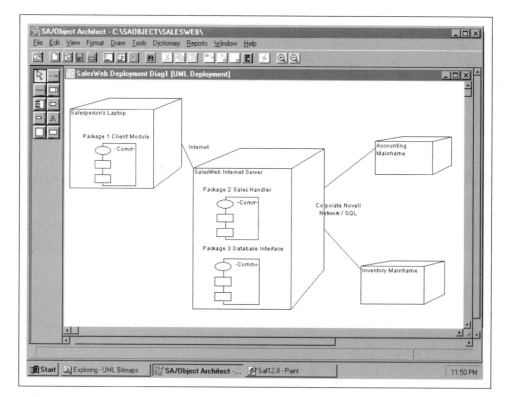

Figure 14.13   *SA/Object Architect screen of the SalesWeb deployment/component diagram.*

main menu screen, pulling down the New Diagram icon, and then choosing Deployment Diagram from the menu and giving it the name SalesWeb Deployment Diagram. This would give us a window with a palette of icons that we would use to create the deployment diagram. Figure 14.13 shows an SA/Object Architect screen with the deployment diagram we drew.

SA/Object Architect also supports component diagrams. We included components inside the nodes of our deployment diagram.

15

Expanding Your Design

Once you have a good idea of the overall architecture of your application, there are still many additional design decisions to be made. We've lumped them under three general headings: (1) expanding your object model, (2) developing user screens or Web pages, and (3) arranging for data access. We've also included a brief note on coding and testing your application.

15.1 Expanding Your Object Model

When you begin the design phase of a cycle, you review each of your earlier UML diagrams and ask more practical questions. In effect, you move from specifying that the *Salesperson* object sends a message to the *SalesOrder* object, to trying to pin down exactly how this will occur. The following tasks will help you accomplish this:

- First, you need to extend your existing diagrams to incorporate infrastructure classes.

- Then you need to determine in more detail how the operations you have identified will actually work. This will generally mean thinking harder about specific data to be manipulated and will involve the development of private operations to assist in processing messages. It also means that you will want to study books on patterns to figure out the most efficient ways to handle certain problems.

- You also need to think about using classes and interfaces in the Java class library or using classes or components from external sources.

15.1.1 *Extending Your Analysis Diagrams*

Recall that in Chapter 8, after we had developed our use case diagram of the SalesWeb application, we went on to develop an OOSE ideal class model. In effect, we inserted interface, entity, and control classes into our Report Sales use case. (See Figure 15.1.)

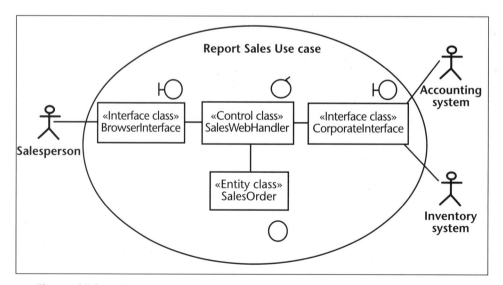

Figure 15.1   *Ideal class model of the Report Sales use case.*

After developing the ideal class model, we suggested that during analysis we would only focus on the entity classes, like *SalesOrder*, and the classes outside the use case, like *Salesperson* and *Accounting*. We ignored the infrastructure classes, including the interface classes and the handlers. Now, as we begin the design phase of our development effort, it is time to insert these additional classes. Before we do, however, let's also think about what our tier model suggests. In Figure 15.2 we have imposed our three-tiered grid over the ideal use case model of the Report Sales use case.

In Chapter 14, when we discussed distributing the different packages on different platforms, we spoke of the need to select a way of linking the different platforms. Linkages do not always imply new classes, but they often do. Thus, looking at Figure 15.2, we can see that if we were to have a Java application on the client and another on the Internet server, we would probably need an interface on both machines. If we

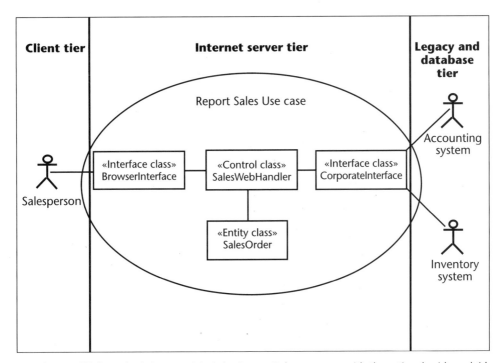

Figure 15.2   *Ideal class model of the Report Sales use case with three-tiered grid overlaid.*

used CORBA, at a minimum we would need stub and skeleton objects on each platform.

On the database side we will probably need one interface object for each of the two legacy/database systems. On the other hand, we probably won't need to create new interfaces for the database tier. Our database interface classes on the Internet server tier will probably be able to generate SQL and thus deal directly with the existing relational databases. You will need to think through the interfaces your application will need to support and create classes to handle them.

Next, consider the handler we showed in Figures 15.1 and 15.2. In analysis we only focused on the abstract relationship between the *Salesperson* and *SalesOrder* classes. Now, as we consider actually implementing the system, we must think about how many salespeople might want to create orders at any one time. We must also consider what would happen if one salesperson started one order, then, without completing it, started another, and so on. Again, there are lots of different ways to deal with this, but a common approach is to create a control or manager class that is designed to handle the overall operation of the Internet server. In effect, this control class (there's a long tradition in OO of calling them handlers) would allocate the resources of the Internet server, accepting incoming contact requests, sending *Salesperson* applets to browsers, creating *SalesOrder* objects, and controlling the overall flow of data to and from the databases. If you decide to create a handler of this sort, you will need to create new sequence and state diagrams to be sure you understand exactly how the handler will respond to the hundreds of different scenarios it might be faced with.

There's no one right answer about any of these matters, of course. Developers working with different platforms would make different decisions. Similarly, depending on the speed required of the application, there could be very different designs. Our only point here is that design is the time when you must face and address these issues.

Different developers would approach the whole process involved in expanding the analysis diagrams into design diagrams in different ways. Some might start, as we did, with the class diagram and expand the number of classes. Then they might proceed to the sequence diagram, inserting the new interface and control classes and reworking the sequence diagram to see how messages would now flow. Others would probably start with the sequence diagrams, adding new objects to see how things might work, move to the state diagrams to work out the details of the new handler class, and return and expand the class diagram as a kind of summary.

When we last considered the SalesWeb application, we ended up with the class diagram that we last pictured in Figure 14.3. If we add a handler and interface classes, we arrive at the class diagram shown in Figure 15.3.

To assure that we understood the SalesWeb class diagram we arrived at in Figure 15.3, we then expanded the sequence diagram we arrived at in Chapter 10 with the new interface and handler objects. This brings us to a new sequence diagram, which is shown in Figure 15.4. To keep things simple,

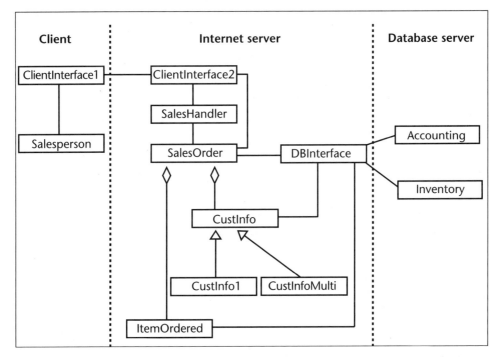

Figure 15.3 *The addition of generic infrastructure classes to the SalesWeb application.*

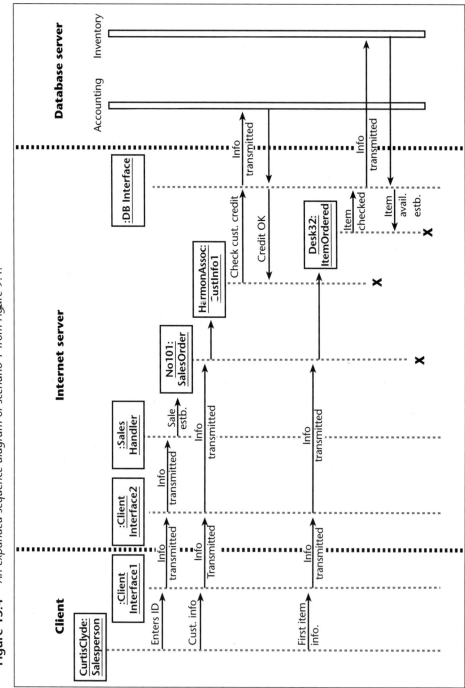

Figure 15.4 *An expanded sequence diagram of scenario 1 from Figure 9.4.*

we haven't shown all the events that would occur, but just a sample to suggest how the new classes will interact with the older business classes.

In preparing Figure 15.4, we are forced to consider in some detail things like which objects will continue throughout the entire transaction and which will be terminated as soon as possible. We also need to determine exactly which objects will be communicating with interfaces.

Notice that we have now resolved the problem with the *Salesperson* class. In the new sequence diagram it doesn't represent the salesperson, as such. It is an applet that is downloaded from the Internet server to the browser on the salesperson's machine. The applet collects information about the order and then transmits all the information, in a single blast, to the *Sales Handler*. There is nothing to keep the salesperson from downloading several different applets, working on each, and then submitting them when they are complete.

15.1.2   *Getting Concrete about Operations*

In analysis, we focused on those attributes and operations associated with business objects. We were primarily concerned with a general description of how the business organization functioned. We wanted to know, in CRC vocabulary, who was responsible for doing what.

During design we need to get much more specific about how things are done. And, as we add infrastructure classes to our model, we need to add new attributes and operations. Just as infrastructure classes are concerned with programming details, the operations and attributes used by these classes are also very practical.

We also mentioned, when we first introduced operations, that some developers distinguish between public operations that are, in effect, visible and available for other objects to contact, and private operations that simply do things inside the specific object. In the analysis phase, we ignore private operations and focus on the operations that make up an object's interface. When we switch to design and begin preparing written descriptions or pseudocode to define exactly what an operation will do, we often find that we would rather divide an operation into several smaller operations. We leave the public operation in place to accept messages and then create private operations to handle different aspects of processing a message or to handle actions (side effects) that the public operation may initiate.

This isn't a book on programming, and we won't go into any details about how to actually code operations. We provide the specific code for the SalesWeb application in Appendix A, and we've annotated the code to suggest why we wrote specific operations in particular ways. More important, however, we can give you very good advice on how to think about operations and the development of interface classes to handle common tasks: Get a book on OO patterns and study it.

15.1.3 *Patterns*

A *pattern* is a standard way of handling some specific task. You rarely think of patterns during the analysis phase of your development effort. Patterns are something you need when you begin to work on the specific design of your application.

Some patterns are large scale and help to solve major problems. Others are very specific and help with more focused problems. In a sense, a pattern is a design for a module or component. You could let someone else implement the pattern and simply buy the component that provided the functionality you needed. Or, if you are working in code or with an OO modeling tool, you study the patterns in one of the books that have been written to describe good OO patterns. In the latter case, you can see exactly how an experienced OO developer recommends you handle a specific problem and decide if it fits your problem. If it does, you simply implement the pattern for your system, incorporating the diagrams provided by the pattern book author and using or converting the code provided by the book into operations in whatever OO language you are working in.

If you are going to be involved in OO development, you should probably buy at least one book on patterns and study it. It will provide you with lots of insights into how developers take advantage of object techniques to solve common programming problems. The best book to start with is *Design Patterns: Elements of Reusable Object-Oriented Software*. It is written by Erich Gamma and three other authors and is listed in the bibliography at the end of this book. It provides a number of solutions to important and recurring problems that every OO developer will encounter. Each pattern is diagrammed using OMT notation, and both C++ and Smalltalk code solutions are provided. (We hope a new edition will be available soon with UML diagrams and Java code.) We list other books on patterns in the bibliography.

Gamma and his coauthors divide common patterns into three groups and define the various patterns appropriate to each group, as follows:

Creational Patterns

Abstract Factory: Provide an interface for creating families of related or dependent objects without specifying their concrete classes.

Builder: Separate the construction of a complex object from its representation so that the same construction process can create different representations.

Factory Method: Define an interface for creating an object, but let subclasses decide which class to instantiate. Factory Method lets a class defer instantiation to subclasses.

Prototype: Specify the kinds of objects to create using a prototypical object, and create new objects by copying this prototype.

Singleton: Ensure a class only has one object, and provide a global point of access to it.

Structural Patterns

Adapter: Convert the interface of a class into another interface clients expect. Adapter lets classes work together that couldn't otherwise because of incompatible interfaces.

Bridge: Decouple an abstraction from its implementation so that the two can vary independently.

Composite: Compose objects into tree structures to represent part-whole hierarchies. Composite lets clients treat individual objects and compositions of objects uniformly.

Decorator: Attach additional responsibilities to an object dynamically. Decorators provide a flexible alternative to subclassing for extending functionality.

Facade: Provide a unified interface to a set of interfaces in a subsystem. Facade defines a higher level interface that makes the subsystem easier to use.

Flyweight: Use sharing to support large numbers of fine-grained objects efficiently.

Proxy: Provide a surrogate or placeholder for another object to control access to it.

Behavioral Patterns

Chain of Responsibility: Avoid coupling the sender of a request to its receiver by giving more than one object a chance to handle the request. Chain the receiving objects and pass the request along the chain until an object handles it.

Command: Encapsulate a request as an object, thereby letting you parameterize clients with different requests, queue or log requests, and support undoable operations.

Interpreter: Given a language, define a representation for its grammar along with an interpreter that uses the representation to interpret sentences in the language.

Iteration: Provide a way to access the elements of an aggregate object sequentially without exposing its underlying representation.

Mediator: Define an object that encapsulates how a set of objects interact. Mediator promotes loose coupling by keeping objects from referring to each other explicitly, and it lets you vary their interaction independently.

Memento: Without violating encapsulation, capture and externalize an object's internal state so that the object can be restored to this state later.

Observer: Define a one-to-many dependency between objects so that when one object changes state, all its dependents are notified and updated automatically.

State: Allow an object to alter its behavior when its internal state changes. The object will appear to change its class.

Strategy: Define a family of algorithms, encapsulate each one, and make them interchangeable. Strategy lets the algorithm vary independently from clients that use it.

Template Method: Define the skeleton of an algorithm in an operation, deferring some steps to subclasses. Template Method lets subclasses redefine certain steps of an algorithm without changing the algorithm's structure.

Visitor: Represent an operation to be performed on the elements of an object structure. Visitor lets you define a new operation without changing the classes of the elements on which it operates.

Figure 15.5 illustrates one of the patterns described by Gamma et al. They call this pattern the Composite pattern, and here's how they describe it:

Graphics applications like drawing editors and schematic capture systems let users build complex diagrams out of simple components. The user can group components to form larger components, which in turn can be grouped to form still larger components. A simple implementation could define classes for graphical primitives such as Text and Lines plus other classes that act as containers for these primitives.

But there's a problem with this approach: Code that uses these classes must treat primitive and container objects differently, even if most of the time the user treats them identically. Having to distinguish these objects makes the application more complex. The Composite pattern describes how to use recursive composition so that clients don't have to make this distinction.

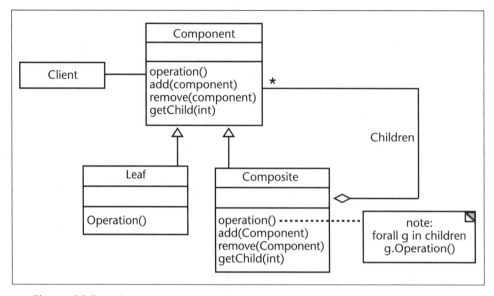

Figure 15.5   *The generic structure of the Composite pattern, modified after Gamma et al.*

We're not going to describe patterns in the detail Gamma and his coauthors do. They not only discuss the generic pattern and how it functions but provide examples and code to show how each operation works. (We have modified the diagram, which was in OMT notation, so that it appears in UML notation.)

15.1.4   *Using Classes, Interfaces, and Components*

At some point in any OO design effort, you should consider what your options for reuse are. If you are using Java to develop your application, you will undoubtedly be reusing some Java classes and interfaces to create your code. All of your classes, for example, will ultimately be derived from the Java object class. More concretely, as you begin to make decisions about architectural interfaces, you may decide to use the Java RMI package to provide you with the functionality of an ORB. In effect, you will incorporate RMI interfaces (sorry about the confusion here, but interface turns out to be a popular term) into your classes to link your classes on different platforms. In a similar way, you may use Java interfaces to help develop user screens or to link to databases.

Figure 15.6 illustrates the *SalesHandlerImpl* class from our SalesWeb application. We have used the lollypop notation to indicate that the class is a composite class that has incorporated interfaces from the Sun's JDK RMI package.

Beyond these basics, however, you will want to check to see if there are class libraries, components, or frameworks of business objects you can use to handle more complex aspects of your application. For example, if you are developing an application in the financial area, you will want to check Java's Web site for financial components you may be able to use. There are components to handle converting from one currency to another, for calculating different kinds of interest, and for providing an on-line link to stock market information. There's no reason to worry about the internal design problems of a class if you can borrow or buy a component that provides the functionality you need. Finding the right components or frameworks can not only reduce your design effort, it can really reduce your coding effort as well.

There is no comprehensive source of components or business frameworks at the moment. We've listed a couple of Web sites in the bibliography that try to keep track of components, but frankly the field is too new and expanding too fast for anyone to stay on top of it at the moment.

The place to begin is to determine whether your company has a library of components or business objects or is part of a

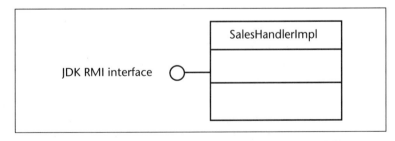

Figure 15.6 *The SalesWeb's* SalesHandlerImpl *class with a lollypop to show that the JDK RMI interface is included in the class.*

consortium that has a library. We've already mentioned that Sun sponsors some Web groups in different industry areas. So do IBM and Microsoft. In addition IBM and Microsoft are both working with consortiums of companies to develop frameworks of components or business objects for a number of major industries. Similarly, some industry groups are working under the auspices of OMG to create business object frameworks for their industries. Getting involved in the OMG and attending some of their technical meetings relative to your industry would be a good way to get up to speed on what's available in your area. If your company isn't part of a consortium, but you discover that there is one in your industry or domain of interest, you should probably correspond or attend a meeting to find out what they offer.

Next, you'll want to talk with people at conferences or via the Web who are developing applications like yours. Similarly, you'll want to look for articles in magazines and newspapers that talk about applications similar to yours and check what components they used. Start keeping track of any mention of component sources that seem likely to provide components you could use.

In addition, a few companies have been set up to sell components. Most are small, and all are rather narrowly focused, but some exhibit their products at conferences and advertise in magazines. You should certainly check out any company that claims to be selling components in your area of interest.

Having said that, we should mention that our SalesWeb used classes and interfaces from JDK and from Sun's AWT (Abstract Windowing Toolkit), but we didn't use any commercial class libraries or components because we did not want you to have to buy any development software in order to modify our SalesWeb example system for your own use.

If you find a class or component that you can use in your core design, you will need to incorporate it into your diagrams. You will need to know what messages (signatures) it responds to and what it returns in response to any messages it receives. Component vendors sometimes provide a detailed description of the source code, and you can treat the component just as you would any other class in your diagram. Other component vendors only describe the interface to the component. In other words, they tell you what messages the component will respond to and what responses it will provide. If the function of the component is clearly specified, an interface specification is usually sufficient.

15.2   Developing User Screens or Web Pages

If your application will have user interfaces, you will need to design the screens. If you are creating a very simple application in Java, you can use Sun and Netscape's Foundation Classes (which supersedes and incorporates Sun's AWT) and create and embed a user screen inside a class like our *Salesperson* class or into an applet. If you are working on a larger application or need multiple screens, this would be a bad idea. In any case, it's rather bad OO design. It's better to keep the interface independent of the class that gathers the information so you can easily modify either without affecting the other. In many applications it's common to have a class for the user interface, which is then subclassed to provide several individual screens or forms.

No matter where you decide to put the code for the screens, creating screens is hard and complex, and most developers avoid the details by using a software tool that allows the screen to be designed at a higher level of abstraction. Many books address the complex technical issues involved in developing software interfaces. We will not go into any details here, but we do want to offer a few general comments with regard to some of the design-level considerations you will face.

From an overall design perspective, as we noted above, the most important thing you want to do is to isolate any user interface from the objects that make up the core of the application. You do this to keep changes in the core system or the interface screens from affecting each other. For example, if you develop for Windows 3.1 and then upgrade to Windows 95, you don't want this to affect your core application. The easiest way to conceptualize this is to have an interface object for the user interface. The screens send messages to that object to pass on to the object that actually manipulates the data (in SalesWeb, the *Salesperson* object) and vice versa.

Thus, if you decide to change the screen layout, you can do it without changing how the *Salesperson* object checked the data and organized it for transport across the Internet. While this is good advice, it would be tedious if you only had a simple system with one screen, like the one we developed for SalesWeb. The idea is to begin by conceptualizing the interface and the data objects as separate classes and then, when you actually begin to write methods, decide if it really makes sense to keep them separate. You may want to break up the user interface object and have more specialized versions of it, or even several different interface objects, but the critical thing is to maintain one or more objects as a layer between the user interface and the core of the application.

When it comes time to develop the actual user interface screens, you should use components or a tool that provides you classes for windows, buttons, text, and so on. There's no point in writing code for interfaces, since others have already written and packaged code for most of the common interface environments. You could work with Sun's Java interface tools, or you could use one of several Java products, such as Borland's JBuilder, Microsoft's Visual J++ Pro, Symantec's Cafe, or Rogue Wave's Jfactory. Each of these products provides interface development support.

If you are using an OO modeling tool, it will probably provide you with a library of interface components. Some developers, however, prefer to leave the OO modeling environment and use a product such as Visual Basic or PowerBuilder to create the interfaces for their applications.

15.3 Arranging to Access Data

Broadly, you could store and access data in a conventional database, or you could store objects. Most objects are transient; they are eliminated as soon as they are used. All of the objects in our SalesWeb application are transient. All of the data created by an interaction between a salesperson and the Sales server is transferred to the relational databases associated with the accounting and inventory applications. Objects that are stored between one session and the next are called persistent objects. We'll consider the problems of storing persistent objects in a moment. First, however, we'll consider the problems of storing data in relational databases.

Most corporate data is stored in nonrelational databases that were established in the 1960s and 1970s. Moreover, early PC databases often used nonrelational techniques. Since the early 1980s, however, most new corporate and departmental databases have been built using the relational model. And, since the beginning of the 1990s, most PC applications have also relied on relational databases. Relational databases are independent of the specific application that uses them, and thus the data can be used by several different applications. The data in relational databases is stored in tables. The various relational database vendors have standardized on SQL (Structured Query Language) as the language to use to access relational databases.

15.3.1 *The Java Database Connectivity Package*

OO systems should be designed so that the objects using data are independent of the objects that interface with databases. Java makes this easy, since JDK provides a package specifically designed to create and support database objects. The Java DataBase Connectivity (JDBC) package allows a developer to quickly create JDBC (Java database) objects. In effect, a JDBC object takes inputs from other Java objects and converts them into SQL, which it then passes to a database-specific relational database driver. Each of the relational database vendors has released a driver that will interface with JDBC. In addition, other software companies are offering database drivers for the more popular relational databases. The same JDBC object can interface with multiple drivers. (See Figure 15.7.)

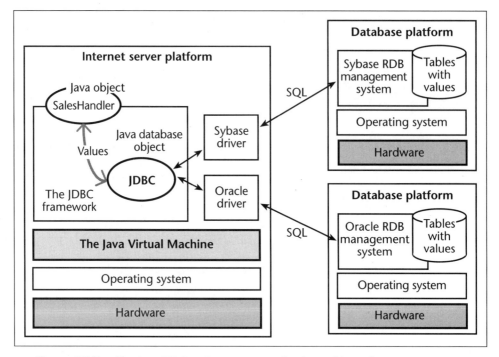

Figure 15.7   *The Java JDBC package supports database objects that can generate SQL.*

JDBC can also generate output that Sun's JDBC-ODBC bridge can use to drive ODBC. ODBC is a database interface developed by Microsoft. ODBC accepts C code and generates SQL. The JDBC-ODBC bridge converts Java to C. Each of the popular database vendors has created a driver that interfaces to ODBC. Thus, if there is a database that you can't reach directly via JDBC, you can reach it indirectly, via the bridge and ODBC. JDBC doesn't even need to be told which database the data is being sent to. It will automatically check through the available drivers to determine which one will access the database it needs.

15.3.2 *Object-Oriented and Object-Relational Databases*

Now let's consider what would happen if you wanted to store a persistent object in a database. You can't store an object directly in a relational database. An object has values, but it also has operations that manipulate those values. Relational databases can store an object's values in a table, but they are forced to store the operations in a file. Thus, you couldn't store an object in a relational database and then send a message to update a value. In order to modify the object, the relational database would have to reassemble the values and the operations. The next generation of relational databases will have OO frontends. In effect, their relational database management systems will be modified so that they can assemble objects in the management system, use the object's methods to change the values associated with the attributes, and then take the object apart and store it again.

Consider what would happen if you wanted to update an object that was derived from a subclass of another class. Also assume that once the object got the message, it would, in turn, send a message to another object to get that object to perform some task and send back the results before it could modify the attributes the original message wanted to change. The object frontend for the relational database would need to get out one object, assemble it, assemble its class and that class's parent to get the operations it needed, and assemble the second object to get it to perform the secondary task, and so on. Relational databases aren't very good at storing objects. Relational databases with OO frontends will be better, but they will never be able to support OO systems the way OO databases will. An OO database (OODB) is a database designed to store objects as wholes. OODBs can store and retrieve persistent objects much faster than relational databases.

Most companies rely on relational databases and will continue to use them. Moreover, object-relational databases will extend the life of relational databases for several years. Indeed, relational databases will probably always be preferred for data, independent of objects. As developers create complex OO applications, especially applications with multimedia objects, they will increasingly find they want to store objects in OODBs. The Internet, with its highly graphical emphasis and with Java, will push companies to experiment with OODBs.

Imagine how much easier it would be if we could simply create *SalesOrder* objects when each sales order came in and then simply store each *SalesOrder* object directly in an OODB. We wouldn't have to worry about moving the attribute values to the JDBC class and changing them into SQL or vice versa. Everything would be objects. This approach wouldn't be appropriate for our SalesWeb application because Watson's already has massive amounts of data stored in their existing DB2 relational databases. Our SalesWeb application isn't important enough to make anyone consider changing that.

If we were creating a new application and were going to create a new database to support the application, that would be quite different. Many new Web site applications, for example, are using OODBs to improve the speed at which they can access and retrieve complex graphical information. (We've included the names of some of the leading OODB vendors in Appendix D.)

15.4 The SalesWeb Design

SalesWeb is a simple application. When we finished our analysis we had nine classes. We decided to make it a three-tiered application and to incorporate the *Salesperson* class into an applet so that it could be downloaded from the Sales Internet server by any salesperson via any laptop. We wrote a small block of HTML code to accomplish the downloading of the applet when salespeople contacted the Sales Internet server Web site.

Once the applet is on the salesperson's laptop, it communicates with the Sales Internet server via RMI. Thus, we needed to add a stub to the *Salesperson* applet and a skeleton to the Sales server package to facilitate this communication. We obtained the needed code from the JDK RMI library.

We also needed to communicate with Watson's existing DB2 databases. In theory, we would have used the JDBC facility from the JDK library to create a database class that would then have communicated with a DB2 driver to access the Accounting and Inventory databases.

We incorporated the order entry form that the salesperson has to fill out and submit into the *Salesperson* applet. If we were creating a complex system with many forms or user interface screens, we would use a separate class for screens and subclasses for each specific screen. However, for a simple system, it makes the example much more straightforward to simply add a small amount of user interface code to the *Salesperson* class. We obtained the classes we need for our *Salesperson* interface from Sun's AWT library. *Salesperson* includes the following AWT classes:

- Panel—Provides an application window and is compatible with the JavaBean architecture

- TextField—Editable text entry form

- TextArea—Multiline output text area with automatic support for scrolling text

- Button—To implement "OK" and other command buttons

In practice, you will want to use a screen development tool to construct user interface screens. However, we wanted to avoid using any commercial software tools for building our example system to assure that anyone with Sun's JDK can modify or rebuild our example. Figure 15.8 illustrates what the user screen on our SalesWeb application would look like, running in Netscape Navigator.

Our SalesWeb application assumes that values are stored in Watson's legacy relational databases. The example system we have developed does not, in fact, implement that database server portion of the system. In a real system, database access would probably be handled by Watson's legacy Accounting and Inventory systems. In our example, the middle tier (the

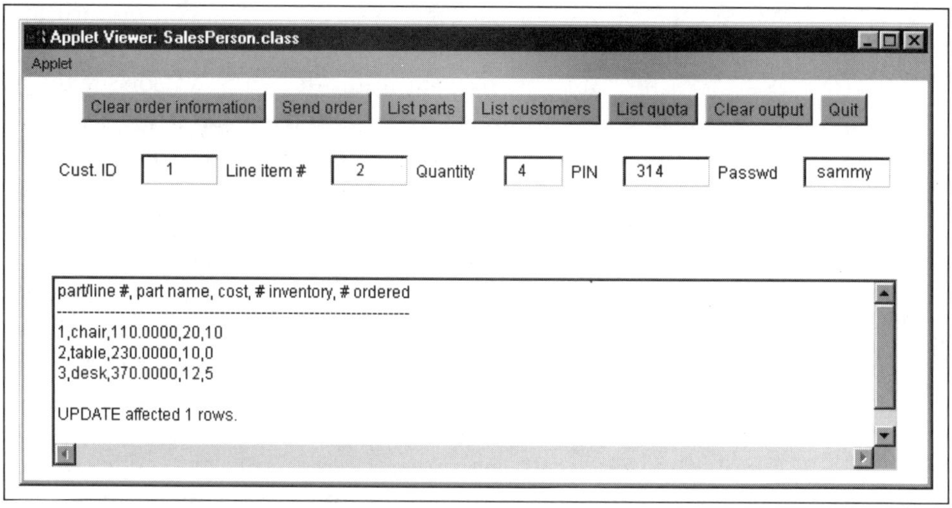

Figure 15.8   *A SalesWeb entry screen being viewed in Java Applet Browser.*

SalesHandler object) simply uses the Java ODBC API to directly access local disk files using SQL. We chose this design to meet the following requirements:

- A simple implementation that can be run on your computer if he or she has the Java development system (JDK 1.0) and any ODBC-compliant database product. (The example code we provide includes a sample Microsoft Access database that works with the example system.)

- The system should be easily extensible to use a legacy database system (that is not written in Java).

- The system provides an illustration of a design that could be implemented on a client/server system and could be modified to work with other client/server applications.

No objects in the SalesWeb application are persistent. The database is used to record all sales and other information. As soon as a given session concludes, all of the objects are placed in garbage.

If we did design the SalesWeb application from the ground up and had to create the databases, we would certainly consider an OODB. As it is, for example, we identified furniture items with a number assigned by the developers of the Watson's relational databases. If we had to do it from scratch, we would create a class hierarchy with furniture as our top class and then proceed to work our way down, identifying the categories and then the specific furniture items. Ultimately, *Inventory* could have persistent objects to represent real furniture items, and orders could send messages directly to furniture items telling them they were to be shipped to specific customers. If we took this approach, we would have developed a much more comprehensive initial business model. Our class diagram would really have modeled the business process, rather than simply using *Accounting* and *Inventory* to stand for complex processes we don't really understand. It's not an approach that's appropriate for the SalesWeb application, but as you become more familiar with OO development and begin to work on new, strategic applications, it will be an approach that will become increasingly appealing.

You can examine the code for the *Salesperson* class in Appendix A and see exactly how the interface, RMI, and JDBC linkages are handled and check the attributes and operations we added to make them all work.

In the early part of this text we described an application that would include three use cases. We then followed only one, Report Sales, through a detailed examination. In the code we developed you can access the complete application, as described in our original use case analysis. Thus, in addition to reporting sales, our salesperson can check on his or her performance. Similarly, sales managers can sign onto the Sales Internet server from their laptops and quickly determine how the salespeople in their regions are doing, either individually or as a group. This additional functionality, which we would have developed during the second prototyping cycle if we had followed the plan laid out in this book, required a new database to keep track of the salespeople in each region and to store information about quota agreements and sales. Thus, the code in Appendix A and the code you can download is slightly more complex than the example we have been discussing up to this point.

15.5 Coding and Testing

There are no UML diagrams that are used for coding or testing. These concerns, in general, lie beyond the concerns of this book. There are numerous books on coding in different OO languages, including Java, and we have mentioned a few of the best in the bibliography, under the heading for Chapter 5.

We do provide all of the Java code for the SalesWeb application we have been discussing in this book. That code includes some comments on why one approach was used rather than another, and programmers should feel free to look at how we completed the SalesWeb application. Information about how to obtain this code is provided in Appendix A.

We want to make just a few comments on testing OO systems. Testing OO systems isn't easy. There are two ways to approach testing: bottom-up and top-down.

15.5.1 *Bottom-Up Testing Starts with Classes*

Because you are developing classes that are independent of each other, there is a sense in which you can test each class by itself. The easy test is to see if a class does what you expect it to do. You plan on sending it a message and asking it for an account number. You send it the message and you get the account number. In effect, by working your way down the object line in an event trace diagram, you should be able to identify each message that an object should respond to and check that it performs as it should.

Of course, if the class is a subclass, then you are only testing a portion of the hierarchy when you test the specific class. Some messages you send to an object of the class will be handled by the operations and attributes defined in the object's parent class. Others will need to be routed up to superclasses. Assuring that a superclass functions correctly with one of its subclasses doesn't assure that it will work with its other subclasses.

The real problem in testing comes when you try to think of all the errors that could result when someone sends an incorrect message or a value that is wrong—larger than you ever expected anyone to send, for example. How will the object respond to exceptions and minor errors? It's very hard to think of all the exceptions that might occur and test to see that your object will handle them as you would like. This has nothing to do with object technology, as such. It's also a problem with conventional systems design. In theory, you could have worked this out by generating lots of scenarios and doing event trace diagrams of each of them. Unfortunately, a scenario that no one imagined often actually occurs, resulting in inputs no one ever planned for. There is no solution for this except to work up lots of scenarios and try to think of all the things that could go wrong.

Once you are satisfied that a single object works, you need to see how it will work when it has to interact with other objects. In effect, you test one object, then several closely related objects, then a large collection of objects, then each module. Problems tend to emerge as you combine more objects. More complex sets of objects generate those exceptions that you failed to think about when you were only focusing on a single object.

15.5.2 Top-Down Testing Starts with Use Cases

Top-down testing can only occur when you have assembled your prototype. If the prototype provides the functionality of a single use case, then you can test the system by working your way through all of the scenarios that you derived from the use case description. The prototype should respond as suggested in the scenario. If it doesn't, you have a problem.

The best thing about OO development is that you can do it incrementally. If you develop a small prototype to begin with, you'll limit the number of objects you need to test. Moreover, you'll complete your prototype in a reasonably short time and will learn if you have problems before developing lots of additional code. It's easier to test and diagnose a moderately sized prototype than it is to test and debug a large system.

You'll also have fewer testing problems if you use interface objects that keep the core of your system isolated from the user interfaces, databases, and other software applications. The interface objects serve as control points that help you locate any problems. On the other hand, even though it's easier to test a smaller prototype, you will have to test it again whenever you finish another cycle and have an enhanced prototype. Adding new objects can introduce new twists to a set of objects that you have already tested.

We tested our SalesWeb application by running several scenarios that we had originally developed when we created use cases, and we were satisfied that it got the results we expected. We have not tested it with enough scenarios to be sure that it would work as a production system in a real sales environment.

15.6 Expanding Your Design in an Object-Oriented Modeling Tool

If you are familiar with an OO modeling tool, everything we've described in this chapter can be done rather quickly. We have included the final SalesWeb diagrams and code we arrived at with SA/Object Architect in a file that you can download from the Internet and examine. By including appropriate references to JDK libraries, we assured that the JDK classes would be incorporated in our skeleton Java code when we generated it. Information about accessing the SA/Object Architect version of our SalesWeb application is described in Appendix A.

Figure 15.9 provides a final summary of the process we went through to develop our SalesWeb application in SA/Object Architect. We began with use case diagrams and

CRC cards (developed in Popkin Software's SA/CRC tool). We could have used Popkin Software's IDEF BPR tool, but used LOVEM modeling instead. From our use case models, we could generate sequence diagrams—the path Popkin Software recommends. The OA UML version of SA/Object Architect doesn't support ideal object diagrams. If we had used System Architect (the pre-OO version) and chosen Jacobson's OOSE method, we could have developed ideal object diagrams and then generated UML class diagrams from OOSE class diagrams.

Instead of moving from use case diagrams to sequence diagrams, we chose instead to begin with a class diagram. Using SA/Object Architect we created a single class diagram and then continued to expand it throughout the rest of the development effort, adding attributes and operations during analysis and then going back and adding infrastructure-related classes and additional attributes and operations during the design phase. Similarly, once we developed the sequence diagram, we used it to generate the collaboration diagram. We also generated a state diagram of one class to study how it worked in more detail. Then, when we moved into design and enhanced our class diagram, we went back and expanded our sequence diagram at the same time to check how the dynamics of our application would work. Finally, we generated deployment, package, and component diagrams.

We used JDK and interfaces to generate our interface and to link to files to simulate a database, so we didn't need to use SA/Object Architect's screen painting or relational database generation utilities, but we could easily have done so.

When we were satisfied with our diagrams, we used SA/Object Architect's ability to generate Java code to produce most of the Java code required for our application. We had to write some additional code for operations by hand, and we had a complete application.

Because our example was so simple we didn't begin to use the capabilities of SA/Object Architect on the SalesWeb example. For example, SA/Object Architect provides a screen painter utility, with an accompanying interface library that would have allowed us to create Windows screens if they had been needed. Similarly, SA/Object Architect could have generated

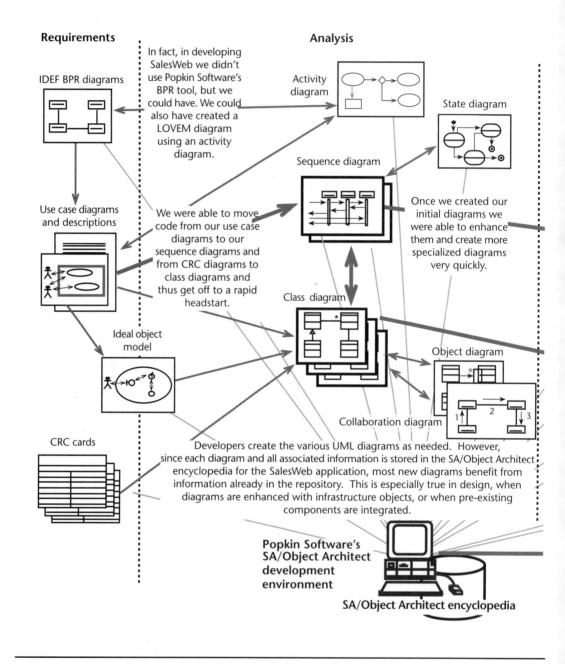

Requirements   **Analysis**

IDEF BPR diagrams

In fact, in developing SalesWeb we didn't use Popkin Software's BPR tool, but we could have. We could also have created a LOVEM diagram using an activity diagram.

Activity diagram

State diagram

Sequence diagram

Use case diagrams and descriptions

We were able to move code from our use case diagrams to our sequence diagrams and from CRC diagrams to class diagrams and thus get off to a rapid headstart.

Once we created our initial diagrams we were able to enhance them and create more specialized diagrams very quickly.

Ideal object model

Class diagram

Object diagram

Collaboration diagram

CRC cards

Developers create the various UML diagrams as needed. However, since each diagram and all associated information is stored in the SA/Object Architect encyclopedia for the SalesWeb application, most new diagrams benefit from information already in the repository. This is especially true in design, when diagrams are enhanced with infrastructure objects, or when pre-existing components are integrated.

Popkin Software's SA/Object Architect development environment

SA/Object Architect encyclopedia

Figure 15.9   *The development of the SalesWeb application using Popkin Software's*

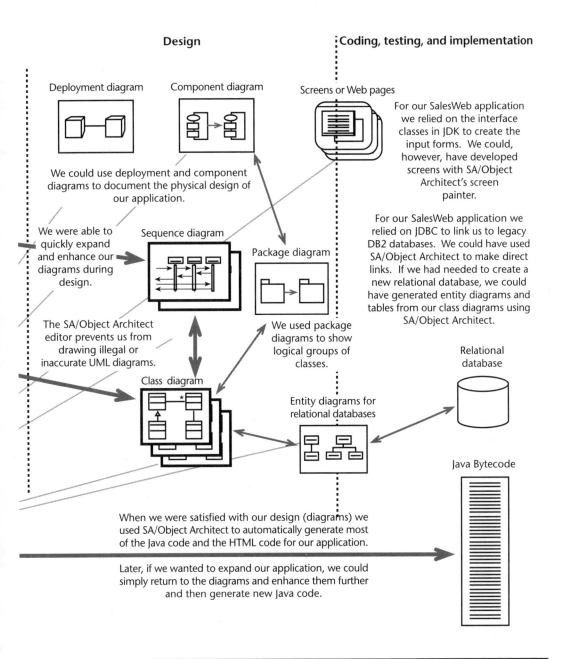

Design   ⋮ **Coding, testing, and implementation**

Deployment diagram   Component diagram   Screens or Web pages

For our SalesWeb application we relied on the interface classes in JDK to create the input forms. We could, however, have developed screens with SA/Object Architect's screen painter.

We could use deployment and component diagrams to document the physical design of our application.

We were able to quickly expand and enhance our diagrams during design.

Sequence diagram

Package diagram

For our SalesWeb application we relied on JDBC to link us to legacy DB2 databases. We could have used SA/Object Architect to make direct links. If we had needed to create a new relational database, we could have generated entity diagrams and tables from our class diagrams using SA/Object Architect.

The SA/Object Architect editor prevents us from drawing illegal or inaccurate UML diagrams.

We used package diagrams to show logical groups of classes.

Relational database

Class diagram

Entity diagrams for relational databases

Java Bytecode

When we were satisfied with our design (diagrams) we used SA/Object Architect to automatically generate most of the Java code and the HTML code for our application.

Later, if we wanted to expand our application, we could simply return to the diagrams and enhance them further and then generate new Java code.

SA/Object Architect.

the CORBA IDL code for our application if we had needed to use CORBA rather than RMI. Also, SA/Object Architect provides Rogue Wave's popular C++ class libraries that can be used to handle more complex tasks and can be incorporated in Java code.

What an OO modeling tool is especially good at is supporting business object reuse. Since an OO modeling tool saves all the diagrams you create, you can easily access past classes from other applications. Moreover, since OO modeling tools are often used by companies that take efficient software development very seriously, companies with OO modeling tools are likely to have libraries of business objects that you can access. Thus, if we had actually been developing an application like SalesWeb with an OO modeling tool like SA/Object Architect, our company would probably have had libraries of previous work. We might have been able to obtain an existing *Sales-Order* or *ItemOrdered* object and incorporate it into our design without having to re-create it.

SA/Object Architect can also generate entity diagrams from class diagrams. Hence, if we had been developing a new application that required that we create a relational database, we could have used the work we did in creating the class diagrams to quickly create and then systematically normalize the relational tables we would need to store data.

As we said at the beginning, using SA/Object Architect was overkill on an application as simple as SalesWeb. Still, at least one author was able to create and modify UML diagrams in SA/Object Architect much more quickly than the other. And, using the tool, we were guaranteed that our UML diagrams were consistent and conformed to UML standards. More important, if we were now to decide to expand the SalesWeb application and incorporate it into a more complex corporate enterprise environment, the author with all his diagrams on SA/Object Architect would have a considerable advantage.

We've tried to keep this book simple. Our goal is to popularize UML. In spite of our effort, we're aware that we've introduced a lot of notations and many different concepts in a reasonably short book. We wanted to give you enough information to get you started. Unfortunately, there's a lot to learn even to get started in a new methodology. Suffice it to say that there's a lot more that we didn't introduce. Moreover, we have emphasized getting started and provided you more information on how to think about your first application and how to analyze it than on how to complete it. If this book helps you get a feel for OO development and makes it possible for you to generate diagrams that will help you analyze a system in OO terms, we've done what we set out to do.

The greatest temptation for anyone beginning to develop OO applications is to think of the problem in procedural terms. It's easy to do, and it will result in bad OO designs. Whenever you find yourself falling back on procedural ways of thinking, recall the CRC card exercise. It's kind of silly, but thinking again of each object as a card and thinking how cards ask other cards for help doing things will remind you of what you are trying to achieve with an OO design.

In the spirit of OO development, we hope you'll start small and work a few simple prototypes through to code. Feel free to start by downloading the code for SalesWeb, in either the straight Java version or in the version running in Popkin

Software's SA/Object Architect environment, and playing with the example until you are sure you understand it. Once you see some results, you'll begin to wonder how to handle more complex problems. At that point, you'll probably want to consult more extensive books on OO methodology and on some of the more specialized design issues. We've included a bibliography to help you find some especially good books to read and some Web sites to check when you need more information.

We hope the UML Job Aid we provide in Appendix B will be helpful if you tackle your first projects by hand and have to draw UML diagrams. It summarizes the various notational elements. Photocopy the Job Aid and use the copy to remind yourself of how to notate things for a little while and you'll have memorized the diagramming techniques with minimal effort.

UML diagrams, especially the use case, class, and sequence diagrams, can help anyone who is trying to create an OO application. Thus, some use of UML can help anyone who is considering a Java application for the Internet.

For larger applications, careful analysis and design phases are the best way to assure that the application will do what you agree to do when you first write a requirements statement. If you are undertaking a midsized to large project, the best advice we can give you would be to suggest you use an OO modeling product to help develop your application. With a tool, you won't need our job aid. You can generate a diagram just by clicking on notational elements on the various menus. And you can use some diagrams to generate others. More important, you can easily modify and extend your diagrams as you move from one prototype to another. Similarly, a tool can create databases and edit your work for consistency. When you are beginning, there's a lot to learn. An OO modeling tool allows you to focus on the real analysis and design issues while it takes care of most of the details.

Java Example Program

This appendix lists the part of the sample program described in the text. We also provide information about how you can download this code and a sample version of Popkin Software's SA/Object Architect with the SalesWeb diagram.

The Java server application is listed with the salesperson client Java applet. This example program is simple, but it provides useful code demonstrating the use of the Java JDBC API for accessing local relational databases and the Java RMI API for building distributed Java applications.

A Zip file containing the Java source code for this example and a test database for Microsoft Access is available at both Morgan Kaufmann Publisher's Web site (*www.mkp.com/umldg*) and Mark Watson's Web site (*www.markwatson.com/uml-book.html*). Popkin Software's SA/Object Architect tool with the SalesWeb diagrams is available at *www.popkin.com*. A link to Popkin's Web site is provided in Morgan Kaufmann Publishers' Web page for this book.

The following files are listed in this appendix:

Server Java application

1. SalesHandler.java—Main Java program that connects to a local RMI ORB and creates an instance of the class *SalesHandlerImpl*.

2. WatsonRMI.java—Interface definition for remote method calls using RMI. This interface is also used by remote clients.

3. SalesHandlerImpl.java—Application code for handling remote requests. This class implements the *WatsonRMI* interface, which is used by remote clients.

4. DBInterface.java—Utility class for using JDBC.

5. CustInfo.java—Small utility class to hold customer data.

6. ItemOrdered.java—Small utility class to hold data for items that can be ordered.

Salesperson client Java applet

7. SalesPerson.java—User interface for the *thin-client* that uses RMI to access the remote *SalesHandler* object through the interface defined in WatsonRMI.java.

Listing 1 shows the implementation of the *SalesHandler* main Java application. The main program creates an RMI security manager and then uses an instance of class *SalesHandlerImpl* to register itself with a local *rmiregistry* object request broker (ORB) using the name *WatsonRMI*. The constructor for class *SalesHandlerImpl* does not return once it is called unless there is a run-time error.

Listing 1   SalesHandler.java

```
// SalesHandler.java

import java.rmi.*;
import java.rmi.server.*;

public class SalesHandler
{
```

```
public static void main(String args[])
{
   System.setSecurityManager(new RMISecurityManager());
   try  {
     SalesHandlerImpl server = new SalesHandlerImpl("WatsonRMI");

     System.out.println("WatsonRMI Server ready.");
   } catch (Exception e) {
     System.out.println("Exception WatsonRMI, " +
                         e.getMessage());
     e.printStackTrace();
   }
 }
}
```

Listing 2 shows the RMI interface that is implemented in class *SalesHandlerImpl* and is used by class *SalesPerson* to make remote method calls to process sales requests. This interface contains the signature for a single method *process*. Method *process* has the following six arguments:

option—integer specifying the desired operation:

    1—process a sales order

    2—list all line items in the database

    3—fetch quota information for *SalesPerson*

    4—list all customers in the database

PIN—access number for a given salesperson

password—password for a given PIN

part—part number

quantity—quantity ordered

customer—customer ID number

Not all arguments are used for every processing option. The *process* method returns a single Java string that contains the results of the processing option.

Design note: *A good alternative to a single method to handle all processing would be to define a method for each processing option in the WatsonRMI interface. This approach would have the advantage of showing clearly which arguments* *are required for each processing option. The advantage of the approach used in the example program is that there is common setup code for all of the options (although this code could have been placed in a separate helper method that called in different processing option methods).*

Listing 2   WatsonRMI.java

```
// WatsonRMI Interface

public interface WatsonRMI extends java.rmi.Remote
{
    String process(int option, String pin, String password,
  String part, String quantity,
  String customer)
      throws java.rmi.RemoteException;
}
```

Listing 3 shows the implementation of the class *SalesHandlerImpl.* The class constructor requires a String argument specifying the service name that is registered with a local *rmiregistry* ORB. The static method *java.rmi.Name.rebind* is used for registering with *rmiregistry*. The method process checks the validity of the password for the requested PIN. Method *process* then uses a switch statement to execute the appropriate code for each processing step. The class *DBInterface* encapsulates the JDBC code for accessing local databases. Method *process* uses the static method *DBInterface.Query* to dynamically execute SQL SELECT query statement and the static method *DBInterface.Update* to dynamically execute SQL statements that modify databases (e.g., UPDATE and INSERT).

Listing 3   SalesHandlerImpl.java

```
// SalesHandlerImpl.java, SalesHandler implementation
//
// RMI implementation class for the SalesHandler class.
// (Implements the WatsonRMI interface)
// (This example is supported from the www.markwatson.com
// web site at URLs www.markwatson.com/books.htm and
// www.markwatson.com/errata.htm)
//
```

```java
import java.rmi.*;
import java.rmi.server.UnicastRemoteObject;

import java.sql.*;

// Design note: for the purposes of a demo, this class
// simply uses JDBC to access a local database when it
// receives remote requests (via RMI).  Unused instances
// of classes SalesOrder and ItemOrdered are created as
// an example of creating data received from RMI method
// calls and locally from a database; in a real application
// these objects might be used for business logic.

public class SalesHandlerImpl extends UnicastRemoteObject
implements WatsonRMI
{
  public SalesHandlerImpl(String name) throws RemoteException
  {
    super();
    try  {
      Naming.rebind(name, this);
    } catch (Exception e) {
      System.out.println("SalesHandlerImpl exception: "
                          + e.getMessage() + "\n");
      e.printStackTrace();
    }
  }

  // The method 'process' is called from remote client applications
  // with all of the "screen information" for a query or a new
  // sales order:

  public String process(int option, String pin, String password,
                        String part_id, String quantity,
                        String customerID) throws RemoteException
  {
    System.out.println("SalesHandlerImpl.process(" + option + ",...");
    String results = "no results....";  // get this from the database
    String url    = "jdbc:odbc:UMLdb";
    String user_id = "Admin";
    String passwd = "sammy";
    // Make sure the password is OK:
    String password_check =
```

```
        DBInterface.Query("SELECT password FROM SalesPerson WHERE PIN = "
                        + pin,
                        url, user_id, passwd);
System.out.println("results from password check=" +
                    password_check);
if (!password_check.trim().equalsIgnoreCase(password.trim())) {
  return "Password does not match";
}

switch (option) {
case 1: // order
  // First, make sure that the customer is in the database:
  String balance =
    DBInterface.Query("SELECT balance FROM Customer WHERE ID = " +
                        customerID.trim(), url, user_id, passwd);
  System.out.println("balance=|" + balance);

  String customerName =
    DBInterface.Query("SELECT name FROM Customer WHERE ID = " +
                        customerID.trim(), url, user_id, passwd);
  float a_balance = (new Float(balance)).floatValue();

  // In a "real application," we would have business logic to
  // check on customer information, etc.  For this example,
  // we simply create a 'CustInfo' object as a useful container
  // for customer information retrieved from a database from
  // the customer ID key value:
  CustInfo customerInfo =
      new CustInfo(customerID, customerName, 0.0f);

  // we need to check the part in inventory:
  // NOTE: it is very inefficient to perform three SQL queries
  //       to fetch three columns from the same table (but
  //       it does make this example even simpler)
  String temp =
    DBInterface.Query("SELECT number_on_hand, part_name, cost " +
                        "FROM Inventory WHERE ID = " +
                        part_id.trim(), url, user_id, passwd);

  String number="";
  String part_name="";
  String part_cost="0";
  int index = temp.indexOf(",");
```

```
if (index>-1) {
  number=temp.substring(0,index);
  temp=temp.substring(index+1);
}
index = temp.indexOf(",");
if (index>-1) {
  part_name=temp.substring(0,index);
  part_cost=temp.substring(index+1);
}

float cost = 0.0f;
if (part_cost!=null) cost=(new Float(part_cost)).floatValue();
int part = 0;
if (number!=null) part=(int)((new Float(number)).floatValue());
int quan = 0;
if (quantity!=null) quan=(int)((new
                              Float(quantity)).floatValue());

// In a "real application," we would have business logic for
// handling the item that is being ordered.  Here, we
// simply create an ItemOrdered object, using it as a useful
// container for all data dealing with an item in inventory
// that is being ordered:
ItemOrdered item =
  new ItemOrdered(part, cost, quan, "no description"); // unused

// In a "real application," we would have business logic for
// handling a sales order (checking credit, etc.). Here, we
// simply create a SalesOrder object, using it as a useful
// container for all data dealing with a SalesOrder:
SalesOrder salesOrder =
  new SalesOrder(customerInfo, item); // unused

// NOTE: This example system is a two-tiered system
// (client applets and a Java server application that speaks
//  directly to local databases via JDBC).  In a
// "real system," we might (as in the discussion in
// the book) use a three-tiered system.  This program
// could be converted to be the second tier of a three-tiered
// system by doing the following:
//
//    1. Add business logic to this program to check on
//       customer credit, etc.
```

```
//     2. Use RMI to pass the SalesOrder (and contained CustInfo
//        and ItemOrdered objects) to the third tier application
//        that connects to local databases.

// For this example, we will simply use SQL and JDBC to
// add an order to the 'order' table in our test database:
String salespersonName =
  DBInterface.Query("SELECT name FROM SalesPerson WHERE PIN = "
                    + pin,
                    url, user_id, passwd);
String a_query =
  "INSERT INTO ORDERS (salesperson, customer, " +
  " partname, numberordered) " +
  "VALUES ('" + salespersonName.trim() + "' , '" +
  customerName.trim() + "' , '" +
  part_name.trim() + "' , " + quan + ")";
results = DBInterface.Update(a_query, url, user_id, passwd);
break;

case 2:
  // List line items:
  return DBInterface.Query("SELECT * FROM Inventory",
                           url, user_id, passwd);

case 3:
  // quota query
  return
    DBInterface.Query("SELECT * FROM SalesPerson WHERE PIN = " +
                      pin.trim(),
                      url, user_id, passwd);

case 4:
  // List all customers:
  return DBInterface.Query("SELECT * FROM Customer",
                           url, user_id, passwd);
default:
  break;
}
return results;
}
}
```

The class *DBInterface*, shown in Listing 4, is a small utility class that encapsulates the JDBC API and simplifies accessing local databases at the expense of efficiency. This class provides two public static methods:

- Query
- Update

Listing 4   DBInterface.java

```
// DBInterface

import java.rmi.*;
import java.rmi.server.UnicastRemoteObject;

import java.sql.*;

public class DBInterface
{
   static public String Query(String a_query, String url,
                              String user_id, String passwd) {
     System.out.println("\n\n+++++++++++++++++++++++++\nQuery: " +
                        a_query + "\n");
     String results = "";

     try {

       doInit();

       // Connect to the JDBC driver:
       Connection con =
         DriverManager.getConnection(url, user_id, passwd);
       checkConnection(con.getWarnings()); // connection OK?

       Statement stmt = con.createStatement();

       // Submit a query:
       ResultSet rs = null;
       try {
         rs = stmt.executeQuery(a_query);
```

THE JDBC API

The JDBC API, which is used to implement the class *DBInterface*, supports sending structured query language (SQL) queries to almost any databases. JDBC uses the low-level Open Database Connectivity (ODBC) API. ODBC was developed by Microsoft and has been adopted as the common, lowest level API for programmatically accessing databases. The HTML documentation for the JDK 1.1 provides full documentation for JDBC. This sidebar summarizes the important API calls that are used in this appendix. All classes discussed in this section belong to the package *java.sql*. The following import statement is assumed in the code examples in this section:

```
import java.sql.*;
```

Driver Manager Class

The *DriverManager* class manages one or more JDBC drivers. In the class *DBInterface,* we will only be using the default Sun/Javasoft driver. The static method *getConnection* establishes a connection to the database:

```
String url = "jdbc:odbc:LocalDatabase";
Connection connection = DriverManager.getConnection (url,
"Admin", "sammy");
```

```
} catch (SQLException se) {
  System.out.println("NO result set");
}

if (rs != null) {
  // Display all columns and rows from the result set
  results = resultSetToString(rs);

  // Close the result set
  rs.close();
}
```

```
      // Close the statement
      stmt.close();

      // Close the connection
      con.close();
   }
   catch (SQLException ex) {
      while (ex != null) {
         System.out.println("SQL error message:   " + ex.getMessage());
         ex = ex.getNextException();
         System.out.println("");
         results = ex.getMessage();
      }
   }
   catch (java.lang.Exception ex) {
      ex.printStackTrace();
      results = ex.getMessage();
   }
   System.out.println("DBInterface.Select() results: " + results);
   return results;
}
```

CONNECTION CLASS

An instance of class *Connection* represents an open session with a specific database. The following code example shows how to get error warnings:

```
SQLWarning warning_list = connection.getWarnings();
```

Any current SQL warnings can be cleared with the method *clearWarnings()*:

```
connection.clearWarnings();
```

```
static public String Update(String a_query, String url,
                            String user_id, String passwd) {
  System.out.println("\n\n++++++++++++++++++++++++\nUpdate: " +
                     a_query + "\n");
  String results = "";

  try {

    doInit();

    // Find a driver:
    Connection con =
      DriverManager.getConnection(url, user_id, passwd);
    checkConnection(con.getWarnings()); // connection OK?

    Statement stmt = con.createStatement();

    try {
      int n = stmt.executeUpdate(a query);
      results = "UPDATE affected " + n + " rows.";
    } catch (SQLException se) {
      results = "UPDATE had no effect on database.";
    }

    // Close the statement
    stmt.close();

    // Close the connection
    con.close();

  }
  catch (SQLException ex) {
    while (ex != null) {
      System.out.println("SQL error message:  " + ex.getMessage());
      ex = ex.getNextException();
      System.out.println("");
      results = ex.getMessage();
    }
  }
  catch (java.lang.Exception ex) {
    ex.printStackTrace();
    results = ex.getMessage();
  }
```

STATEMENT CLASS

An instance of class *Statement* is used to execute a static SQL query and to fetch the results in an instance of class *ResultSet*. The following code example shows how to create an instance of class *Statement* from an instance of class *Connection* and to make an SQL query:

```
Statement statement = connection.createStatement();
ResultSet result = statement.executeQuery("SELECT * FROM
                                                  NameTable");

// Use the result set here...
result.close();
statement.close();
connection.close();
```

```
   System.out.println("DBInterface.Select() results: " + results);
   return results;
}

static private boolean needToInit = true;

static private void doInit() {
   if (needToInit) {
     try {
       // Load the JDBC driver
       Class.forName("sun.jdbc.odbc.JdbcOdbcDriver");
       //DriverManager.setLogStream(System.out); // uncomment for
                                                   // debug printout
     } catch (Exception e) {
       System.out.println("Could not set up JDBC: " + e);
     }
     needToInit=false;
   }
}


static private String resultSetToString(ResultSet rs)
                  throws SQLException {
```

```
    int i;
    StringBuffer outputText = new StringBuffer();
    int numCols = rs.getMetaData().getColumnCount();
    boolean more = rs.next();
    while (more) {
      for (i=1; i<=numCols; i++) {
        if (i > 1) outputText.append(",");
        outputText.append(rs.getString(i));
      }
      if (i!=numCols)  outputText.append("\n");
      more = rs.next();
    }
    return new String(outputText);
}

static private boolean checkConnection(SQLWarning warning)
                       throws SQLException  {
    boolean ret = false;
```

EFFICIENCY

You can use the class *DBInterface* shown in Listing 4 to easily access local databases, but you should also consider the following to make your Java-based database applications more efficient:

- Use the interface *java.sql.PreparedStatement* when making many repetitive queries to avoid repeating the overhead for creating multiple *java.sql.Statement* objects (which will happen if you use *DBInterface.Query* multiple times with similar queries against the same tables).

- Use stored procedures in a database by using the *java.sql.CallableStatement* interface.

```
    if (warning != null) {
      System.out.println("\n *** Warning ***\n");
      ret = true;
      while (warning != null) {
        System.out.println("Message " + warning.getMessage());
        warning = warning.getNextWarning();
      }
    }
    return ret;
  }
}
```

The class *CustInfo* is shown in Listing 5. This class encapsulates the data required to represent a customer.

Listing 5   **CustInfo.java**

```java
//
// Simple class that represents Customers
//

public class CustInfo {
  public CustInfo(String an_ID, String a_name, float a_balance) {
    ID = an_ID;
    name=a_name;
    balance=a_balance;
  }
  public CustInfo() {
    name="";
    balance=0;
    ID="";
  }

  public String getName() { return name; }
  public float getBalance() { return balance; }
  public void setBalance(float b) { balance=b; }
  public String getID() { return ID; }
  protected String name;
  protected float balance;
  protected String ID;
}
```

The class *ItemOrdered* is shown in Listing 6. This class encapsulates the data for representing an item in inventory that can be ordered.

Listing 6   **ItemOrdered.java**

```java
// ItemOrdered.java
//
// Simple class that represents parts in inventory
//

public class ItemOrdered {
  public ItemOrdered(int num, float a_cost, int quant, String desc) {
    part_number=num;
    cost=a_cost;
    quantity=quant;
    description=desc;
  }
  public ItemOrdered() {
    part_number=-1;
    cost=0;
    quantity=0;
    description="";
  }

  public int getPartNumber() { return part_number; }
  public float getCost() { return cost; }
  public int getQuantity() { return quantity; }
  public String getDescription() { return description; }
  public void setCost(float c) { cost=c; }
  public void setQuantity(int q) { quantity=q; }
  public void setDescription(String d) { description=d; }

  protected int part_number;
  protected float cost;
  protected int quantity;
  protected String description;
}
```

The class *SalesPerson* that is shown in Listing 7 implements a thin-client for accessing a remote *SalesHandler* object. The class *SalesPerson* runs as an applet and presents a simple form for entering orders and querying the status of customers, inventory, and sales quotas. The form generated was picture in Figure 15.8 in Chapter 15.

- The method *SalesPerson.setupRemote* makes a connection to a remote *SalesHandler* object by using the RMI API. The class variable remote (*interface WatsonRMI*) is initially null when the applet starts. The method *SalesPerson.setupRemote* initializes the value of the variable remote if it is null by setting its value to the results of calling the static method *java.rmi.Naming.lookup* with the desired remote server name. Note that the remote server name is formed by concatenating three strings:

```
"rmi://"
getCodeBase().getHost()
"/WatsonRMI"
```

- The method *java.applet.getCodeBase* fetches the code base for the applet that contains the host name where this applet is stored. This code allows this applet to correctly call the remote *SalesHandler* object that must execute on the same machine as the Web server that stores the *SalesPerson* applet. Once the variable remote is set, the following method call can be made transparently on the remote *SalesHandler* object:

```
remote.setup
```

The method signature for *process* is defined in the *WatsonRMI* interface that is shown in Listing 2.

Listing 7 SalesPerson.java

```
// SalesPerson.java
//

import java.awt.*;
import java.util.*;
import java.applet.Applet;
import java.rmi.*;
import java.rmi.server.*;
```

```
// Design note: This thin-client applet contains no
// information concerning business objects (i.e., SalesOrder,
// Customer, and ItemOrdered).  It provides a simple data entry
// form and sends the data entered in the form as Java strings
// to the remote server.

public class SalesPerson extends Applet {

    int width = 680;
    int height = 290;

    protected TextField part_number_1;
    protected TextField customer_number_2;
    protected TextField part_number_2;
    protected TextField quantity_2;
    protected TextField name_3;
    protected TextField billing_address_3;
    protected TextField telephone_3;
    protected TextField PIN;
    protected TextField Password;

    protected TextArea outputText;

    protected Button inventoryButton;
    protected Button customersButton;

    public String getAppletInfo() {
        return "Sales Client.  By Mark Watson";
    }

    public static void main(String args[]) {
        SalesPerson sc = new SalesPerson();
        Frame f = new Frame("Sales Person");
        f.add("Center", sc);
        sc.init();
        sc.start();
        f.show();
    }

    public void init() {
        resize(width, height);
```

```
Panel globalPanel = new Panel();
globalPanel.setLayout(new GridLayout(2,1));

Panel topPanel = new Panel();
topPanel.setLayout(new GridLayout(3,1));

Panel panel1 = new Panel();
panel1.add(new Button("Clear order information"));
panel1.add(new Button("Send order"));
panel1.add(new Button("List parts"));
panel1.add(new Button("List customers"));
panel1.add(new Button("List quota"));
panel1.add(new Button("Clear output"));
panel1.add(new Button("Quit"));
topPanel.add(panel1);

Panel panel3 = new Panel();
panel3.add(new Label("Cust. ID"));
customer_number_2 = new TextField("   ", 5);
panel3.add(customer_number_2);
panel3.add(new Label("Line item #"));
part_number_2 = new TextField("   ", 5);
panel3.add(part_number_2);
panel3.add(new Label("Quantity "));
quantity_2 = new TextField("   ", 3);
panel3.add(quantity_2);
PIN = new TextField("314", 6);
panel3.add(new Label("PIN"));
panel3.add(PIN);
Password = new TextField("sammy", 6);
panel3.add(new Label("Passwd"));
panel3.add(Password);

topPanel.add(panel3);

outputText = new TextArea("", 8, 60);

globalPanel.add(topPanel);

globalPanel.add(outputText);
```

```java
  //this.setLayout(new FlowLayout());
  this.add(globalPanel);
}


public boolean action(Event evt, Object obj) {
  System.out.println (evt.id);
  if (evt.target instanceof Button) {
    String label = (String)obj;
    if (label.equals("Send order")) {
      System.out.println("Run button pressed\n");
      doQueryOrder();
      return true;
    }
    if (label.equals("List parts")) {
      System.out.println("Run button pressed\n");
      doListLineItems();
      return true;
    }
    if (label.equals("List customers")) {
      System.out.println("Run button pressed\n");
      doListCustomers();
      return true;
    }
    if (label.equals("List quota")) {
      System.out.println("Run button pressed\n");
      doListQuota();
      return true;
    }
    if (label.equals("Clear order information")) {
      customer_number_2.setText("");
      part_number_2.setText("");
      quantity_2.setText("");
      return true;
    }
    if (label.equals("Clear output")) {
      outputText.setText("");
      return true;
    }
    if (label.equals("Quit")) {
      System.exit(1);
      return true;
    }
  }
```

```
      return false;
    }
    private WatsonRMI remote=null;

    protected void setupRemote() {
      if (remote==null) {
        System.out.println("Setting up remote WatsonRMI");
        try {
         String hostName=getCodeBase().getHost();
         String serverName="rmi://" + hostName + "/WatsonRMI";
         remote = (WatsonRMI)Naming.lookup(serverName);
         System.out.println("after setting up remote...");
        } catch (Exception e)

         System.out.println("Error setting up remote: " + e);
         remote=null;
        }
      }
      if (remote==null)
          System.out.println("setupRemote(): error remote==null");
    }

    protected void doQueryOrder() {
      String results="error";

      //try {
      //  System.setSecurityManager(new RMISecurityManager());
      //} catch(Exception e)

      //  System.out.println("OK if already set: " + e);
      //}

      setupRemote();
      try {
        System.out.println("before RMI call...");
        results=remote.process(1, PIN.getText(),
          Password.getText(),
          part_number_2.getText(),
          quantity_2.getText(),
          customer_number_2.getText());
        System.out.println("... after RMI call");
      } catch(Exception e)
```

```java
      System.out.println("Exception from WatsonRMI: " + e);
    }

    outputText.append(results + "\n");
  }


  protected void doListLineItems() {
    String results="error";
    setupRemote();
    if (remote != null) {
      try {
        results=remote.process(2, PIN.getText(), Password.getText(),
          part_number_2.getText(), quantity_2.getText(),
          customer_number_2.getText());
      } catch(Exception e)

        System.out.println("Exception from WatsonRMI: " + e);
      }
    }
    outputText.append(
      "part/line #, part name, cost, # inventory, # ordered\n" +
      "_____-\n");
    outputText.append(results + "\n\n");
  }

  protected void doListQuota() {
    String results="error";
    setupRemote();
    if (remote != null) {
      try {
        results=remote.process(3, PIN.getText(),
                                  Password.getText(),
                part_number_2.getText(),
                                  quantity_2.getText(),
                customer_number_2.getText());
      } catch(Exception e)

        System.out.println("Exception from WatsonRMI: " + e);
      }
    }
```

```
    outputText.append("ID, PIN, name, password, region\n" +
        "――――――――――――――――-\n");
    outputText.append(results + "\n\n");
}


protected void doListCustomers() {
  System.out.println("Entered SalesPerson.doListCustomers()");
  String results="error";
  setupRemote();
  if (remote != null) {
    try {
        System.out.println(
          "SalesPerson.doListCustomers(): before RMI call");
      results=remote.process(4, PIN.getText(), Password.getText(),
        part_number_2.getText(), quantity_2.getText(),
        customer_number_2.getText());
    } catch(Exception e)

      System.out.println("Exception from WatsonRMI: " + e);
    }
  } else {
    System.out.println("doListCustomers(): remote ==null");
  }
  outputText.append("ID, customer name, balance\n" +
      "――――――――――――――――-\n");
  outputText.append(results + "\n");
  }
}
```

A Zip file containing the Java source code for this example and a test database for Microsoft Access is available at both Morgan Kaufmann Publisher's Web site (*www.mkp.com/umldg*) and Mark Watson's Web site (*www.markwatson.com/uml-book.html*). Popkin Software's SA/Object Architect tool with the SalesWeb diagrams is available at *www.popkin.com*. A link to Popkin's Web site is provided in Morgan Kaufmann Publishers' Web page for this book.

UML Job Aid

I n the following pages we've summarized the key notational symbols used when developing UML diagrams. You can copy these pages and keep them on your desk when you undertake your first UML analysis effort. They will remind you of any diagramming details you may have forgotten.

Figure B.1a *UML Job Aid.*

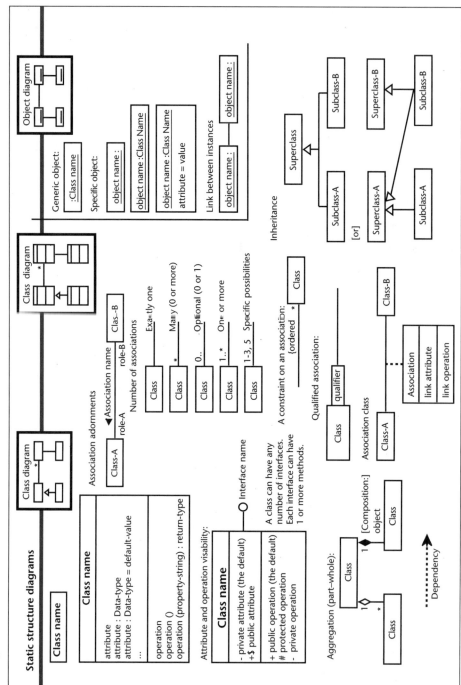

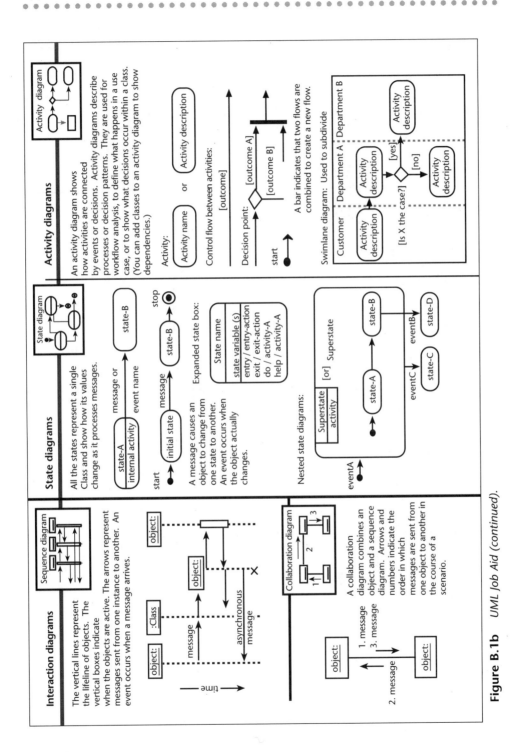

Figure B.1b *UML Job Aid (continued).*

Figure B.1c *UML Job Aid (continued).*

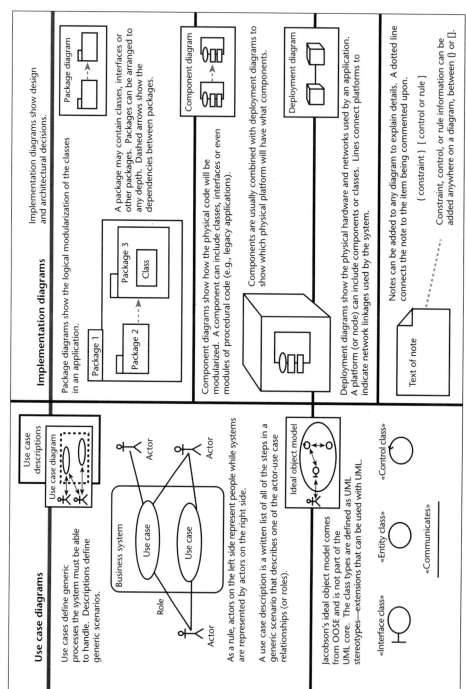

Use case diagrams

Use cases define generic processes the system must be able to handle. Descriptions define generic scenarios.

As a rule, actors on the left side represent people while systems are represented by actors on the right side.

A use case description is a written list of all of the steps in a generic scenario that describes one of the actor-use case relationships (or roles).

Jacobson's ideal object model comes from OOSE and is not part of the UML core. The class types are defined as UML stereotypes—extensions that can be used with UML.

Use case descriptions · Use case diagram · Actor · Business system · Use case · Role · Ideal object model · «Interface class» · «Entity class» · «Control class» · «Communicates»

Implementation diagrams

Implementation diagrams show design and architectural decisions.

Package diagrams show the logical modularization of the classes in an application.

A package may contain classes, interfaces or other packages. Packages can be arranged to any depth. Dashed arrows show the dependencies between packages.

Package diagram · Package 1 · Package 2 · Package 3 · Class

Component diagrams show how the physical code will be modularized. A component can include classes, interfaces or even modules of procedural code (e.g., legacy applications).

Components are usually combined with deployment diagrams to show which physical platform will have what components.

Component diagram

Deployment diagrams show the physical hardware and networks used by an application. A platform (or node) can include components or classes. Lines connect platforms to indicate network linkages used by the system.

Deployment diagram

Notes can be added to any diagram to explain details. A dotted line connects the note to the item being commented upon.

Text of note

Constraint, control, or rule information can be added anywhere on a diagram, between {} or [].

{ constraint } [control or rule]

Comparison of UML, Booch, and OMT Notations

O ver 60% of the developers currently using OO notations use either OMT (developed by Rumbaugh and others) or Booch notations. The rest of the developers use a wide variety of notations, including Responsibility Driven Design (CRC cards) and Jacobson's Objectory Methodology (use cases, ideal object diagrams). To make it easy for readers who are familiar with Booch or Rumbaugh notations to determine the equivalent notation in UML, we've included the following tables that compare the notations. As in the body of this book, we have not included all of the details of each notation, but only the important features that readers will need to handle most applications.

A Comparison of UML, OMT, and Booch.

Notational item	UML	OMT	Booch
Class and Object diagrams			
Class	Solid rectangle	Solid rectangle	Dashed cloud
Sections of class rectangle	Top: name Middle: attributes Bottom: operations	Name Attributes Operations	Name All members
Attribute characteristics	Name : type = initial value	Name, type, initial value	Name, type, initial value
Operation characteristics	Name (argument list) : result_type	Full signature	Full signature
Visibility	+ public # protected - private null unspecified	+ public # protected - private	null public I protected II private III implementation
Parameterized class	Class rectangle with a smaller dashed rectangle overlying the right corner with the list of template arguments in attribute format	C++-like syntax with a list of parameters and their types	Class cloud with a smaller dashed rectangle
Object	Solid rectangle (same as class) but with object or class name underlined	Solid rectangle with object name: class	solid cloud
Object attributes	Name = value	Name = value	Name = value
Instantiation	Dashed line from object to class	Dashed arrow from object to class	Dashed arrow from object to class
Inheritance	Line from subclass to superclass with open triangle pointing to superclass	Tree from triangle fanning out to subclasses	Solid arrow from subclass to superclass

A Comparison of UML, OMT, and Booch *(continued)*.

Notational item	*UML*	*OMT*	*Booch*
Nested class or object diagram	Nested class rectangle within superclass box	None; discouraged	Nested cloud within superclass cloud
Sequence diagram	Sequence diagrams are like message trace diagrams in both OMT and Booch.		
Collaboration diagram	Shows object diagrams with arrows and numbered messages superimposed to show message flow and sequence. New in UML. Not previously used in either OMT or Booch.		
State diagram	Basic Harel diagrams are used in all three.		
Activity diagram	A special variation of the state diagram that shows activity flows internal to a class. New in UML. Not previously used in either OMT or Booch.		
Package diagram and component diagram	File folders represent logical modules of code called packages. Rectangle with oval and two small rectangles crossing left side used to represent a component.	No equivalents	Rectangle with oval and two small rectangles crossing left side used to represent a module. No distinction between package and component.
Deployment diagram	Cubes used to represent processors or other hardware devices	No equivalents	Cubes used to represent processors or other hardware devices. Called a process diagram.
Use case diagram	Use cases and use case descriptions incorporated into UML from OOSE. OOSE also supports ideal and actual object (class) diagrams and many other conventions not directly incorporated into UML. UML allows "stereotypes" or extensions of the notation. In effect, ideal object diagrams are a stereotype of UML class diagrams.		
Misc. notations	Notes: dog-eared rectangle attached to element by dashed line	Text in braces near the target	Dog-eared rectangle attached to target by a dashed line

Products Mentioned in This Book

At various points in the book we've mentioned specific organizations or products, or referred to groups of products. Here we've listed contact information for many products or organizations we've mentioned.

Chapter 3: A Simple Object-Oriented Methodology

More information about IBM's San Francisco Project Java components can be obtained from IBM's Web site: *www.ibm.com/java/sanfrancisco.*

Chapter 5: Coding Applications in Java

The key product here is Sun's Java Development Kit (JDK), which includes a Java compiler and interpreter and the libraries. JDK 1.1 can be downloaded free from Sun's Web site: *www.sun.com/java*.

Chapter 6: Development with an Object-Oriented Modeling Tool

The OO modeling tool that we feature in this book is SA/Object Architect from Popkin Software & Systems:

Popkin Software & Systems Inc.

Product: SA/Object Architect, SA/BPR, SA/CRC Cards
11 Park Place, New York, NY 10007
Phone: 212-571-3434, Fax: 212-571-3436
Web site: *www.popkin.com*

We cannot list all of the many OO CASE vendors, but here are a few of the more popular ones.

Advanced Software Technologies (AST)

Product: Graphical Designer Pro (GD Pro)
Phone: 303-730-7981, Fax: 303-730-7983
Email: infor@advancedsw.com
Web site: *www.advancedsw.com*

Aonix

(Formerly Interactive Development Environments [IDE])
Product: Aonix 007 (StP & ObjectAda)
Phone: 415-543-0900, Fax: 415-543-0145
Email: info@ide.com
Web site: *www.ide.com*

Cayenne Software

(Formerly Cadre and Bachman)
Product: ObjecTeam, GroundWorks, Terrain
Phone: 617-273-9003, Fax: 617-273-9904
Web site: *www.cayennesoft.com*

i-LOGIX

Product: Rhapsody
Phone: 508-682-2100, Fax: 508-682-5995
Internet: *www.ilogix.com*

Microsoft

Product: Visual Modeler
(lightweight version of Rational's Rose)
Phone: 905-568-3503
Web site: *www.microsoft.com*

ObjecTime

Product: ObjecTime
Phone: 613-591-3535, Fax: 613-591-3784
Internet: sales@objectime.on.ca

Platinum Technology

(Formerly Protosoft)
Product: Paradigm Plus
Phone: 630-620-5000, Fax: 630-691-0710
Internet: info@platinum.com
Web site: *www.platinum.com*

Rational Software

Product: Rational Rose, Objectory
Phone: 408-496-3600, Fax: 408-496-3636
Internet: product_info@ rational.com
Web site: *www.rational.com*

Select Software Tools

Product: Select Enterprise
Phone: +44-1242-229-700, Gen. fax +44-1242-229-701
Web site: *www.selectst.com*

Sterling Software

> Product: KEY: Workgroup (Activity Flow Modeler [BPR tool]), KEY: Analyze (ADW/Analysis), KEY: Construct (ADW/Construction Workstation)
> Phone: 214-891-1000, Fax: 214-980-1255
> Sterling Web site: *www.key.sterling.com*
> TI Software Web site: *www.ti.com/software*

> *Note: Sterling owns the ADW product that KnowledgeWare (the largest of the old CASE vendors) used to sell. They have just agreed to acquire TI Software, for its Composer product. Composer evolved from TI's old CASE product, IEF. It was TI software that worked with Microsoft to design their OO repository.*

Repository Products

Here are the three best known OO repositories designed to hold information about OO applications.

IBM

> TeamConnection for OS/2
> Phone: 919-254-4760

Microsoft

> Object Repository
> Web site: *www.microsoft.com/repository*

Unisys

> Universal Repository
> 714-380-6460, Fax: 714-380-6113
> Web site: *www.unisys.com*

Microsoft's ActiveX-oriented repository will undoubtedly play a growing role in the market, but at the moment, the most advanced of these repositories is the one from Unisys.

The OMG is working on an OO repository standard. For more information, contact Sridhar Iyengar at 714-380-5692, or send email to siyengar@po7.mv.unisys.com.

Chapter 7: Business Process Reengineering

The following companies offer LOVEM tools:

Proforma

Product: ProVision Workbench
Phone: 810-443-0055, Fax: 810-443-0506
Email: proforma@proformacorp.com

IBM

Product: Business Process Modeler
For information, contact: Karl Van Leuven at
kvl@raleigh.ibm.com

Holosofx

Product: Workflow*BPR Modeler
Web site: *www.holosofx.com*

The person at IBM responsible for developing LOVEM is Alan Brown. You can send email to him at alan_brown @vnet.ibm.com. Phone: 905-316-3093, Fax: 905-316-2535.

Chapter 8: Use Case Diagrams and Ideal Object Models

The most systematic approach to developing OO applications via use cases was Objectory's Objectory OO CASE tool. Objectory was acquired by Rational Software when they hired Jacobson and may still be available from Rational, although Rational has indicated that it will not be pushing it. Instead, they are promoting the Rational Rose OO CASE line. (Rational is listed with the OO CASE vendors under products mentioned in Chapter 6.)

Most OO modeling tools, such as Popkin Software's, support a use case utility of some kind. Check the list under Chapter 6 for OO CASE vendors.

Chapter 9: CRC Cards

Popkin Software has a product available, SA/CRC Cards Modeling Tool. (See Popkin Software under listing for products mentioned in Chapter 6.)

Chapter 14: Choosing an Object-Oriented Architecture

Here are some of the leading Object Request Brokers.

Java Remote Message Invocation Java RMI) comes packaged with Sun's JDK and can be downloaded from the Sun Web site: *www.sun.com/java*.

Microsoft's DCOM is included in Windows95 and WindowsNT operating systems. For more information, check *www.microsoft.com*.

The OMG's CORBA is sold by the following vendors:

BEA Systems

Product: ObjectBroker (formerly sold by Digital Equipment)
Phone: 800-817-4232
Email: info@beasys.com
Web site: *www.beasys.com*

Expersoft

Product: PowerBroker
Phone: 669-546-4100
Email: powerbroker@expersoft.com

Hewlett-Packard

Product: HP ORB Plus
Phone: 408-447-5526
Email: witham_r@apollo.hp.com
Web site: *www.software.hp.com*

IBM

Product: SOMobjects
Phone: 512-823-5992
Email: chrisvs@austin.ibm.com
Web site: *www.austin.ibm.com/developer/objects*

ICL Object Software Labs

Product DIAS Object Request Broker
Phone: 800-868-3427
Email: dias@wg.icl.co.uk
Web site: *www.icl.com/dias*

IONA Technologies

Product: Orbix
Phone: 617-949-9000
Web site: *www.iona.com*

Sun

Product: NEO, Joe (NEO is the ORB, Joe is a Java implementation)
Phone: 512-345-2412
Web site: *www.sun.com/sunsoft/index.html*

Visigenic

Product: Visigenic (The Java ORB that Netscape and Oracle are using.)
Phone: 415-286-1900
Web site: *www.visigenic.com*

Chapter 15: Expanding Your Design

The Java development environments or tools keep changing and we can hardly list them all. Following are a few of the best.

Borland International

Product: Latte
Phone: 800-790-3366
Web site: *www.borland.co*

Bulletproof Corp.

Product: JDesignerPro
Phone: 800-505-0105
Web site: *www.bulletproof.com*

IBM

Product: VisualAge for Java for Windows, WebRunner
Web site: *www.software.ibm.com/ad/vajava*

Microsoft

Product: Visual J++ Pro. Ed.
Phone 206-882-8080
Web site: *www.microsoft.com/visualj*

Next Software (a division of Apple)

Product: WebObjects
Phone 415-366-0900
Web site: *www.next.com*

ObjectShare (formerly ParcPlace-Digitalk)

Product: Parts for Java
Phone: 408-970-7280
Web site: *www.objectshare.com*

Rogue Wave Software

Product: Jfactory
Phone: 541-754-3010

SunSoft

Product: Java Workshop
Phone: 415-960-1300
Web site: *www.sun.com/java*

Symantec Corp.

Product: Symantec Cafe, Visual Cafe
Phone: 408-253-9600
Web site: *www.cafe.symantec.com*

The best general source of information on Java tools and components is Gamelan, which maintains an on-line directory of Java products. Contact: *www.earthweb.com*.

There are several OODB vendors and we can't list them all, but here are a few that are popular. Each of these OODBs support the storage and retrieval of Java applications.

GemStone Systems

Product: GemStone/J (A Java OODB and Web server for high-end applications.)
Phone: 503-629-8383
Email: info@gemstone.com
Web site: *www.gemstone.com*

O2 Technology

Product: O2
Phone: 415-842-7000
Email: o2info@o2tech.com
Web site: *www.o2tech.com*

Objectivity Inc.

Product: Objectivity/DB
Phone: 415-254-7100
Email: info@objy.com
Web site: *www.objy.com*

Object Design, Inc. (ODI)

Product: ObjectStore
Phone: 800-962-9620
Email: info@odi.com
Web site: *www.odi.com*

Poet Software

Product: Poet (Most popular inexpensive OODB product for Windows.)
Phone: 800-950-8845
Email: info@poet.com
Web site: *www.poet.com*

Versant Object Technology

Product: Versant
Phone: 800-837-7268
Email: info@versant.com
Web site: *www.versant.com*

Popular databases that combine some OO features with a relational database include:

Informix

Product: Informix-Universal Server
Phone: 415-926-6300
Web site: *www.informix.com*

Oracle

Product: Oracle8
Phone: 415-506-7000
Email: info@us.oracle.com
Web site: *www.oracle.com*

Unisys Corp.

OSMOS
Phone: 714-380-6999
Email: osmos@mv.unisys.com
Web site: *www.osmos.com*

Bibliography, Notes, and Web Sites

As we finish this book, the Object Management Group is just about to publish its official UML standard. At the moment, the best way to get a detailed description of the new UML standard is either to go to the Rational Software Web site and download their description of version 1.0 of UML (*www.rational.com*), or to go to the OMG Web site and download their official version of the new notational standard (*www.omg.org*). Both are available without charge.

In the next few months there will probably be several books published on the new UML standard. Among the most comprehensive and authoritative will be books by Booch, Rumbaugh, and Jacobson. In addition, other methodologists, such as James Odell, who cochaired the OMG standardization task force, are likely to write authoritative books. Most books will probably mix a presentation of the UML notation with an OO development methodology.

It's hard to keep up with the rapid, ongoing changes in the object technology market. The senior author of this book edits a monthly newsletter that is designed to help managers stay on top of new development in all areas of object technology. For more information, check out the Cutter Web site and download a copy of the "Object-Oriented Strategies" newsletter: *www.cutter.com.*

In the meantime, we have listed books here that discuss older methodologies and notations that led to UML, including books on Booch, OMT, and OOSE methodologies. These books will soon be out of date as far as their notation goes, but they will continue to be a source of good advice on the OO development process. Unfortunately, all of these earlier methodology books were written before the internet and Java achieved their current popularity, and thus, they don't tend to discuss internet-based approaches to application development.

This is not a scholarly book, so we have avoided footnotes and are not including an extensive bibliography. We have included references to the books we would recommend you to look at next if you want more information on any specific chapter. The books we list provide a lot more detail than we do and provide bibliographies that will allow you to pursue specific ideas much further. We have also provided a few Web site (URL) listings that will provide you with more information about indicated topics. The books and notes are organized by chapter.

Chapter 2: The Vocabulary of Object Technology

The best book we know that introduces object technology to managers is this one:

> Taylor, David. *Object-Oriented Technology: A Manager's Guide.* Reading, MA: Addison-Wesley, 1992. ISBN 0-201-56358-4.

The next two books provide slightly more detailed introductions to object technology:

Khoshafian, Setrag, and Razmik Abrous. *Object Orientation.* 2nd ed. New York: John Wiley & Sons, 1995. ISBN 0-471-07834-4.

Taylor, David. *Object-Oriented Information Systems: Planning and Implementation.* New York: John Wiley & Sons, 1992. ISBN 0-471-54364-0.

This is a good introduction to OO technology and the best introduction to components, compound documents, and distributed computing, including ActiveX, DCOM, and CORBA.

Orfali, Robert, Dan Harkey, and Jeri Edwards. *The Essential Distributed Objects Survival Guide.* New York: John Wiley & Sons, 1996. ISBN 0-471-12993-3.

If you are new to OO development and would like some examples of the kinds of applications that were developed by companies who won recognition in the OMG's annual contest for the best OO applications, consider this book:

Harmon, Paul, and William Morrissey. *The Object Technology Casebook: Lessons from Award-Winning Business Applications.* New York: John Wiley & Sons, 1996. ISBN 0471-14717-6.

In addition, most of the books about OO methodologies will provide a more or less general introduction to object technology.

Chapter 3: A Simple Object-Oriented Methodology

As we finish this book there are no good books on methodologies specifically for UML, but there soon will be.

Jacobson, Ivar, Grady Booch, and James Rumbaugh. *The Objectory Software Development Process.* Reading, MA: Addison-Wesley, 1997. ISBN 0-201-57169-2.

This book will be part of the three-volume description of UML from the gurus at Rational Software. As the title suggests, this will be Jacobson's version of a methodology. Jacobson usually isn't very concise, but he always has lots of good, pragmatic suggestions.

Meanwhile, the reader should consult one of the books listed below to get an in-depth discussion of either analysis, design, or an overall approach to OO development.

Booch, Grady. *Object-Oriented Analysis and Design with Applications*. 2nd ed. Reading, MA: Addison-Wesley, 1994. ISBN 0-8053-5340-2

This describes Booch's methodology, which is slightly different from OMT, but it also provides lots of practical advice about designing OO applications and getting them to work.

Martin, James, and James Odell. *Object-Oriented Analysis and Design*. Englewood Cliffs, NJ: Prentice Hall, 1993. ISBN 0-13-630245-9

Rumbaugh, James, Michael Blaha, Williama Premerlani, Frederick Eddy, and William Lorenzen. *Object-Oriented Modeling and Design*. Englewood Cliffs, NJ: Prentice Hall, 1991. ISBN 0-13-629841-9

This is the source of information on the OMT methodology. Since this book has been published, James Rumbaugh has published a number of articles suggesting modifications to this book. Some people refer to these articles, collectively, as OMT-2.

Shlaer, Sally, and Stephen J. Mellor. *Object Lifecycles: Modeling the World in States*. Englewood Cliffs, NJ: Yourdon Press/Prentice Hall, 1992. ISBN 0-13-629940-7

Yourdon, Edward. *Object-Oriented Systems Design: An Integrated Approach*. Englewood Cliffs, NJ: Yourdon Press/Prentice Hall, 1994. ISBN 0-13-636325-3.

We haven't said much in this book on managing OO projects. If you are going to use a modeling tool, you will probably face management and coordination problems. The best book on how to plan and manage OO projects is

Goldberg, Adele, and Kenneth Rubin. *Succeeding with Objects*. Reading, MA: Addison-Wesley, 1995. ISBN 0-201-62878-3

Booch, Grady. *Object Solutions: Managing the Object-Oriented Project*. Reading, MA: Addison-Wesley, 1996. ISBN 0-8053-0594-7.

This book isn't very systematic, but it provides lots of good advice.

Chapter 4: The Unified Modeling Language

At the moment, there are no books on UML. The best source of detailed information on UML is either the UML 1.0 documentation, which can be found on the Rational Web site, or the documentation on the work of the OMG A&D task force, which can be found on the OMG Web site.

Rational Software has announced books in a series on UML that should come out about the time this book is published. The OMG has not announced a book, but around the end of the year, after the OMG board has finally approved the OMG analysis and design standards, the OMG will undoubtedly publish its final specification. The easy way to get it will be to go to the OMG Web site after January 1998 and download the official specification. The books by Booch, Rumbaugh, and Jacobson will constitute an informal but comprehensive description of UML. The specification by the OMG will constitute the official specification that OO modeling tool and repository vendors will want to use.

Booch, Grady, James Rumbaugh, and Ivar Jacobson. *Unified Modeling Language User Guide*. Reading, MA: Addison-Wesley, 1997. ISBN 0-201-57168-4.

This book, along with its companion volume by the same three authors, with Rumbaugh in the lead, will constitute Rational Software's official description of UML. Anyone serious about using UML for large projects will want to obtain and study these books.

Rumbaugh, James, Ivar Jacobson, and Grady Booch. *Unified Modeling Language Reference Manual*. Reading, MA: Addison-Wesley, 1997. ISBN 0-201-30998-X.

This book, along with its companion volume by the same three authors, with Booch in the lead, will constitute Rational Software's official description of UML. Anyone serious about using UML for large projects will want to obtain and study these books.

Booch, Grady, James Rumbaugh, and Ivar Jacobson. *The Unified Modeling Language for Object-Oriented Development*. Documentation Set, Version 1.0. Available from Rational Software, Santa Clara, CA, 1996 (Web site: *www.rational.com*).

Chapter 5: Coding Applications in Java

We've included a few of the many books on Java and Java application development that are especially outstanding. Two Web sites provide good Java book reviews if you want to search the latest literature: *www.cbooks.com/java.html* and *www.webreference.com/books/programming/java.html*.

Cornell, Gary, and Cay S. Horstmann. *Core Java*. 2nd ed. SunSoft Press/Prentice Hall, 1997. ISBN 0-13-596891-7.

A very detailed and clear explanation.

Daconta, Michael C. *Java for C/C++ Programmers*. New York: John Wiley & Sons, 1996. ISBN 0-471-15324-9.

A good book for those who are making the transition between C and Java.

Flanagan, David. *Java in a Nutshell*. O'Reilly & Associates, 1997. ISBN 1-56592-183-6.

A nice introduction if you like lots of code.

Gosling, James, Bill Joy, and Guy Steele. *The Java Language Specification*. Java Series. Reading, MA: Addison-Wesley, 1996. ISBN 0-20163-451-1.

Watson, Mark. *Intelligent Java Applications*. San Francisco: Morgan Kaufmann Publishers, 1997. ISBN 1-55860-420-0.

An advanced book for those who want to extend their Java applications with AI techniques.

Obviously, the documentation for Sun's Java Development Kit is a must for understanding what you can do with Java. Both the JDK and documentation can be downloaded from the Sun Web site: *www.sun.com*.

Chapter 6: Development with an Object-Oriented Modeling Tool

There are no good books on the range of OO modeling tools currently on the market or on the specifics underlying OO modeling tools. Most books on modeling focus on older CASE products that were in use before 1990. Expect some new books on visual modeling tools and OO repositories as Microsoft steps up the promotion for its OO repository.

The best way to come up to speed on Popkin Software's SA/Object Architect is to read the documentation available from Popkin. For more information, contact the Popkin Web site: *www.popkin.com.*

Chapter 7: Business Process Reengineering

There are lots of general books on BPR and only two books on object-oriented BPR. We've listed a few of the general books and Jacobson's book on a use case-based approach to BPR. What's needed is a good book that ties BPR process workflow diagrams and tools to OO tools.

Davenport, Thomas H. *Process Innovation: Reengineering Work Through Information Technology.* Harvard Business School Press, 1993. ISBN 0-87584-366-2.

Forget about Hammer and Champy. This is the real classic that described the impulse from which BPR derives.

Fischer, Layna, ed. *The Workflow Paradigm: The Impact of Information Technology on Business Process Reengineering,* 2nd ed. Future Strategies, 1995. ISBN 0-9640233-2-6.

Grover, Varun, and William J. Ketiner, eds. *Business Process Change: Reengineering Concepts, Methods and Technologies.* Idea Group, 1995. ISBN 1-878289-92-2.

Jacobson, Ivar, Maria Ericsson, and Agneta Jacobson. *The Object Advantage: Business Process Reengineering with Object Technology.* Reading, MA: Addison-Wesley, 1995. ISBN 0-201-42289-1.

Taylor, David. *Business Engineering with Object Technology.* New York: John Wiley & Sons, 1995. ISBN 0-471-04521-7.

IBM's LOVEM

The best book on LOVEM is the book that IBM's methodology was ultimately derived from:

Rummler, Geary A., and Alan P. Brache. *Improving Performance: How to Manage the White Space on the Organization Chart.* San Francisco: Jossey-Bass, 1990. ISBN 1-55542-214-4.

Tkach, Daniel, Walter Fang, and Andrew So. *Visual Modeling Technique.* Reading, MA: Addison Wesley, 1996. ISBN 0-8053-2574-3.

This book has a section on LOVEM and information about how LOVEM diagrams relate to use cases.

Alan Brown at IBM's Toronto Labs is responsible for LOVEM at IBM. His phone number is +1-905-316-3093. His email address is Alan_Brown@vnet.ibm.com.

Chapter 8: Use Case Diagrams and Ideal Object Models

The best book on use cases and the only good book on ideal object models is Jacobson's:

Jacobson, Ivar, Magnus Christerson, Patrik Jonsson, and Gunnar Overgaard. *Object-Oriented Software Engineering: A Use Case Driven Approach,* 4th Revision. Reading, MA: Addison-Wesley, 1992. ISBN 0-201-54435-0.

The best explanation of use cases and ideal object models and a very good introduction to object development.

Chapter 9: CRC Cards

There are two good books on CRC cards. One by Wirfs-Brock is more oriented to methodology and theory. The other, by Wilkinson, is very pragmatic and a must-read book for anyone serious about CRC cards.

Wilkinson, Nancy M. *Using CRC Cards: An Informal Approach to Object-Oriented Development.* New York: SIGS Books, 1995. ISBN: 1-884842-07-0.

The best practical introduction to using CRC cards.

Wirfs-Brock, Rebecca, Brian Wilkerson, and Laura Wiener. *Designing Object-Oriented Software.* Englewood Cliffs, NJ: Prentice Hall, 1990. ISBN 0-13-629825-7.

A good description of the RDD methodology with lots of information on CRC cards.

Chapters 10, 11, and 12: UML Diagrams

When it comes to the UML diagrams, the source is the Rational UML documentation, version 1.0, cited earlier, under Chapter 4.

Chapter 13: Designing an Object-Oriented System

The place to start looking for information on OO design is with the same methodology books we cited under Chapter 3. They are increasingly dated, however, because the internet and the use of components were not available and hence not adequately considered when they were developed. This isn't a systematic book, but it presents some interesting ideas:

Coad, Peter, and Mark Mayfield. *Java Design: Building Better Apps & Applets.* Yourdon Press/Prentice Hall, 1997. ISBN 0-13-2711494

Chapter 14: Choosing an Object-Oriented Architecture

Once again, the place to start is with the basic OO methodology books. Then for the more specialized aspects discussed, consider the following:

> Linden, Peter van der. *Not Just Java.* SunSoft Press/Prentice Hall, 1997. ISBN 0-13-864638-4.

This book is excellent, although brief, on Java libraries, security, tiered systems, RMI, CORBA, and JavaBeans. In fact, there is a whole series by Sun called the Java Series, and they all seem very authoritative.

CORBA and Object Distribution Systems

> Orfali, Robert, and Dan Harkey. *Client/Server Programming with Java and CORBA.* New York: John Wiley & Sons, 1997. ISBN 0-471-16351-1.

> Siegel, Jon, ed. *CORBA: Fundamentals and Programming.* New York: John Wiley & Sons, 1996. ISBN 0-471-12148-7.

The best advanced book for programmers who are going to design a distributed system that will rely on CORBA.

> Vogel, Andreas, and Keith Duddy. *Java Programming with CORBA.* New York: John Wiley & Sons, 1997. ISBN 0-471-17986-8.

DCOM and ActiveX

> Chapman, David. *Understanding ActiveX and OLE: A Guide for Developers & Managers.* Redmond, WA: Microsoft Press, 1996. ISBN 1-57231-216-5.

The best introduction to ActiveX.

If you're working on a large system that will include legacy applications and databases, you should certainly check out this title:

> Brodie, Michael L., and Michael Stonebraker. *Migrating Legacy Systems: Gateways, Interfaces & the Incremental Approach.* San Francisco: Morgan Kaufmann, 1995. ISBN 1-55860-330-1.

Chapter 15: Expanding Your Design

For writing Java code and incorporating JDK classes and interfaces in your applications, check the books we recommended under Chapter 5.

Patterns

The best general source on what's happening in patterns is the Patterns Home Page: *st-www.cs.uiuc.edu/users/patterns/patterns.html.*

> Beck, Kent. *SmallTalk Best Practice Patterns.* Englewood Cliffs, NJ: Prentice-Hall, 1996.

> Coad, Peter, David North, and Mark Mayfield. *Object Models: Strategies, Patterns, and Applications.* Englewood Cliffs, NJ: Prentice-Hall, 1995. ISBN 0-13-108614-6.

> Gamma, Eric, Richard Helm, Ralph Johnson, and John Vlissides. *Design Patterns: Elements of Reusable Object-Oriented Software.* Reading, MA: Addison-Wesley, 1995. ISBN 0-201-63361-2.

The best source of descriptions of patterns.

> Mowbray, Thomas J., and Raphael C. Malveau. *CORBA Design Patterns.* New York: John Wiley & Sons, 1997. ISBN 0-471-15882-8.

Pree, W. *Design Patterns for Object-Oriented Software Development*. Reading, MA: Addison-Wesley, 1995. ISBN 0-201-42294-8.

Components

Jacobson, Ivar, Martin Griss, and Patrik Jonsson. *Software Reuse: Architecture, Process, and Organization for Business Success*. New York: ACM Press/Addison-Wesley Longman, 1997. ISBN 0-201-92476-5.

Watson, Mark. *Creating JavaBeans: Components for Distributed Applications*. San Francisco: Morgan Kaufmann, 1997. ISBN 1-55860-476-6.

Sun maintains chat groups where people working in specific domains in Java can exchange ideas and Java components. Two are:

www.jtone.com—for people in telecom services and equipment manufacture, and

www.jfox.com—for people in the financial industry.

Database Access

There are lots of good books on relational databases, and any OO design book will discuss how to link to a relational database. As Oracle begins to promote Oracle8, there will probably be lots of new books on object-relational databases. The best book on the advantages and disadvantages of OO vs. object-relational and relational databases is

Barry, Doug. *The Object Database Handbook: How to Select, Implement and Use Object-Oriented Databases*. New York: John Wiley & Sons, 1996. ISBN 0-471-14718-4.

More information is available from the Object Database Management Group's Web site: *www.odmg.org,* and Barry publishes an expensive but very authoritative report comparing

OODBs. For more information on that, send email to Doug-Barry@aol.com.

Graphical Interfaces

Geary, David M., and Alan L. McClellan. *Graphic JAVA: Mastering the AWT.* SunSoft Press/Prentice Hall, 1997. ISBN 0-13-565847-0.

Paul Harmon is the editor of "Object-Oriented Strategies," a monthly newsletter that he writes for corporate managers and developers who want to keep abreast of the latest developments in OO technology. He is the past editor of "CASE Strategies" newsletter. He is on the program committee of the OMG's ObjectWorld Conference, and he is chairman of DCI's OO CASE Conference. Mr. Harmon consults with large companies about using new software technologies. He has written several books, including *The Object Technology Casebook* (with Bill Morrissey) and *Objects in Action* (with David Taylor).

Mark Watson has started his own company that provides Java tools for natural language interfaces to relational databases. Mr. Watson is the author of eight books dealing with Java, C++, distributed systems, and artificial intelligence. He is also an employee consultant for SAIC.

Index